AMBASSADOR FOR CHRIST

Ambassador
for
Christ

Mary Lar's reflections
on
Nigeria, Past and Present

Foreword by Monica Hill

Published by the British Church Growth Association,
Bedford, England, in association with Kingsway Trust.

First published in England in 1997

© Mary Lar, Jos, Nigeria

British Library Cataloguing-in-Publication Data
A catalogue for this book is
available from the British Library

Unless otherwise indicated, biblical quotes are from the New
International Version © 1973, 1978, 1984 by the International Bible
Society.

ISBN: 0-948704-373

Typeset by Andrew Lewis, PWM Trust

Printed in Great Britain by Cox and Wyman Ltd, Reading

Front Cover picture: Solomon and Mary Lar

Back Cover picture: Mary Lar

Dedication

This book is dedicated to my late parents,
Mr Nansep Lar and Mrs Mbai Lar,
and to my father's father, Lar Mbamzhi,
an early Christian in Tarok land.

Contents

Plate Section Contents

Acknowledgements

I thank God for the Revd Dr Clifford Hill and Mrs Monica Hill, who inspired the writing of this book. They were visiting Nigeria in April 1991 and spent Easter with us in Jos. At that time the Lord used them to minister to thousands of Christians who were going through a period of great persecution in Northern Nigeria. Churches had been burned down and many Christians killed.

One evening as we were talking together, I was telling them something of my family history, and it was Monica who encouraged me to put pen to paper, so that my story could be shared with others. She generously offered to help in the practical details of editing the manuscript and presenting it for publication.

My husband Solomon did all he could to help me, and my children Chalya, Beni, Mark and Debbie contributed in various ways, particularly during my illness. There has also been much support from my extended family. I praise God for them all.

Thanks are due to my typist, Azi Musa, who worked so tirelessly to see that the original manuscript was typed on time to send to England and to Liz Baker and Ruth Addington in England, who retyped the first draft.

My gratitude goes to Joyce Milverton and K Maxwell for providing some of the photographs of Gindiri days and also to Joyce Milverton and David Williams for commenting on some of the draft manuscript.

I particularly want to acknowledge the dedication of Dorothy Richards who undertook the major task of editing and reordering the manuscript. Monica and Clifford Hill did the final editing and Andy Lewis of PWM did the layout and preparation for the printer. I am most grateful to them and to Prophetic Word Ministries and the British Church Growth Association for their invaluable help in publishing the book in association with Kingsway Trust.

God bless you all!

Mary Lar
October 1997

Foreword

It has been both a personal pleasure and a privilege to know the whole Lar family and especially Mary Lar whom I count as a friend and sister in Christ. Over the past ten years I have come to know her and other members of her family, especially Debbie and Mark during their schooling in England, and to share in some of the events that have affected their family.

Through our ministry in London we have had connections with Nigeria for more than 30 years - we had a Nigerian Fellowship in our church in Tottenham when Mary was a student less than half a mile from our church, although we did not know her in those days.

We met Solomon before we met Mary when he came to Port Harcourt where we were addressing a conference. He had just been released from prison in 1987 and we shared in the rapturous welcome he was given by the Christian leaders gathered there. Prior to that we had been communicating with him during his years of detention through our good friend Austin Ukachi who introduced us to the Lar family.

Mary Lar is a unique and highly talented lady who makes things happen. She has made an outstanding contribution to the status of women and the provision of education in Nigeria. Her influence has gone beyond her own country and has contributed positively to the changing African scene. She has supported her husband fully through the different phases of his involvement in the complexities of Nigerian politics including being the First Lady of Plateau State during his Governorship and carrying out her duties as the wife of a Government Minister. Through all the pressures of public life alongside her husband and caring for a growing family, she nevertheless found time to live a life of her own and make a unique contribution in her own right.

Her story told in this book shows triumph and determination in the face of adversity. Mary had to struggle even to obtain the most elementary education which was not thought appropriate for girls in the remote northern village where she grew up. Against all the odds she fought her way through to achieve a College and University education and finally a Doctorate in Education. Her thesis was a study of education among nomadic peoples reflecting her passion for helping the underprivileged and marginalised in society.

Mary has been responsible for instituting a major literacy programme and for developing her native Tarok tongue into a written language. Her major motive in this has been to enable her own people to read the Scriptures in their own language. Indeed her Christian faith has been the prime motivating force behind all her social activity - her faith shines through her own account of facing hardship, danger and adversity both in her childhood and latterly as the wife of a prominent politician in turbulent times.

When I sat with Mary in her home listening to her recollection of some of the dramatic incidents in her life, I felt it was important that she should write about these things so that her testimony could help and encourage others. Now that she has done this I am amazed at the detail of her memory and the extent of her achievements. Her insights into the complex problems facing the continent of Africa make fascinating reading. This is a book which will be of great interest to all who love Africa and who long to see that continent achieve its true potential. Mary Lar sees this as both possible and practicable through Christian principles becoming part of the culture of a nation. Her story is one of faith triumphing over adversity and will be an inspiration to all her readers. Kingsway publishers have already asked Mary to write a sequel to this fascinating book.

Monica Hill
October 1997

Chapter 1

THE MISSIONARIES

The nineteenth century and early twentieth century missionary movement changed the course of history in the continent of Africa. The coming of the missionaries to Nigeria not only brought the Gospel, but opened the way for educational and economic advancement. Prior to this period, the land was dominated by ignorance, illiteracy, diseases and superstitious beliefs. Infant mortality and some diseases like meningitis, small pox, measles, malaria and tuberculosis were appallingly shortening the lives of children and adults.

God raised up people like Herman Karl William Kumm, who was born in Germany in 1874, and prepared him to take a lead in bringing the gospel to my people, the Tarok, of Plateau State in Nigeria. Kumm's life was influenced by Mr Glenny, who spoke about his work in North Africa at a Mission Hall service. Kumm realised that he could help in taking the gospel to Africa, especially to the Sudan, which was then the land covering Dahomey (now the Republic of Benin), Nigeria, Chad, Cameroon, and the present Sudan.

Mungo Park's discoveries of the land beyond the river Niger helped to extend the British colony of Nigeria to the Northern part of the country. The Union Jack was hoisted in Northern Nigeria on the 1st January 1900 (*The Road to Freedom*, Wrights (Sandbach) Ltd, Cheshire, England; Sudan United Mission, 1968).

The Lord gave Kumm the vision of a mission, which he called 'The Sudan Pioneer Mission'. He rallied support from Britain and on 15 June 1904, a meeting of interested men was held with Protestants of all denominations. They called the mission 'The Sudan United Mission' (SUM). One of the first to volunteer was Mr J Lowry Maxwell, who already knew something about Nigeria. Other young men were Dr Ambrose H Bateman and Mr John G Burt. After a farewell by the brethren in England, the four young men sailed out to the unknown on 23 July 1904.

They travelled up the Niger in a river steamer to Lokoja, where they spent a few days with the Niger Trading Company. Dr Kumm went alone to Zungeru, the then Government Headquarters of Northern Nigeria, in order to discuss the mission's future with His Excellency the Commissioner, Sir Frederick Lugard. He returned to them after ten days with the news that they should start their work among the people around Wase in Plateau State, instead of the Bauchi hills as originally planned. They journeyed by boat, about 225 miles, from Lokoja to Ibi, along the river Benue. At Ibi they spent a few days with the Trading Company before taking off for Wase (about 80 miles from Ibi) on foot, which was very exhausting. Mr Burt, Dr Bateman and Mr Maxwell became ill on the way and most of their helpers caught Malaria. Dr Bateman was so ill that he had to return to England. There were no roads, only footpaths although in some places they were able to get horses to help with the journey. The other missionaries eventually reached the foot of Wase Rock (Gobron Dutse) on 12 October 1904.

The First Settlement

They built their first home near this conical hill but none of them knew how to build, nor how to communicate with the people in the region. In 1905, Dr Kumm went back to England (and later America) to appeal for men, funds and prayer partners. He came back with three workers, Messrs Aust, Ghey and Young. They were all engineers, so they helped to set up some more permanent buildings, which improved their health.

Soon they were frequenting Ibi for their supplies. The Chief of Wukari, near Ibi, was very receptive to them, so they established a mission there and Mr Maxwell and Mr

Young were left to be pioneers of this section of the mission. One day when they went to replenish their stocks they returned to find that their house had been razed to the ground. This was thought to be the work of Islamic zealots. That same day, in 1907, they packed up and came to Langtang, my home village, where they were warmly welcomed by the *Ponzhi Tarok*, who allowed them to settle in the area of the present mission house.

This marked the beginning of important changes in Tarok land. Superstition, fear, ignorance, disease and poverty were on their way out. Activities started in earnest in Langtang in 1908 with the Revd H J Cooper and his wife.

God works in a mysterious way and the candle that was lit on 15 June 1904, was the one that cleared darkness out of millions of Nigerians today, including me.

The SUM became indigenised and now has its own pastors and evangelists in Nigeria and the Sudan. It is popularly known now as the Church of Christ in Nigeria (COCIN), which has the largest membership of any church in Plateau State. If it had not been for the missionaries' sacrifices, many Nigerians would not be Christians today. The Lord used them to call many from darkness into His glorious light. Most of the early missionaries have now been called to glory but their work is still being passed on (*Half a Century of Grace*, L Maxwell, SUM 1954).

The Influence of the Missionaries

Old and young people were trained by the missionaries. Some became teachers, evangelists, carpenters, builders, para-medics and pastors. The first pastor from among the Tarok people was the late Pastor Bali and the second was the late Pastor Damina Bawado. Pastor Damina started as a teacher, who worked hard and zealously to promote education for both boys and girls. The author is indebted to him for encouragement in her pursuit of education. Mallam Domven Rimdan was another favourite Tarok teacher under whose influence many Tarok people turned away from idol worship and became Christians. This exposed them to a new standard of life.

My Father's Family

My father is from Gaban in Gazum chiefdom, of Langtang Local Government Area. His family lived up on the hill, ie the Gazum Hills. Many people rejected the God of the white man but my grand-father Lar Mbamzhi received the word through a friend in Langtang, who invited him to consider the truth of the Gospel. He was one of the very early people who received that grace of God. He did not find it easy because others made him a target of attack. He was encouraged by the constant visits of the Revd and Mrs H J Cooper. They worked with their whole hearts and became especially loved by the Tarok people for their love of the Lord, which radiated their lives. They shared the sufferings and the joy of the people and would visit them when they were sick, when there was a death in the family, or when there was a birth. They would share Jesus Christ during such a visit and share an appropriate word of God from the Bible.

The village people were very jealous of my grand-father and set fire to his house in the middle of the night, hoping the entire family would perish but the Lord worked a miracle. The youngest child in the family, Fakcit Lar, woke her mother up for a drink in the night and so the mother saw that the house was on fire. She shouted for help and all were saved.

Out of consideration for the Lar family, the Revd H J Cooper offered to take their youngest son to live with him in Langtang. Lar did not hesitate to give him his son, Nanshep, who happened to be my father. His elder brother Zingpyen Lar insisted on going with them, so the Revd and Mrs Cooper had two boys to look after.

Their new home exposed them to many things that qualified them for the elite way of life. They were taught how to read and write, cook, wash and iron. In addition, Mr Cooper made them join the adult classes he had established in Langtang. After their graduation they were given jobs. Nanshep, my father, became a teacher in Garkawa Shendam Local Government Plateau State from 1930-1935. His brother Zinpyen joined the Native Authority and was made a road overseer for the Langtang area.

My father used to wear shoes and this annoyed some of the missionaries, who came after the Revd Cooper. This brought some disagreement which led my father to travel to Jos, where he joined the SIM (Sudan Interior Mission – mainly missionaries from the USA sent to urban areas) and worked in the Niger Printing Press that used to print Hausa hymn books and other Christian literature. For a time our family lived in Jos, where my father was active in the SIM Church and when I grew up they used to send me to Sunday School and I owe a lot to the SIM.

If it were not for the Gospel, my father would never have had any contact with civilisation, or have been able to introduce it to us. It was because of the attack on their house that they prospered more than any other family and became the most enlightened and educated. Lar Mbamzhi himself did not witness it, but the Lord blessed his children, grand-children and great-grand-children. Some have good jobs, some education, some are blessed in their businesses and above all, there are some who are strong in the Lord, carrying on the light which their great-grandfather received.

My Family

I was born in 1935 into the family of Mr Nanshep and Mrs Mbai Lar Mbamzhi, at Garkawa. When my father met my mother, Mbai Dadi, at church, she was suffering a lot of persecution from her own family for joining the Christians. She was denied food whenever she went to church, yet this did not discourage her. I was their first child, then others followed – Lillian, Esther, Stephen, Sunday and Kefas. Mother died on 2nd September, 1983, aged 65 and my father died on 5th February 1991, aged 82.

In Tarokland Christians are the medium for spreading modern civilisation to the rest of the community. Before she died, my mother was able to help train her sister's children, some of whom now occupy elitist positions in the country.

My mother trained us all to work hard, even during illness. She was not a farmer but was known for cooking and selling food so there was food to sell all day long in our house. The local people nick-named her *Mai Alele* – the woman who makes the food. She sold a kind of steamed beans pudding and we were all involved in the making and selling of it.

After my father left the SIM he worked with the Vom dairy and later gave some service at the Bible Translation Centre, where he found great comfort and joy and finally died. I shall always be grateful to the staff there for the care and love that they gave my father while he was with them.

Chapter 2

YOUTH AND SCHOOL DAYS

I was born in May 1935 – or at least that is what my father had always told me, although when I saw the entry in the church records I noticed that 1938 was given as the year of my birth. To us that does not really matter, the important factor is the person brought into the world.

The Revd H J and Mrs Mary Cooper, the missionaries for whom my father had worked for many years as a house boy, were a godly couple. They were childless and gave themselves to a life of service. My father named me Mary, after Mrs Cooper, and explained to me that 'Mary' meant 'one who does not use vain words'. Although I sometimes wondered if that were really true, I wanted to live up to this name which I had been given. More than that, I wanted to meet this woman whose namesake I was. I was told that she had returned to her home in England long ago, and in my mind's eye I would picture this white lady who had been such a blessing to the *Tarok* people, teaching them to read and write and sing songs. I wondered if I could ever have such a profound influence on people when I grew up.

Local School

My father told me that girls did not need to be very educated; it was enough just to be able to read the Bible in Hausa. So when, at the end of Primary Two I was able to achieve that, I had to leave. This was a source of great disappointment to me and every morning I would stand outside the house and watch the children in their neat uniforms on their way to school; then I would run back into the house and cry, but nothing I could say would persuade my father to change his mind. I remember one day when my mother found me crying, instead of comforting me she gave me a good beating. Often I would kneel down and pray before getting on with helping in the house.

The irony was that earlier, when I had been at school, I had often played truant, and spent days with a friend, deceiving my parents by leaving home in the morning at the right time and returning with my school bag at the same time as all the other children. School had been a miserable experience because the teacher never took any notice of me. Lessons were in English, which I did not understand, and all the learning was by rote. Incorrect answers resulted in pupils being reported to the Headmaster and we used to wait miserably for the moment when he would appear with his *dorina* (long leather whip) and hit us in accordance with the number of times table we had failed. Added to this was the problem that St Luke's School, Jos, was dominated by two ethnic groups, the *Igbos* and *Yorubas*, and as I was from neither of those groups, I was considered to be of inferior intelligence, so loneliness was a real problem.

Sunday School

In marked contrast to this experience was the care and concern of my Sunday School teacher, Mrs Collins, whom we fondly called *Baturiya Larai* (white woman, born on a Wednesday). She was always cheerful, caring and eager to be sure that all the children under her instruction understood her. If for any reason I was unable to attend on Sunday, she would visit me at home to make sure that I was all right. I loved the cards she gave us – old Christmas cards – on which I would boldly and deliberately write 'Mary'. I did not want anyone else to touch my cards. In fact, I never wanted to share my things with anybody. I was full of self.

I eagerly looked forward to Sundays and listened attentively to the stories which Mrs Collins used to tell us. I remember one was *Pilgrim's Progress*, written long ago and in another culture, and yet the story greatly appealed to me. It was illustrated by flannelgraph pictures and I clearly remember the joy I felt when Pilgrim arrived at the cross of Jesus and finally dropped his heavy burden. But I also remember the horrors of the Valley of Death and all the trials which Pilgrim went through, which reminded me vividly of some of the trials and temptations in my own young life. Most of all I remember the day when the teacher placed a picture of the celestial city on the board, and we learned how heaven was waiting to welcome Christian, the pilgrim – in fact the beauty of that city kept me smiling all the way home! Despite being greatly impressed by the story I never at the time really understood its relevance to my young life.

Conversion

One Sunday there was no Sunday School, and all the children were asked to join the adult service. I was about 12 years old and was glad that Dr Stirret was going to be the preacher. He was a medical doctor who was running the SIM (Sudan Interior Mission – now known as ECWA – Evangelical Churches of West Africa) clinic in Jos and people used to call him *Bature Mai Magani* (the white man with the medicine). He used to sing and preach whenever he could gather a crowd – at the market place and railway station as well as in the hospital.

That Sunday morning he was preaching from John 1:12-29. He told us that all those who receive Jesus Christ have the power to become sons of God. This impressed me greatly because I really wanted to be God's child. But it was verse 29 which really pierced my heart, 'Behold the Lamb of God who takes away the sin of the world.' I began to tremble like Christian in Pilgrim's Progress and I saw myself as a sinner who was carrying a heavy load and seeking to drop it at the cross of Jesus. My thoughts were interrupted by *Bature Mai Magani* saying 'Is there anyone who is burdened by sin and wants to get rid of it? Come to Jesus now!' I wanted to move forward, but hesitated as I wondered what my friends would think of me. Maybe they would mock me or call me names, like masu tsarki (the clean one). There was a battle going on

21

inside me, but in response to the preacher's second call I could resist no longer – it was as if I were moving forward to receive something more than gold. I was afraid of being left out when the Son of Man came to take away the sin of the world, so why should I hang on to my sins? He said that if we were ashamed of Jesus, he would be ashamed of us on the last day. To my joy I saw that some of my friends were moving forward too, but my focus was on Jesus alone. I was the one who had to make the decision for myself. The preacher prayed for us and later presented each of us with a Hausa New Testament. What a joyful experience! As I hurried home there was some name-calling but I hardly noticed. I was praising the Lord for the greatest thing that had ever happened to me – my sins had been washed in the blood of Jesus and I was a new creature. I was bubbling over with joy beyond description. This happened in Bishara Church Number One, formerly SIM church in Jos.

Early Discipling

Mama Milkatu was an elderly woman who lived on the church premises. She was a jolly lady, full of the joy of the Lord. I used to imitate her speech and laughter and would often join her preaching team in the hospital or the market place, learning all the time from her teaching and lifestyle. She was a woman of prayer and I was impressed that she seemed to know all the songs in the hymn book! I joined her Sunday School class in the afternoons and was soon busy memorising the hundred questions and answers of the catechism. Her praise and encouragement were a great help to me in my early Christian life. She presented me with my second Bible, this time both Old and New Testaments. I only regret that today few Sunday School teachers take such an interest in the progress of their pupils as Mama Milkatu did.

As I look back, I can see how God brought to me many of his servants whose lives have had considerable influence upon me. Mama Amina Kadong was one. She had married my uncle, Baba Nimmel Kum and they were in Gindiri to train as pastors. He was a real disciplinarian whom I much respected. He had even taught his wife to read and write before they went to Gindiri so that she would be able to cope with her new studies. As they were travelling home for their first Christmas vacation they were involved in a terrible accident in which my uncle and three others were killed. Amina had a broken arm and lost the control of both hands. Despite her great loss the cheerful and patient way in which she carried on was a great inspiration to me and I often turned to her for advice. Many other tragedies were to come her way – including the death of two of her children and that of her second husband – and yet it was her love for the Lord which always shone through.

The Reverend Damina Bawado was a COCIN (Church of Christ in Nigeria) pastor in Langtang and Chairman of the Regional Church Council. He did a great deal to encourage female education and his positive influence enabled many girls, including myself, to benefit from the opportunity of going to school at Gindiri. He knew that my parents were not in a position to pay school fees, and so they were no longer interested in my education. He approached my father's senior brother to take over my education and so it was that Baba Bennim Lar, my uncle, took over. At that time he was an evangelist with the SUM church in Gazum, and because he was a church worker all his children and wards, including me, were entitled to a rebate on the school fees.

Mrs Darmicit Tintin, my auntie, along with my mother, taught me that it was a sin to sit idle. They encouraged me to work hard from childhood.

The late Mrs Mokem Janfa was my cousin, a prayer partner and confidante, and a church elder for many years in COCIN, Langtang. The late Mallam Domven Rimdan was my teacher in Langtang, who wrote to the Tarok girls at Gindiri, giving us much encouragement and telling us to work hard and prove the value of Tarok women.

Going to Gindiri

At last the list with the names of the girls who were going to Gindiri Girls Boarding School was announced. There were six girls from Langtang: Darmicit Tyemlong, Larai Ndam (whose father, Mallam Ali Ndam, was a teacher at the Boys

23

School, Gindiri) Larai Zhembin, Julcit Shikji, Yankat Dala and myself.

An impressive crowd gathered at the SUM primary school to see the first group of girls going away in January, 1950. It was the first time anyone had left our village to go away to obtain an education. We were considered the stars of the village and my mother was proud to see me among the first to receive senior primary schooling. People were pointing at us as if we were more than mere mortals!

Just before I left for Gindiri, God used me to help my family in a particular way. I had noticed that my mother always found it difficult to save money. This had made me feel rather insecure, even though I knew that the Bible tells us in Matthew 6:25-34 that we are not to worry about tomorrow. I devised a plan, which I felt God was encouraging me to do, and started to put aside a tiny fraction of the proceeds of whatever was sold each day, and gave the rest to my mother as usual. In time I was able to save about six shillings. When I was leaving for Gindiri I gave the saved money to my aunt to buy some guinea corn, requesting that she should keep it for mother in case things got difficult for her. Later that year, while I was in Gindiri, I heard that there was a famine in the area where we lived, so I was able to write to my mother and tell her to collect the corn from my aunt. That was an absolute life-saver for her and I learned later that she wept for joy when she received it. God taught me through this that it is important for children to respond to God's promptings and to take their part in family responsibilities, not acting selfishly. God knows our hearts and will bless whatever steps we take in faith.

It was not difficult to pack my wooden box, which I had got ready for school. In it were two dresses, underwear and a knitted vest given me by my auntie Mama Darmicit Tintin. She knitted this vest in the women's school, where Mrs Jump, a missionary's wife, taught them.

I went round to my relatives and friends to bid them good-bye, and they gave me gifts to help me as a student. I collected up to ten shillings. On my arrival at Pankshin, I bought some brown canvas shoes for six shillings. I bought a small bottle of pomade for nine pence and some soap for six pence - in short I spent the rest of the money buying things I needed for my school days. All I had left to get me to Gindiri was nine pence: I had forgotten that I needed money to pay for transport to Gindiri!

Before going to Gindiri Girls' School, we were expected to have a medical examination. Others were examined under a special doctor in Langtang, who was sent from a hospital in Vom but I lost the opportunity of being examined there. I travelled with the group going to Gindiri and stopped off at Pankshin General Hospital to have my medical examination.

The medical examination took three days, so I lived with my uncle and his family Mr Shetur and his wife Mama Christiana Shetur. Because of my training in housework from childhood, I became so used to doing it that even while in other people's houses I would get up very early in the morning and work. The obvious job I could do was to help them sweep the house, the entire compound, wash the pots and dishes and also fetch water. They were not strange jobs, so I happily participated, to the joy of my uncle and his family. They soon grew very fond of me.

After the medical examination, I regretted spending all the money I had been given. I wished someone had advised me to set some aside. As a young girl, I got excited about my looks and forgot the important things. I knew I was in trouble but I did not tell anybody. Instead, I prayed, and the Lord answered my prayer for soon I was told that my uncle, on my father's side, Sergeant Emmanuel Kadong Lar, was a physical instructor at the Pankshin Central School, so I visited him and informed him that I was going to school in Gindiri. Without my mentioning my problem, he gave me two shillings and urged me to work hard, because our family members are not associated with failure and I should not be an exception! Prayer had now swollen my purse by two shillings. I needed one shilling more to cover my fare, so I prayed again. To my surprise, when I got back to Uncle Shetur's house, he had heard of a prison vehicle which would be conveying some prisoners to Jos early in the morning and he had asked them to give me a lift to Mangu.

Then I could take another transport to Gindiri, which is only nine miles from that town. I was very grateful. I woke up early in the morning and started my normal housework that day, when someone came running looking for the girl going to Gindiri. I had to stop sweeping, wash up quickly and go for my box. My uncle, obviously touched by my zeal to serve the house, gave me another shilling. I now had three shillings and nine pence to get me to Gindiri.

It was a real answer to prayer that the prison vehicle was made available to convey us to Mangu town. I got in the strong heavy lorry with the prisoners, and the cold that I experienced from the movement of the lorry was enough to freeze me to death. But as I shivered with the cold, I was talking to my Lord. I started singing to take my mind off the cold and in a way to let the prisoners hear the word of God in my song. I sang such songs as John 3:16 in Hausa and many others that I had learnt in Sunday School. Some of the prisoners asked where I was going. I told them I was going to school in Gindiri. One of them commented on the changing world - who would have thought of sending a girl like me to a school so far from home, if it were not for the white man and his ideas?

It happened that Mallam W Zitta and his family were also going to Gindiri in the same vehicle. He was going to the men's school. After we got off at Mangu, they decided to trek to Gindiri on foot. Both my mother and auntie used to send me to nearby markets about 12-15 miles on foot, and I would do both journeys on the same day, so trekking nine miles to Gindiri was no problem at all. I took my wooden box and even added some of their load to mine, because they had little children with them.

We arrived at Mangu quite early and we trekked to Gindiri in about three hours. They first accompanied me to the girls' school and then went on to settle at the family student's quarters. They were grateful for my help and for me their company was most appreciated because I would not have known what to do on arrival in Mangu. The Lord was with me through my silly youthful behaviour with money and He provided more that I had asked for. I reached Gindiri with more money in my purse and with almost everything I needed as well.

Because of my contribution to the housework, my auntie Mrs Shetur used to look forward to having me during the holidays. Whenever the Langtang students were going back to school or coming on holidays, the vehicle normally took a break in Pankshin. Sometimes we would spend days before we would finally get a vehicle to complete the journey.

Life at Boarding School

I used to have a friend, whom I love. Her name was Titi Bawado (later Titi Rindip). She used to say that as a girl I should not be free with boys, because boys are horrible and could ruin my life. She said it would be best to keep away from men and boys as much as possible and not even speak to them. It would be even worse when I was away from home. Men would find me easily, she said and I would be at a very dangerous age. I was shocked but I heeded her advice because it was sincere and meant for my good. When I arrived in Gindiri I would put my head down and pretend not to notice the boys or the men. I followed this advice so well that my behaviour seemed strange to most people. Soon they started to shower criticism on me. They said that I was proud and arrogant - that I was imitating the Europeans instead of behaving like a Nigerian. This criticism made me very sad. I became confused and worried. It did not occur to me that anybody would misinterpret my efforts to live a decent young girl's life.

After two years, my mother and father parted. Since she allowed me to go to school against my father's wishes, she had been my main provider. The clothes I first brought to school were now torn and I naturally needed some new ones. I did not know whether to send to my father or my mother, knowing that my mother had done so much for me. I felt my father too should meet some of my needs but I was not sure he would be pleased with me. I decided to write to both of them. I said how much I was enjoying my school work but that I was in serious need of some clothes: I had only one good dress - the other two were worn out. I used to

27

wash that one dress at night, then hope that it would be dry enough to iron and wear to school the next day.

My mother responded immediately by sending me two outfits that I liked so much. To my great joy my father also replied to my letter, much later, and enclosed a one pound note for me to sew my own dresses the way I liked them. This to me was his acceptance of my continuing education. I expected my father to ask why I went to Gindiri, after he had told me not to pursue further education as a girl. The Lord had put things right for me even without my taking the necessary steps. He knew my heart and so He acted on my behalf. With such an encouraging letter from my father, my poverty came to an end. I was able to sew two more dresses and even have some extra money left. I was better dressed than some girls in the school, so friends started borrowing from me. God really blessed that one pound. We used to wear each others clothes joyfully. We were all acting as members of the same family. Whenever any of us wished to dress well for any reason, we would borrow clothes from each other. Before the advent of uniforms, this was quite natural.

After some time the school authority decided to make uniforms for the girls in order to minimise borrowing. They told us of the dangers of borrowing clothes, but none of us listened or paid any attention. Then a girl came back from holidays with ringworm. And then we listened, because we were afraid of having patches on our skin, either on the head or the body. People started to hide their clothes, so that they would not be borrowed randomly. When the uniforms were made, everyone had clothes to wear.

I started to learn how to plait hair and became good at it. The girls would book me. Some would offer to carry out my work for me, so I could be free to plait their hair. Some would go to the market on my behalf, when it was my group's turn to go. Some would wash my few clothes, and others would iron them for me. So my whole weekend, including part of Sundays, was used for plaiting hair. My own hair remained unplaited. Some girls started learning the skill and later became experts too. We then had several plaiters and my plaiting load was lessened.

The Dream

One Sunday afternoon in Gindiri, I was tired and I decided to have an afternoon sleep. It was a visiting Sunday and female friends could visit us in the hostel. I slept so soundly that even though my next door neighbour had visitors and some of them were sitting on my bed I did not notice them. That afternoon I had a dream about my uncle Mallam Nimmel Kum, who had died in an accident when we were travelling home for the Christmas holidays in 1952 from Gindiri while he was training to be a Pastor. He appeared to me in the afternoon dream. I could only see his head high on the wall of a house in which I had never been before. He said he wanted to speak with me, and another girl from Langtang in the college. The two of us knelt before him. He said: 'You two girls, do you want to prosper in all you do? Then love the Lord and walk in his ways. This is all you need for your life'. He kept on repeating this. The other girl got up and walked away, while I continued to listen to him. In the end he said to me 'the Lord knows you, He has seen you, so keep on loving Him and obeying Him and walking in His ways. Go in peace my daughter'. I woke up from that afternoon's sleep and saw two Mwahavul women by my bed and my friend's. I greeted them but I was puzzled by the dream, so I went to a quiet place to read my Bible. After I had prayed, I opened my Bible to find words of comfort. I came to Deuteronomy 10:12 'And now, O Israel, what does the Lord God ask of you but to fear the Lord your God, to walk in all His ways, to love Him, to serve the Lord your God with all your heart and with all your soul'. This verse made me even more scared. I said to myself, perhaps I have not pleased my Lord and He is warning me. I fell on my knees and prayed that He should forgive me and put me on the right path. By the evening, my peace was restored and I carried on normally – praising the Lord but I was filled with a new joy.

Growing in Maturity

The school authority invited one Mr Piepgrass from the

Baptist Mission in Kaduna for a revival week. Many students gave their lives to Jesus. I was worried by my recent experience with my uncle in the dream and was not sure myself so said I needed to confess my sin in a more serious way. I could not think of anything in particular, but I believed I must have wronged my Lord. Mr Piepgrass's message was on repentance and at the end, he called for those who would like to receive the Lord as their Saviour to move forward. I did. As he listened to me, he said 'you are already a Christian, why did you come?' I told him how worried I was about the possibility that I might have wronged my Lord. 'I sincerely do not want to annoy Him in case He takes away His love from me. I want to live absolutely within His will for me. How can I do that. How can I be sure that I am a Christian?' I asked. Mr Piepgrass asked me to read Ephesians 1:8 'For it is by grace you have been saved through faith - and this not from yourselves, it is the gift of God, not by works, so that no one can boast.' With these verses he made me realise that it was not because I was good that the Lord had saved me, but by grace. The devil wanted me to doubt what the Lord had done for me and I should not doubt. I felt great relief and left Mr Piepgrass full of joy, because I had been assured that the Lord will never change or revert from saving me because I may have wronged Him. I should keep trusting and loving Him with all my heart and all my soul as He instructed me through my uncle in that dream.

Ruth Bincan (now Mrs Ruth Yamusa) was a girl who loved the Lord. She was very mature in her approach to life and close to me. We went through school together from 1953-1959. We were open with each other, and like all girls, we discussed our futures together. We were concerned about having good homes after our school career. She used to discuss with me some of the Jukun customs relating to marriage. In their custom, a girl whose virginity is not seen by her wedded husband is a disgrace to her and her family. When her husband meets her as a virgin, the sheet of her virginity would be taken to her mother with a token of appreciation from the husband and the news would get round to the other relations and friends. In this way the girl's prestige would be built or ruined depending on how pure she had kept herself or how spoilt she had been. Ruth and I grew to appreciate one another more and more as we shared in prayer. I was married before Ruth; she was my chief bridesmaid.

Some of us were sure of going to University, whilst I could not imagine life very far ahead without getting married. All we needed to do was to trust the Lord completely as a child would trust his father (Matthew 6:34).

My favourite song in the school at that time was "make new friends but keep the old, one is silver the other is gold". Good friends are a great treasure and should be chosen carefully. One of my friends was Clara Kitchener. Our friendship lasted a very long time and started at Gindiri. I visited her several times in Zaria and she visited me several times in Langtang. She has now been called to glory; I attended her funeral in Wusasa.

My Teachers

Long before I ever reached Gindiri I had heard about the headmistress there, a Miss Elsie Rimmer. Her reputation was well-known and I was half-scared, half-eager to meet her. However, the day we arrived it was Mama Bako who greeted us and made us welcome. Our proper accommodation was not yet ready so we were taken to a temporary hostel where we spread out our sleeping mats on the ground. There were 15 girls in all and Mama Bako was our first matron/cook who had the job of supervising us as we cooked our own meals.

It was after our first meal that Miss Rimmer arrived. I studied her in detail and concluded that she was a woman of integrity, a Christian woman whose Christian life radiated from her. She was firm and I instinctively knew that she was a woman to be obeyed. I was scared – and happy at the same time. Scared of myself in case I couldn't meet her standards, but happy that I was in the hands of a Christian who was a great disciplinarian.

Miss Rimmer was a slim, elegant elderly woman whom I greatly admired, in fact I even used to copy the way she walked! She was firm and knew just what she wanted and how her instructions were to be carried out. She was constantly inspecting the girls' hostels, and whenever she was starting her rounds news would spread like wild-fire and we quickly rushed to put our things in order. It wasn't that she was austere – rather that we were eager to please her for we loved her very much. She was always friendly to us and it was a constant source of amazement to us that she had never married. We wondered how such a nice woman could have remained single. It was only later that we realised that many white women at that time were prepared to give up the prospect of marriage in order to serve God as teachers and missionaries.

Classes were held in her house, for part of it had been converted into a classroom. We had a busy daily timetable, but nevertheless life at Gindiri was easier for me than it had been at home where I had always had to work hard. At home I also had to work without supervision so it was natural for me to do the same at school. Before long Miss Rimmer had picked me out as one of those in whom she could see leadership potential and Elizabeth Genka (now Mrs Elizabeth Dimka) and I were made prefects. Our happiness was complete! Mr and Mrs Ikan, who were acting as our house parents, also seemed to have a special liking for us.

But we weren't always perfect! One day when Miss Rimmer came on her inspection rounds, she caught Elizabeth and me hiding envelopes under our pillow cases. She considered this a serious crime because it looked as if we were being deceitful. A few other girls were also found out and we were told to move to a different room, away from the other girls. I was mortified and the experience affected me deeply. I never imagined that I could be a problem child after all the training that I'd had from my mother and auntie, and I hated myself. But eventually I went to the Lord in repentance and later summoned up the courage to go and see Miss Rimmer to tell her how sorry I was. I think she realised that her punishment had been unduly hard and she was apologetic too! She tried to encourage me by saying that it was important that all the girls should realise that none of us were above punishment if we deserved it, but that she held no grudge against us. She knew really that we were good girls. I thanked her and left, somewhat relieved and yet still there was a sadness inside. I prayed often that I would not fall into anything like this again. The Lord heard my prayer and I always managed to behave myself after that. By this time eighteen more girls had joined us at the school and it was becoming increasingly difficult to be tidy in the restricted space that we had. I suppose it was inevitable that Miss Rimmer had to become more strict with us, and really her discipline was a joy.

Some years after she left, I was called upon to play her part at an Open Day in 1959. I dressed up like her and talked like her. I wanted to grow up to be able to teach like she did.

I used to enjoy all my classes but some were more enjoyable than others. Miss Rimmer. was firm when necessary, yet she could be very relaxed with her pupils. She was a mother in the real sense. She took an interest in each student, praised where it was due and blamed when necessary, although even then she would take time to redirect that student.

Miss Blenko was our physical education teacher in early 1950. Most of us admired her walking style - she used to move with such dignity. She did not speak much, but taught her lessons very well. She made sure the girls did what she wanted. Anyone who got things wrong was called forward to watch the rest do it well, so that they could improve. Sometimes she would call a person who was good at an exercise to come forward and perform so that the others could copy. There were times when she would go round assisting individual girls to do better. However, I could never understand when she was pleased with us or not so pleased. She would praise or remark 'good' but would still remain calm. She had no favourites – she seemed to like us all equally.

Saturday inspections were something to look forward to because marks were added on the notice board, so that each group's performance was noted. The students knew that a total mark at the end of the year meant the whole group parading on the stage and the group leader receiving the school shield in front of the entire Gindiri population at the school's prizegiving day. Parents and visitors came from all over Nigeria to see the performances put out on display and these days left very happy memories of my time at school.

Girls used to go for a walk with the teachers on Sunday evenings, before singing songs from 5.00 - 6.00 p.m. On one of these occasions in 1950 Mr Morris, Miss Spencer and Miss Milverton were to take us for a walk. The two ladies were both very tall and the girls started to call Miss Spencer 'Gongola' (a tall bamboo). At the slightest thing Miss Milverton would say 'Oh dear!' Good or bad was all 'Oh dear, dear!' but from the tone in which she expressed herself you could tell whether it was joyful or otherwise. Our attention was all on the new teachers. We were not told where they were going to teach and we were anxious, for we wanted more contact with these smart teachers.

One evening Mr Morris, who in 1952 became the principal of the Teacher Training College, made me very happy. He arrived riding a bicycle, greeted the girls and called out 'Mary could you look after my bicycle please!' There were two Marys then, one was identified as Mary Pankshin, daughter of the late Mallam Ilya Kyauta, a prominent Christian man, who was then working as a teacher in Pankshin. I was known as Mary Langtang. The girls found it easier to identify us by our towns than our family's names. When Mr Morris called out for Mary, I was hesitant to move forward, until he qualified the name with Langtang - then feeling uplifted and important, I moved forward to look after the bicycle. I had never handled a bicycle before, so it was a real struggle for me to walk with it without getting into anybody's way; yet the joy that I was called upon to take care of the bicycle was worth the struggle. Girls looked at me and wondered, the same as I did, how this new teacher came to know my name. That kept me rejoicing for a long time. When I met him later in the English class at college I felt at home and faced him with much confidence. I appreciated very much his way of encouraging me. He taught us only for some months before

Miss Esler took over from him.

During my school years, as well as praying a good deal on my own, I had two special prayer partners, Victoria Job (later Dalaham) and Kwarama Bisalla (later Matta). We often went into the assembly hall for our prayer times together.

The Girls' Brigade

As a former captain of the 3rd Plateau Girls' Brigade Company in Langtang, I naturally yearned for Girls Brigade activities at Gindiri. On my own I mobilised the girls in Gindiri Girls' School and I was the Captain in command. I instructed them in marching, wand drills, and skipping and some other outside activities. Miss Rimmer came late one night at about 7.30 pm and Girls' Brigade activities involving more than sixty girls was in full swing. She stood behind the door watching us, and when she came out to us, she was full of praise. 'Perhaps we should have a Girls' Brigade company in the school' she suggested. I was delighted with the idea but it did not take off immediately.

Belonging to the Girls Life Brigade (as the Girls' Brigade was then known) was one of the highlights of my young days at Langtang. My first Girls' Brigade officers were Mrs Jump and Miss Kay Maxwell, daughter of one of the early pioneer SUM missionaries. She was always a great encouragement to me in many ways, not least from the Scripture verses we used to learn and the stories she told us. The instruction we received was wide-ranging, from laundry, cookery, hygiene and child-care to signalling and figure-marching. I always managed to do well and was often called out to demonstrate exercises to the other girls, and in fact my promotion to the rank of Commissioner was remarkably fast before I left for further training in the UK in 1962.

Chapter 3

COLLEGE LIFE 1952-1959

In 1952 we joined classes with the boys as the 3-year Elementary Teacher's Course was done together. I graduated in December 1955 with the Grade III Teachers' Certificate. I give God the glory for all of this because I know He helped me to trust Him and keep close to Him during that time. I was the second Tarok girl to have gone through the Elementary Teacher's Course and I became a teacher in the Junior Primary School at Langtang for two years from January 1956.

Queen Elizabeth II Visits Nigeria

In January, 1956, the Queen of England, Queen Elizabeth II, visited Nigeria. The preparation was exciting. School children from both primary and secondary schools were conveyed from all the northern part of the country to greet the queen. Before we left Gindiri, Ruth and I were asked to accompany the primary children from Plateau State to Kaduna. Both of us were new teachers and new to Kaduna but we accepted the responsibility. We met at St Theresa's Primary School in Jos, a day before we took off and were instructed by the Provincial Education Officer that about sixty children were entrusted to our care. They instructed the children to obey us and that all would be well with them. That night Ruth and I slept at the SUM Headquarters. In the morning we committed the journey and the children to the Lord in prayer.

The children behaved very well, with the exception of

some of the girls from the South who felt that they were more civilised than their teachers. We took our stand firmly and insisted on things being done the way that we had chosen and they began to understand that we were not stupid as they took us to be.

After a day's journey, we arrived at Kaduna and the vehicle that came to meet us at the train station took us to the Sacred Heart College, Kakuri, Kaduna, where we slept on the floor in our wrappers in one of the classrooms without any food. The next day, we were fed from the college's dining hall. The Queen's visit was in three days time, so we spent the week-end in Kaduna. On Saturday, some of the girls wanted to go into Kaduna, but we did not allow this.

On Sunday after breakfast we were encouraged to attend the school's chapel, which was a Roman Catholic service. It was the first Catholic service I had ever attended and I did not understand anything. After the service, they blew a whistle for all of us to go to the games field – we wondered if it were to give us some information. But then the Sister and some of the students arrived with balls, skipping ropes, etc. for games. I said that we were not used to playing games on Sundays and that we would not play, basing our argument on Exodus 20:8. The Sister insisted it was good for the children as they would have a long day, the next day, and that they needed able bodies to get them ready. So Ruth and I had some discussion and said that we would allow the children to play but that we could not. We stood at the side and watched them. Some of the girls stood by us, while the majority of them went to play. When the games were over, we accompanied the pupils to the hostel where we ate and slept.

The next day was the great day. We were all excited about meeting the Queen. We had an early breakfast and went to the big square, where we lined up. We were there for a long time. At last the Queen arrived, our tiredness was gone, we held our flags, the Union Jack of Great Britain, and waved a welcome to the Queen. All spoke of her beauty, and she greeted us with a wave of her hand.

On our return to Jos, parents were waiting to meet their children. We took our leave of them and went to our lodgings, thanking the Lord for helping us look after the children. It was a very happy memory.

After two years' teaching I went back again to Teacher Training College for the Grade II course (1958-59).

My College Teachers

My Domestic Science teacher, Miss Joyce Milverton, was British. She was a hard worker as well as caring for us on a personal level. We responded well to her teaching and in quite a short time we became good at Domestic Science. Miss Dinnick Parr, an examiner who used to come once a year from Kaduna, as external examiner for the final year students, always gave an excellent report about the Domestic Science classes at Gindiri, even writing on one occasion 'Anyone who wishes to observe excellent Domestic Science Classes should visit Gindiri'. I was proud to have been taught by Miss Milverton and to be part of this community which was so highly commended.

Cleanliness was high on her list of priorities. To me dirt was anything sticky or muddy, but Miss Milverton's description of dirt was anything which was in the wrong place. Thus, grease and mud in the right place were not dirt. She hated seeing soap wasted when washing. She explained that the more water we added to soap while washing, the more soap it consumed. I used to wonder why she was so concerned about wasting water, when it came from a well and was not bought with money, but later I realised she was right when some of the wells dried up!

She taught that we should care for the sick with smiling faces and encouraging remarks. When giving them food we should serve it in attractive dishes, serving only the best food to entice them to eat. Their rooms should be well aired, dust free and beautified with flowers. She taught us how to use tinned food - to open it and use it quickly, not to warm it in the tin as we used to do previously. We should fill a hot water bottle by bending the neck to let the air out and then to wrap it in towels, so that it was not too hot to handle.

Miss Milverton was interested in us but she wanted everything done perfectly, which was very demanding. If we made a mistake it was 'Oh dear, dear, dear!' Yet she encouraged us with 'good, that's very good, that's right'. We used to feel that some mistakes in knitting could be pardoned, so we would cover it up and carry on, but Miss Milverton would insist that we undo the whole thing and put it right. Realising she was like this I soon tried not to make any mistakes.

Miss Milverton encouraged us to consult her at any time, including in her house. Domestic Science classes therefore took place anywhere. Many girls used to visit her after school and she never complained about being disturbed. I would have been very slow at this subject if I had relied solely on class teaching but in the end I passed it with merit.

I found Miss J E Spencer a great disciplinarian. I had my moments of joy with her but also moments of doubt. There were four girls in our class, Ruth Bincan (the favourite), Lydia Imande, Virginia and myself. Amongst the boys we thought Thomas Kola Adeyanju was her favourite because she called on him a great deal in class. I kept Miss Spencer's notes until I was teaching my Grade II students at Government Teacher's College in Jos in 1976 as they were still relevant. She was good at mathematics and used her eyes to control the class, which method I later copied for my Sunday School.

Miss Pixie Caldwell taught us English and also to trust God with every detail of our lives. I used to be very fearful, so much so that the girls called me *mai tsoro* (the fearful), but we can be bold and courageous in Jesus. She said that if we trust in the Lord, then we need not fear anything. Fear is doubt she explained, then she gave me a tract entitled 'Fear' that helped me.

I consider myself very fortunate to have been exposed to such a good all-round education. This is a special inheritance and I pray that the Lord will make it possible for me to pass it on to the younger generation. I have a burden to establish a college for girls that will take the same form of training girls for academic, physical, social, spiritual and emotional efficiency.

I value all the people who taught me, who gave not just abstract knowledge but imparted some quality of life as well and advised and guided us to a better future. I give praise and thanks to God for each one of them.

Cameroon Visit

In my final year, December 1959, I was elected head girl. The majority of the girls co-operated with me, so the responsibility was easy. I was also picked by my Principal to represent my college in Cameroon for a Man O' War Bay course. We were the first women participants in such a course for girls from the colleges of Nigeria, and it was quite an adventure for me as I had never before travelled outside Northern Nigeria. It was a long train journey and other girls joined us on the way. That in itself was quite a culture shock as the Nigerians further south seemed equally primitive. There were some unkind words spoken but I tried to avoid the disputes about which people were the more progressive.

As the miles passed and the distance from home became greater, a loneliness and insecurity stole over me. Seeing the peasants on a market day in Ogoja with their bodies decorated with red and white designs, and feathers sticking out as if for some kind of festival, made me quite fearful. I was told they always dressed that way, but I could not wait for the white ladies who were with us to finish taking their photographs so we could get away. I prayed silently, fearful of being attacked. In my heart I recited Psalm 23 and I felt God was encouraging me to trust Him.

At last we reached the town of Mamfe on the border of Nigeria and Cameroon. By this time I was totally overcome with weariness and utterly homesick. We spent the night at the Catholic Compound School. We were awoken at 5.00 am the next morning. The land was thickly forested and I feared wild animals. My continuing fear did not stop the journey, however, so I determined to set my eyes on Jesus and not on the forest! Eventually we arrived at Kumba and were given some money to buy food in the market. Even as we got out of the lorry the Kumbians started to stone us shouting,

'Nigerians go. Go back to your country. We don't want you here!' We hastily got back into the lorry and it was explained to us that their behaviour was due to some local political conflict with Nigeria of which we had not been aware. We travelled on to the next town where it was more peaceful, and ultimately arrived at Victoria, by which time it was late at night. Thankfully we were made welcome and given a meal of rice and plantain before being shown to our rooms.

The next day we were given Man O' War Bay attire. This was my first experience of wearing trousers and I felt as if my status had been changed to that of a man! Soon I made friends with the other girls – especially when they knew I could plait their hair! Everybody was divided into groups, or houses, and I was in Mary Slessor's. All that we did as individuals counted as points for the house so everybody had to behave well in order to score marks for their group. Hard work and efficiency in all activities and service was recognised and marks assigned accordingly. Marks were also subtracted for lateness or bad behaviour such as untidiness, carelessness with property etc. The overall winners would be announced at the end of the course.

Seeing the Ocean

The hostel where we lived was a tall building right on the sea and we had a wonderful time, only spoilt by the sandflies which tried to make our lives miserable during the day. They were different from the ones we had back home, probably because of the coastal location.

I had never seen the sea before and I marvelled at it. In fact in my dreams I saw it coming towards me. I enjoyed the evenings too when we would relax and learn Man O' War Bay songs. We were encouraged to teach one another songs from our own home areas, and as Christian choruses were the only ones I knew, I taught them some of those, which seemed to be appreciated just as much as the others.

I had always liked physical activity so I enjoyed taking part in the vigorous training we had in canoeing, swimming, mountain climbing, rope climbing, sport and games. On the first day when we arrived, the girls from

Lagos and Ibadan, who were bigger than us and better off than we were, mocked those of us who were smaller and from the villages. They even said 'Who brought such a thing here? Who brought this weak, primitive girl to come and die here?' I did not say a word but I determined to show them!

I excelled in most of the activities. Swimming and canoeing I found most difficult, but I prayed God to help me and within two weeks I was participating in a hundred yard swimming race and came third out of the fourteen competitors. By His grace I had also conquered my fear of the sea as I participated in canoeing. The big girls from Lagos and Ibadan who had been so full of themselves tried to dodge most of these activities!

Climbing the Mountain

On one memorable occasion we set out to climb Mount Cameroon. I had spent much time in prayer asking the Lord to help me so that the abuse of the other girls would be thrown back at them. We trekked to the mountain base which was tiring enough. With our haversacks we climbed the mountain and by the evening we arrived at a camp built by the Germans on the mountainside. There we ate and relaxed and played games together. Although we knew there were wild animals on the mountain, we only saw harmless ones like baboons and chimpanzees. The next day we continued our climb and my feet and thighs ached. It was tough and many of the girls gave up. I knew the Lord was supporting me and renewing my strength, giving me the ability and energy to climb, especially when it was really difficult.

Thirsty, hungry and cold, we arrived at the second mountain camp where the whole area was black from volcanic eruptions. A strong cold wind was blowing and we were told that the girls who had got this far would be awarded high marks, as if they had reached the summit. Seven of us determined to struggle on with the instructors, one of whom was Miss Gentle who was then Principal of Queen's College, Yaba. The instructors encouraged us and helped me whenever I felt like giving up. 'Yes, Mary, you have done it, just take one more step, now another. You are there.' And so, one step at a time, I eventually managed to reach the very top of the mountain. All over the area were deep pits caused by the volcanic eruption. The wind at the top was so strong that I was afraid of being blown away! I remembered how Jesus stopped the winds that disturbed the boat when He was crossing the lake with His disciples. But that was in a situation where the wind just suddenly arose against them, whereas up there in the mountains there is always a strong wind. Should I pray to the Lord to stop the winds? 'No,' I concluded. Instead of doing that I would trust Him and pray that He would keep me firm. I remembered the words to Joshua in Joshua 1:9, 'Have I not commanded you? Be strong and courageous. Do not be terrified; do not be discouraged, for the Lord your God will be with you wherever you go.' I suddenly became bold and strong. I started moving without fear. I realised that it was the Lord who had given me His strength and my heart was overjoyed. Our instructors were able to go over to help and encourage some of the other girls who were lacking in confidence.

Eventually I turned out to be an instructor myself and was able to encourage others in the same way. It is good to know how true the Bible is when it has encouraging words like those in Isaiah 40:31, 'Those who hope in the Lord will renew their strength. They will soar up on wings like eagles, they will run and not grow weary, they will walk and not faint'.

Back to Base

Cameroon mountain is 13,353 feet high, the highest in West Africa. It took us a much shorter time to come down the mountain but it was a dangerous descent as the slightest mistake could result in a big tumble from top to bottom. Our legs were shaking with fatigue and by about 4.30 pm we arrived at the first base and were joined by those whom we had left there. Many of those were the big girls from Ibadan and Lagos who had mocked me. They could not believe that I had reached the very top of the mountain! I told them I did it because 'I could do everything through Him who gave me strength' (Philippians 4:13).

That evening our achievements were on the Cameroon radio. As usual the news was that African girls are now proving equal to the men. It was the first time that Nigerian and Cameroon girls had climbed the Cameroon mountain – previously only European women had done it. The wife of the premier of Western Cameroon, Her Excellency Mrs Endele was full of praise for us. She entertained us in her house which was quite an experience! The house was so magnificent I could hardly describe its beauty, and I was so proud to be able to be there.

The next day the seven of us were in the newspaper. They called us 'the seven exceptional girls who reached the very summit of the mountain', and there was a picture of us at the bottom of the article. This event enabled me to earn high marks for my house, Mary Slessor, and the others were really pleased. All the instructors and staff were involved in the evaluation. On the last day of the Man O' War Bay event all the marks were added together and there was a big celebration for the winning house. Kingsley's house came first and my house, Mary Slessor, was second. Praise the Lord! Marks were also awarded to individuals and the one with the highest marks was Habiba Isah from the Women's Teachers' College, Kano. She was a gifted sports girl and had the advantage of coming from Shendam where she had learnt to swim in the Shendam river.

I did not score very highly in swimming or canoeing but improved my position by my success in mountain climbing. I was also able to score highly in service. The instructors noticed that I spent a lot of my time plaiting hair and they awarded marks to me for this. How true it is that even the world wants us to behave the way the Bible tells us, so that whatever we find ourselves doing, eating or drinking, we should do it with all our might and to the glory of God (1 Corinthians 10:31). Whoever would have thought that marks would be awarded for hair plaiting! We take these small things for granted.

We were at the Man O' War Bay camp in Cameroon for just three weeks. It was a wonderful experience for me and kept me happy for a long time. My report was sent to Miss J

E Spencer, my Principal in Gindiri. When she read it she sent for me from class and praised me highly. 'Well done, Mary!' she said. 'You have not shamed the college. The leadership course you attended in Cameroon spoke well of you.' I scored 'A' for everything which both pleased and surprised me. I gave thanks to God and left the Principal's office with much joy in my heart. I told my parents the news and of course they were happy too.

Home Again

During the holidays I went to inform my chief in the village, *Ponzhi Garba Wuyep* and he was glad that I had been able to be a representative for our area, and he was glad I had been a good ambassador for Langtang. When the Bible tells us that we are to be the ambassadors of Christ, we can be either good or bad ambassadors, representing Him in whatever we are doing. Every detail of our lives is seen daily by the world – not just our academic achievements. At the end of our lives we will be judged by what kind of ambassadors we have been for Him. It will be a day of great joy for some – and great sorrow for others.

The pastor of our church in Langtang, the Revd D Bawado, asked me to give an account in church of my experiences, to encourage the other girls. They were amazed and full of admiration for me, even though I did not tell them about the excellent report that I had had. That a girl could go so far away and come back safely was a new experience for the whole village.

The leadership course taught me a number of things. Prior to that time I used to see achievement only in terms of academic performance. Now I realised that physical and social achievements could be equally important. Also I recognised the value of the early training I had had at home, having to help with the physical work and take responsibilities in the family. I realised that such training is a great help in coping with more demanding things later in life. For myself, I just praise the Lord for preparing me and giving me the ability to fulfil all that I set out to do. The underlying secret is in maintaining daily contact with Him.

After Cameroon I had only one more year to finish my Higher Elementary Teachers' Course. I settled back into college work but was still always afraid of failure. In fact fear was my greatest enemy and I had constant battles to conquer it. What caused the fear? I had a great many responsibilities at that time. As well as being Head Girl I was second to Miss Summerville in charge of the Sunday School in the chapel. I was secretary of the African Challenge Magazine, secretary of my house, Maxwell House, and I participated in the Drama Club and the Debating Society. All of this involved a good many meetings and so I was afraid that I might not get through my examinations – which after all was the main reason for my being at Gindiri. My one comfort was the Lord who always assured me that He was with me and He helped me when I retired to do my homework after late meals.

Soon we were waiting for the result of our year's work. To my great surprise my results not only showed that I had passed in all the subjects, but also that I had three credits. This was an extra bonus for me. When the Lord blesses, He blesses abundantly!

The Higher Elementary Training Course at Gindiri was very highly thought of at that time. There were only three girls in my class at Gindiri. Most of the rest were young married men, although there were a few who were single. We respected the married ones and in a way they acted like parents to us. One Sunday afternoon each month we were allowed to visit our colleagues in the compound and we used to visit the married ones in their compound. That way we had the opportunity to get to know the families of our colleagues, and their wives kindly cooked meals for us.

Chapter 4

THE MAN GOD HAS CHOSEN FOR ME

When I attained the age of 16, society expected me to get married and to start raising a family but I was not ready for this. It was my greatest desire to further my education, taking the opportunity which God had so generously offered me although it was not that I could not find a man to marry me.

It got to the point when my parents threatened they would withdraw me from school to give me away in marriage to a most prosperous man, whom they considered right for me! My desire for school was so strong that it became difficult to maintain our relationship and my parents sadly watched as I left home. But the Lord, who knows and plans all our lives, gave me the grace to cope with the bad feelings resulting from this. It was a period of great concern to my parents, who felt I was getting too old and perhaps not likely to marry well, but I trusted the Lord and my heart was at peace. I carried on joyfully at school. All my interest was geared towards education. There were those who praised me for my courage but others made very discouraging remarks, that I was wasting human seed, or that I was getting too old and would probably not find it easy to get married at all.

One of the customs of the Tarok people was to sing songs about people and when I returned home for the holidays the local people would sing that I was as beautiful as a teacher's wife! That was great praise because teachers were the elite of society at that time. They sang that my beauty qualified me to be driven in a car! However, by the time I became a primary school teacher the tone of the songs had changed. They sang that Mary was destroying seeds by not getting married, and other such damaging things. I was really angry and determined that I would never marry a Tarok man. In fact I didn't even wish to remain in the Tarok community.

God Overrules

By the time I was 18, I was more mature and started to make moves of my own to settle down into marriage. I considered marrying someone from outside my own ethnic group. I wanted to move away from a society that had disturbed me so much, and secondly I wanted to marry someone from a more civilised society. But God, who knows the future, controlled everything for me. As I was planning to be married to a non-Tarok man at Easter, I received a letter from my former teachers in Gindiri, Mr and Mrs J S C Farina. In it they expressed concern about this marriage. They said that it would thwart the objectives for which they had trained me, ie to serve my own people. They promised they would work for me to take the Grade II entrance examination, if I would reconsider the step I was about to take.

At the same time a letter came from Zaire urging me to get married quickly, because the man I was about to marry would not take it kindly if I refused him at the last hour. I was worried and confused, so I took the two letters to my church to be alone with God and prayed over each letter. I wanted God to show me clearly his will for me. Nothing seemed clear, so I decided I would take the Grade II entrance examination and if I should pass, then I would go for the course, while I would continue to pray. I said 'Lord, I am waiting patiently for you to provide a good husband for me'. Even though I prayed this prayer, I did not actually wait for long.

Meeting Solomon

I had heard about Solomon Lar and what I had heard had endeared him to me but I had no opportunity to come closer to him, until, one Christmas holiday in 1956, when we went to Gindiri for a Christian leadership course. This course used to bring students and former students from all over Nigeria for a spiritual revival. That year most teachers from Langtang were reluctant to attend the course, but I insisted that I had to go. At the same time, Solomon also insisted that he had to go, despite the transport and other difficulties that we faced. Without any prearrangement, we found ourselves the only two people who were bent on attending the course. Because we travelled with a common objective, we kept together. Solomon took care of me and I found my heart warming towards him.

On arrival at Mangu, we both spent the night at the house of friends. This family had two former students: the young man was a friend of Solomon's at Gindiri and his sister was also my friend from school.

The next morning, we found a vehicle that conveyed us to Gindiri. The course, which normally lasts a week, provided me with a good opportunity to see more of Solomon's spiritual side. He played an active role in the course, eg reading the scriptures, leading the services or doing most of the translating from English into Hausa. I watched him with great admiration.

After the course, I was planning to get transport to travel back home, but Solomon told me he had already made arrangements for our return journey. It was such a relief and I was very grateful. The vehicle took us to Pankshin and terminated there. We got into another one which took us through Dengi, Bashar and Wase before reaching Langtang. This was a longer route, but as it was the only transport available we joined it happily. Solomon bought us some food in Dengi and the last bit of the journey was full of emotions - we found ourselves holding hands together from Bashar to Langtang. At the end of the journey we bade each other goodbye but I found my heart constantly reflecting on the journey.

We heard nothing else from each other for a long time, but when I arrived home for the next Christmas holiday, Solomon sent some money to my mother saying that it was to help her to look after her visitor - and that visitor was me! Solomon invited my friend Ruth Bincan and me to his house for supper on Christmas Eve, with some of his friends. The meal was full of fun and then they escorted us back home. We continued to live separately and yet our hearts were now together.

Marriage Proposal

Several of us took the entrance examination for the Grade II course and three of us from Langtang district passed. In my first year, Solomon wrote and congratulated me for making such a wise decision. I was the first Tarok girl to achieve this status. During this period in Gindiri, I received more proposals, which made me more and more confused. Solomon had never really come out openly to express his intentions about me, so I was not sure of the type of relationship he had in mind, yet he frequently wrote me letters which were inquisitive and encouraging. I usually replied to his letters instantly. This went on until the end of the year when we went home for the Christmas vacation. It was his senior brother, the late Mallam Ibi Nimak Lar, a Church elder, who visited my mother's house and released the news of his brother's intentions towards me. Although within me I was certain that this was the man I had grown to love more than all who had come my way, I still hesitated to give an instant reply and asked for time to think it over. He left us with a gift that solved much of my mother's financial difficulties at that time.

A Fleece to the Lord

I tried to control my feelings to allow me to get a clear assurance from the Lord. After some days of prayer, I decided to ask the way Gideon did in the Bible. I knew that as a Christian I should walk by faith and not by sight but this to me was urgent and I felt that God must do something to assure me of the step I should take. I could not go on waiting for life. Surely God wanted me to get married but to whom? I did not want to make mistakes all my life. I said to my Lord 'You have led me thus far - now please put an end to the matter concerning the choice of a husband'.

One evening as my mother was preparing some Sudan potatoes *risga* for supper, the Lord put into my mind to take four of the potatoes of various sizes and to label them with the names of those who had proposed marriage to me and on the fourth to put 'wait', meaning that none of the other three were to be for me. I left the potatoes all night in the path of the rats and asked the Lord to allow the rats to eat a bit of the one that was his choice for me and to leave the rest untouched. I went early in the morning to the 6.00 am prayer meeting and when I came home I went to check on the potatoes. A miracle had happened. Three were left untouched whilst the one bearing Solomon's name had completely disappeared! This was a miracle because normally nothing would have been left uneaten in the rats path. I had my answer!

The Answer is 'Yes'

After this joyous experience, all became clear. I would wait for Solomon's brother to call again and then I would give a positive reply. I said 'God has been preparing us for a long time, without our knowing it, and I believe Solomon is my chosen husband'.

From that day on the courtship began. I introduced him to my mother as was the custom. Solomon's family tried to satisfy my mother's requirements eg farming various crops for her and building some female huts for her. Then they asked her to introduce them to my father's people, so that they could also meet their requirements in preparation for the wedding. My mother did not hesitate and they built male huts for my father and farmed male crops for him. This is usually compensated for with money. In the next year, all requirements were met, both from my mother's and my father's side and the 30 January 1960 was fixed for the wedding. I was married at the age of 23.

The Wedding

It was not surprising that the wedding was the best ever witnessed in Tarok land up to that time. I had 12 bridesmaids and I sewed all their dresses - they were in pink and the two flower girls were in blue. Flash photographs were taken and an organ was played in church. It was the first wedding that had a wedding cake in the area. The first wedding that witnessed the church full to the brim, with people all but sealing the windows. It was also the first wedding where a large sum of money was collected at the marriage ceremony and gifts sent from far and near, including gifts from the missionaries. In short, it was a grand wedding. All our relations were present. My mother was very pleased and proud of me that day. Our Pastor, the late Revd Damina Bawado did not hide his joy over our coming together. He said to us that he could see that God would use us greatly in the future; he was content that both of us were Christians and also teachers. He advised us to live in the fear of the Lord and the Lord would bless us.

There was no way we could sleep on the day of the wedding. There were dances and merriment until dawn in the new home. The next day, visitors started arriving as early as 6.00 am. Sleeplessness went on for about a week and I was getting tired but I could not say so because Solomon had earlier reminded me that as his wife, I had to be prepared to respect people. He could pardon anything but giving offence to the poor. I was impressed by his love and concern for the less privileged, which I associated with the love of Christ for the poor and needy. We were cooking and serving all the time. Sometimes, when people were not around, he would say 'cook enough food and keep it for when they come'.

When we got married, we moved into an apartment given to us by his relation Baba Bincan. Because of this I was not privileged to have all the early morning wake-up and serving of my in-laws, even though the usual *amora* was cooked and sent round to our relations and neighbours. After a month, I returned to my parents' home to prepare for a permanent life in my husband's house. This was the custom.

After I had completed my Grade III Teacher's course, I taught for two years before I left for further studies in Gindiri. I used to receive £12 per month, which was split three ways. £3 to my mother, £4 to my uncle (the one who sent me to school) and £5 to myself. I was able to buy all my dishes and a sewing machine, ready for when I would move into my husband's house. Relations contributed grains, dishes and soup ingredients and together with friends, they conveyed all these items to my new home. This meant another ceremony. They had to sweep the whole compound and share *amora* food again. Then my husband had to give back to them a token of appreciation.

I soon settled in to my husband's house. People came to advise us. Outstanding amongst them was the late Baba Ladapo, a Yoruba businessman in Langtang, who was highly respected for his Christian ideals and his ability to mix with the Tarok people. He said 'Now that you are happily married, there are people who are not happy to witness this successful wedding, and they would do anything to break your house down. You should watch them. Do not listen to anything said about each other without proving it for yourselves. Some of these sayings are intended for evil'. He prayed for us and left.

My auntie Mama Darmicit Tintin, invited me to her house and gave me some advice too. She said I should know that many marriages are broken because of the wife's personality. The wife may fail to respect her husband, especially in front of his friends; she emphasised that men do not like that. She warned me against being rude to my husband, or saying things contrary to my husband's views. I thanked her and left for my new home. I had no cause to be rude to my husband because I loved him and I considered myself very fortunate to be given a man like him, well liked and respected by his people, who had elected him to represent them in the House of Parliament. I could not think what might cause me to be rude to a person like this. We went for a honeymoon in Lagos. It was the first time I had been up in an aeroplane. It was a great experience.

Our First Child

After a year people were expecting the blessing of my marriage. They looked forward to me having a baby, but there was no sign of this. Some people made discouraging statements like 'Mary will never have a baby - she is one of these girls who may never have children'. They said Solomon had married me for my education and that that would be his only gain from me. He should not expect any children.

Dr Hartley in Vom Christian Hospital removed a cyst from one of my ovaries and conception took place soon after the operation. Our first child, a daughter Chalya, arrived almost two years after our marriage. The Lord has wiped away our tears. We praise Him always.

An Opportunity to Study in the UK

I was quite contented after my Grade III just to live happily with my husband but because I had earlier prayed for education, the Lord continued to open doors for me. My husband suggested that I should apply for a scholarship to study in the United Kingdom. That was a high ambition, I thought. The newspapers advertised that they needed qualified women to be trained abroad, so that they could come back and man our schools. I reluctantly gave my consent as there were no higher institutions in Nigeria with the same training facilities, only the Advanced Teachers College in Zaria, which was opened the same year I left for Britain. Solomon went to Kaduna to obtain the scholarship forms.

It was like a joke when we saw it in the papers and then heard that I had been admitted into St Katherine's College in Tottenham, London. I could not believe that this was happening. I really wanted to carry on having my home and my children but Solomon felt that opportunity comes only once and that we should not miss it. He organised a party for me and Chalya in Langtang, which was well attended by prominent Tarok and non-Tarok people. Many gave advice that helped me. They said I should work hard and come back well equipped to make a positive contribution to my country. Some gave me verses in the Bible like Joshua 1:9. I should remember the Lord my God would be with me, wherever I go. Songs were sung. At the end I shed tears of joy for the overwhelming support given to me by my people, and the fear of the unknown. I felt elevated in spirit and very important. Some said 'you are the first Tarok girl to come out with a good Grade II Certificate; the first Tarok to have such a wonderful wedding and now the first Tarok woman to be trained abroad'. How wonderful! I quickly bowed my head and said 'Lord humble me. I do not deserve your many blessings upon me, except by your grace'.

We had to be vaccinated against small pox, yellow fever, cholera etc and to get a passport. Our relatives were not happy. Some bade us a final goodbye because they feared we might not meet them when we came back after three years. The goodwill of the people and the memory of them all was such a treasure. I needed it all to keep me going in a foreign land. My chosen husband is very much a progressive husband. He believed he would rise in status and that his wife must be able to climb with him. Obviously full of the love of Christ, he too waits on the Lord for everything. The missionaries knew this, so they took a special interest in him.

The Lord knows where His children are and works out how to bring them together in His own time and in His own way. All we need to do is to submit ourselves to His purposes and will for us. I believe my greatest blessing here on earth is the gift of my husband Solomon. He has been very supportive in every way. The American doctor said 'Mrs Lar, you are very lucky to have such a good husband'. The people of the world describe such a situation as 'luck' but truly it is God's gift and His continuous love for me. I can only say 'thank you Lord for answering my prayers'.

Chapter 5

LONDON 1962-1965

It was in September 1962 that I and Chalya, my daughter, who was ten months old, left Langtang with Solomon to travel to Lagos. We stayed in the Leggico flat, assigned to Members of Parliament, while we made our final preparations for London . We bought what we thought was warm clothing for the winter but we discovered later that it was too light to stand the cold in London.

We left about the middle of September, on a midnight flight for students, arriving in London in the morning. I had my baby in a cot, my own bag and one for her. I could not manage everything on my own but there was no one to help. The Nigerians merely pushed past me but many English people who were working at the Airport recognised that I needed some help and ran to assist me. One of them said to the Nigerians 'you guys came with this woman but could you not help her?' I felt good that there were people there not only to sympathise and help me but to rebuke on my behalf. I saw the Englishmen as kinder than my fellow countrymen. We were received by the Nigerian High Commissioner and were taken to the British Council hostel. I was overwhelmed by my first sight of London!

My first surprise was the uniformity of the houses. I had never seen anything like it. Then I was shocked to see the rampant smoking everywhere. I had come from a missionary background, strictly absenting ourselves from habits that are harmful to our bodies such as drinking and smoking, which were termed as worldly. The white people I had seen back home were mostly missionaries, who kept off these things. Like them, we believe our bodies are the temple of God and we should honour God with our bodies as instructed in I Corinthians 6:19. For me to see the whites making nonsense of my belief was a great shock. I had not understood that all English or white people are not necessarily Christians. It took me a long time to realise that.

Dr Striesow, who had offered to arrange for foster parents for my daughter, met me at the British Council and took Chalya away from me to a Mr and Mrs Gilmour in Forest Gate, London. I became lonely and sleepless thinking of my daughter and how she was faring.

At the British Council hostel we had some three days orientation in London, then we were given the addresses of our colleges to go to on our own. I thought it would be easy. My college was in White Hart Lane, Tottenham, so when I saw Tottenham Court Road on the tube map, I did not know the difference. I just jumped out of the tube and found myself in London's West End. I started to ask outside where St Katherine's College was but nobody knew and there was no sign of a college. I came back to the tube station where I was advised to telephone the college and find the directions from them. I had never used a telephone, so I could not do it. I asked a lady to help me but she could not get through so she returned my fourpence and walked away. People were walking as if they were pursuing something. I stood there cold and tired. I clung to a lady who seemed kind, she telephoned a taxi and the taxi took me to the college. It cost me about £4.00! Whatever the cost, I was delighted to arrive at my college. I was shown to my room. It was on the ground floor of Devonshire Hostel. I saw many papers on my door, each with my name on. Each was welcoming me and informing me of certain activities in the college - trying to win membership from new students. I read each one and was particularly delighted to have a special Christian welcome from the Christian Union of St Katherine's College. I decided to try the Christian Union, the choir, country dancing (for exercise) and the children's club. The Christian Union invited me to coffee/tea in one of the hostels. I responded and soon discovered that they were real Christian people, with love and care for others.

I soon discovered that some English people were good at the first meeting but after that they changed. They would give a false smile; they were often racist and hardly accepted foreigners, especially blacks. I started to prefer my own people - those whom I had heard an Englishman describe as 'inconsiderate gentlemen' at the airport, but they could be kinder. I was so lonely! I kept on my knees all the time and asked so many questions. 'Is this London?', I said to myself 'Then I would rather be back home' - but I was too far away now to do that.

The Striesaws telephoned the hostel and told me I could visit my daughter. It was not easy finding the way. I was delighted to see Chalya but she was crying for food and the house did not look clean. Mrs Gilmour had two children of her own and was expecting a third, so she did not find it easy to look after the house as well. Her husband, a seaman, spent weeks or months away from home. Her house was so disorganised. I felt uncomfortable leaving my daughter with her but I had no choice. The college was designed only to meet the needs of students, rooms and beds were only big enough for one person - there was no extra room. I took the matter to the Lord and left it there.

I felt lonely in this college, even though I found another Nigerian girl, Joanna Ibimidun, on arrival. She said she sat near me on the plane but that I was deeply involved then with my daughter. She saw my struggle with the baby but as she did not know who I was, she went her way. Joanna was from Kwara State but she lived and went to school in Lagos, so she was more exposed to civilisation than I was.

We went for registration and I wanted to register for divinity but the reverend gentleman who was the head of that department rejected me. He said 'No you cannot do it, you have no background in it'. I am glad I did not register for it, for in the end I discovered that it was not the type of Bible knowledge that we were taught at home. They did not even believe in some portions of the scriptures but I still took it as a second subject. The lectures were boring and occasionally ridiculous. For instance they would take a subject like Christmas and start to argue whether Christmas day was indeed the date of the birth of Christ. I thought to myself 'if this is what they style divinity, then I can do without it'! But as the teaching got deeper, we started taking the major and minor prophets, parables and their meanings. These were more like the divinity I expected and the subject became more interesting. But the reverend gentleman who was teaching it lived a life contrary to his teaching - he was smoking and exhibiting the greatest racism I had ever seen. On some occasions I prayed for him and on some occasions I got angry and left. When I attempted to speak to him, he would not listen. I was the only non-white in that class but I managed to complete his course, which lasted two years. They had suggested that I should register for fine arts, English, divinity, integrated science and social studies, which I did.

Fellowship

I was fortunate to be in England the same year as some of my townsmen. People like Domkat Bali, who was at Sandhurst Army College, Nanven Garba, who was in Kent and Mallam Ezekiel Yusufu who was in Swansea. Lawal Abdullahi, who was a Law student and Bitrus Gani. Sussannah Alheri, who was together with me in Gindiri, was in Salisbury and Mr and Mrs B Kato were in London studying for his BD at the University. It was a comfort that some people I knew were near by. I used to feel at home when they visited me at college. We would discuss home until we all became homesick.

Miss Joyce Milverton, my domestic science teacher at Gindiri Teacher's College, now at home to look after her mother, lived in Cockfosters not too far from my college. She wrote and invited me to her house. It was a real joy for me to have someone in London I knew I could run to at anytime. This gave me more confidence at college.

I worked very hard in all my subjects and I was happy, despite the loneliness I was going through. I derived great joy from the marks obtained for my work. I expected little or nothing from people around me but I tried to give my own services. No one had the time in the early mornings to find out how anybody was faring, like we do at home. No one knocked at the door to say 'come let's go, it is time for this or that' like we do at home. The practice at home was to ask somebody to wake one up in the morning, but here I was advised to buy an alarm clock to do the job, which I did! Actually what I really wanted was the human sound of being woken up.

My contact with Miss Joyce Milverton made all the difference to my stay in London. She offered me a room in her house where I could go at anytime. I used to spend my week-ends visiting my daughter at Forest Gate or visiting Miss Milverton, where I was introduced to the Farrows, her neighbours, and Mr and Mrs Bryan and Connie Calkin. Cockfosters became my home in London and I really praised the Lord for that.

As Mrs Gilmour's pregnancy drew nearer to delivery, she found great difficulty in looking after the children. Whenever I visited them I found Chalya unwashed and she appeared hungry. I used to buy her biscuits and sweets. She seemed to know that they were from her mother, so she would hold tight to them and not want to share them with Mrs Gilmour's two other children, but after a show, she willingly shared them.

I was getting more concerned and wanted a change of place for her but I did not know where to take her. It got so bad that I went quietly and brought my daughter to the college but that was not realistic. The students came round admiring Chalya. They asked many questions like 'Where are you going to keep her'? It was night time and I did not know what to do, with no mother and no auntie to turn to. I remembered Miss Milverton and so I rang her up and told her of my difficulty. She asked me to come immediately. I stayed with her for one week and she was able to find a nicer home for my daughter. The new home that Joyce Milverton found was good and more caring. She was obviously very well looked after and one could see a great difference. The foster parents already had two other children from Barbados. They invited me to stay with them for a week so that I could decide whether Chalya would be happy with them. Although I paid for my week with them I appreciated the opportunity to stay with Chalya and this provision gave me peace of mind.

Joyce Milverton was a God-given guardian to me in England as she took my burden as her own. She took great delight in catering for me, without charging me anything for it. I was challenged by her concern and love in many ways. While the cold in England slowed me down, she was very energetic and could get on with all the housework and look after her mother in the most loving and efficient way. I noticed that she had her devotions three times a day. It had never occurred to me to have devotions in the afternoons. It made me reflect on the Lord at such odd times too. It had been my practice to have my devotions in the morning and in the evening but Miss Milverton showed me a third way. I believe the Lord prefers us to come to Him even more than three times a day. With Miss Milverton I learnt some more cooking and she gave me good Christian books to read. She was always cheerful. We would attend her church services at Christ Church, Cockfosters, which I grew to love very much. She took me to SUM Summer Camps, where I received many blessings from the fellowship. It seemed I was in London to receive more training from her. She did not hesitate to teach me even the simplest things that I appeared to be ignorant about. For instance, how to pack glass tumblers or china cups for a journey to arrive safely. It was a very appreciated relationship.

I watched Joyce Milverton with great admiration the way she looked after her mother, who was, through old age, becoming disabled. She could not move on her own. Joyce would bathe her, dress her, feed her and put her to bed. When her mother needed anything at night, Joyce would be down to offer her help. Whenever she went shopping or to church and prayer meetings, she would hurry back to be sure her mother was not in any difficulty. I had never seen such care and love for aged parents. Usually children get too busy to cater for their parents but Joyce had withdrawn from missionary service to care for her mother. She did that faithfully - her reward is in heaven. I felt sad that I could not offer this service to my parents before their home calling.

But I did not feel comfortable adding more burdens to Joyce. She had got enough to do but she insisted that I should come to her home whenever we were on break or holidays. What I did to ease her burden was to accept the invitations of friends from college and other missionaries I knew from Gindiri. I planned my holidays so that I travelled round to many of them.

Visits Around Britain

I stayed with Lillian Blenko - my former physical education teacher in Gindiri. I learnt that she was the only keen child of God in her family; her parents were not totally committed to Christ. I also stayed a week with Mr and Mrs Crow and a week with Mr and Mrs Potter, both former missionaries to Langtang. I spent one week with the Mackays, former missionaries in Gindiri. This was where I learnt to be patient with teenage children!

I stayed a week with Maureen Parry and her parents. Maureen became a personal friend, who went as a missionary to Gindiri and later worked with the Institute of Education of Ahmadu Bello University, Zaria. I thank God for her.

I visited Mr and Mrs Burrough - former missionaries in Kabwir, Mrs Burrough was the first to start the Girl's Brigade in Nigeria. For about two weeks I stayed with Mr and Mrs Morris in Taplow, the teacher who showed me great favour by asking me to look after his bicycle in 1950 in Gindiri. It was at Taplow that I first saw snow. During the Christmas of 1962 Mr Morris invited several of us from Nigeria - Mr Bitrus Pam was in the UK studying accountancy, Mr Barnaba Dusu and Mr Ayuba Tense, who later joined the army, married a school friend Sussanah Alheri and later died. It was alleged that he was involved in a Government coup attempt against General Obasanjo, so she lost her young husband, by then a Colonel, in 1976.

That Christmas of 1962 in Taplow was very cheery, it

brought all the memories of Gindiri back to us. We remembered Mr Morris's stories of his experience in the army, and he told me how he came to know my name. He said he was leading a sing-song evening with all the Gindiri schools brought together. He chose a hymn and forgot the tune. While he stood in front of the congregation, worried about how to get around his difficulty, he heard a voice humming the tune from the direction in which I was seated. This was such a relief for him that at the end of the sing-song he asked for my name, and was told I was Mary from Langtang. Because of that he remembered me. He said that in England the organist would start the tune and the congregation would join in but in Gindiri there was no organist to help him.

We were helped to make snow men and we thoroughly enjoyed ourselves. We had Christmas turkey, Christmas pudding and Christmas carols - just a real English Christmas.

I visited the families of Christian friends at college. Barbara White at St Albans, who was the head girl of the college when we arrived - she was such an efficient student, calm, loving and caring for all, irrespective of where you came from. We found great comfort in her. I discovered that her parents were not Christians. Christine Grundy from Canterbury offered me a home for a week and I simply enjoyed her and her entire family. Evelyn Rowley in London had a wonderful Christian family - they too offered me their home twice. Her mother whom I called Mama Rowley was free with me and I enjoyed her company. Phyllis Chamberlain was totally committed to the Lord, likewise her mother and sisters. When I visited them I found it was a house where there was always a cup of tea. I enjoyed it because it was cold in December 1963.

The Reverend and Mrs Cooper (who took my father Nanshep from his father's house in order to provide him with security and training, and whose wife I was named after) were then very old. They had retired into an old people's home in Rickmansworth but had heard that I was in England, so they wrote that they would like to see me, if I could spare the time. I was very excited, I rang Miss Milverton, who directed me how to get there and Mrs Mary Cooper was at the station to meet me. I felt she was my mother. She took me to the old people's home and into their room. They were in a one roomed apartment, with twin beds. Mr Cooper was older and weaker. Mrs Cooper was stronger and more lively. My heart went out to them. I did not know how to express my joy. I had heard about them and I had longed to see them. It was a great favour from the Lord that He made it possible. They both asked about people they knew while in Langtang - some were alive and some dead.

Mary Cooper asked about my family. I told her Chalya was with me in England and she expressed a desire to see her. She asked me how I spelt her name and I wrote 'Chalya'. She said 'No, that is the wrong way to spell her name - it should be written Calya'. I knew she was right and I appreciated the correction. I remembered that she had taught our people to read and write in our own language many years back. She was to me an authority in Tarok orthography but we were so used to spelling it Chalya that it was not easy to change. She asked their nurses to offer me tea and biscuits, which I received with much delight because it was offered by someone I considered as my mother. I marvelled at their devotedness to each other. Usually in Nigeria not many people would stick together in a marriage where there were no children. That this couple kept to each other and would only be parted by death made me shed tears of joy. The excellent care by the younger people of the home left me touched and thankful. This made me recall my auntie Mama Damicit Tintin, who was also childless but the love of God kept her and her husband together, until death parted them at a good age. They were wonderful Christians. After some weeks, I took Chalya to see the Coopers and they blessed her. They served the Lord with all their hearts and with all their souls and minds. I prayed to the Lord to use me like He had used them.

Other Christian friends I found companionship in from the college were Janet Wigley, Kathleen Groves, Christine

Ray and others. The memory of these students is a great joy to me. They not only made me feel at home but cared so much for my well being. They made it worth my while to stay in England.

Joining the Christian Union was the greatest thing that made me enjoy England. Outside this circle some people were mean and spiteful asking me derogatory questions like 'What sort of house do you live in back in Nigeria?' 'Tell us about the snakes we hear about. Is it true that people live on trees and mountains together with monkeys?' One student asked me how I managed to get my skin so brown! Someone else interrupted with 'The colour of your skin is a better one' 'Why is it better?' I asked. She said 'Because when you blush no one can tell, but if I blush I go red all over and I find it embarrassing!'. 'Thank God I have the right colour skin then' I replied.

The years rolled by. My moments of anxiety were during the holidays when I had no one to stay with. It meant I had to rent a room or a flat somewhere in the town. Then one summer, I was invited to spend the long holiday, except for three weeks, with Sussanah Alheri. When we got to the house in London, we found there was room for only one, so Sussanah occupied the room because she arrived first. They found me another place, where some Igbo people charged me £20 per week. The area was not very decent, full of notorious black people, so that I was afraid to go out in the evenings. Sussanah taught me a dance called the twist. I spent the evenings practising the twist for exercise, without any music. I rang Miss Milverton and told her about the area and she told me to come to her house immediately which I did. This was the only time I spent completely on my own throughout my stay in the UK.

My studies went well. I spent time on my books. I used to take all my books with me wherever I went in heavy suitcases. I almost lost the use of my arms carrying the heavy cases.

In my second year I was too homesick to stay away, so during the summer holidays, I was allowed by my scholarship to go home to Nigeria. It was as though I had been to somewhere very important and come back again - some saw me as having fallen from the sky! Many greeted me with excitement. I did not want to go back to the UK, but Solomon persuaded me to try and finish my studies because I would find it useful later in life. In any case I had to go back for my daughter!

Teaching Practice in the UK

I found the children more accommodating than many adults as they did not see the difference between white or black. Once a teacher was able to handle them, they were very responsive. I enjoyed the children more than anything else in the UK

I received such high marks for my teaching practice that news started to go round the college that I got on well with the children. Meanwhile we had a new English teacher at college who taught speech to overseas students. He concluded my speech was the best of all the overseas students because I was privileged to have been taught by English teachers in Gindiri. He happened to know Dr Striesow, who helped find a foster parent for Chalya. This English teacher told the Striesows about me and they invited me for supper and congratulated me on my achievement.

One evening after a visit to Miss Milverton, I was going back to college, when a white lady sat by me on the tube. This lady asked me what I was doing in London. I told her I was at St Katherine's College in White Hart Lane. 'Are you Mary Lar' she asked. I almost fainted - how could anyone know me in the heart of London? Her daughter was in the college and used to tell them about a Mary Lar from Nigeria. So people were watching me and knew me even though I did not know them.

College Meetings

Every Friday was a college meeting at which all students and staff were expected to be present. The students put forward some of their problems and the authorities responded to them. They would also inform students of their programmes and plans, and the students would react to them. It was a meeting of sharing; whenever staff travelled they brought back slides to share at the college meetings, such occasions were very educative. This type of interaction between the school and the students I found very useful and it prevented riots and misunderstandings. I would recommend such interaction to other colleges.

One summer, Miss Sylvia Huggler, one of the staff teaching English (she was my tutorial teacher) went to Ahmadu Bello University, Zaria, Nigeria for a summer programme. She took several pictures of snakes and people. She reported at the college meeting that she saw people praying in the dust, eating from the dustbin, vultures all over the place, flies uncontrollable and the heat unbearable. The two of us who were Nigerians were taken aback by the ridiculous way she presented the country to the college. This report caused the students to ask us more spiteful questions. The report from Nigeria had upset us but the Lord helped us to bear it.

Life at college was detestable during this period. I spent more time with the Lord, and I visited Joyce Milverton more frequently. It was during this period that Joanna, the other Nigerian girl, had to undergo an operation and was in hospital for about two weeks. She had uncles and cousins in London who used to visit her. I remember Joanna was so enraged with the attitude of some of the students that she had reacted angrily. She accused them of being racist, but when Joanna was in hospital, she was surprised that the students were so concerned about her. They went to see her and took her flowers. We concluded that we did not understand the English people.

Student Stress

Ade, another Nigerian girl, joined us in our third year. She was from Lagos and was in Britain for her 'A' levels. Her mother had a girls' college in Lagos and wanted Ade, her only daughter, to be trained as a teacher so that she could take over the school from her. Ade arrived at college and was delighted to see us. We were equally happy to see her but felt that she had her priorities wrong. She spent so much time going to town to look for recommended books that she never had time actually to read them. Then she would spend her evenings chatting in Joanna's room or mine or with other students. We were final year students and we had a lot to cover. It was a big sacrifice on our part to spend so much time with her to help her to adjust. I sometimes wondered how the English students got on so well with their studies without much reading. I would fail if I did that. They seemed to spend more time on recreation that on academics - but when the examinations came round they all seemed to do well. One day Ade came to my room. She told me that these 'Oyibos' (the name Nigerians used to describe Europeans) were wicked. She said they discriminated against her in class, so much so that she could not bear it anymore. I advised her 'just go to your lecture and when it is over leave for the next one'. 'Learn to work alone'.

I invited Ade to join me one evening for devotions but she stood up, furiously snatched my Bible from my hands and threw it at the door. 'Why?' I asked. 'Haven't you got your god back in Nigeria', she fumed. 'Why do you worship these people's God? We have our own god in Yoruba land, if you do not have one of yours, you can join and worship the Yoruba gods'. I quietly went for my Bible first, then I said to her 'Ade, the tension you are going through is as a result of discrimination. I also went through this but I conquered it with what is contained in this Bible. But you have thrown your strength away by throwing away the Bible, so I have nothing left to comfort you with'. I did not say any more. She stood up from my bed, gave a big hiss of disillusionment and resentment and left. I pitied her and prayed for her. I knew she had a stronger battle to fight than I did because she was fighting it alone.

Barely one week after that I met Ade at tea in the dining hall. She looked tense and she was doing funny things, like going for a cup of tea but not drinking it. Gradually the others moved away and I was left with her. I pleaded with her to go to lectures but she refused to respond. I felt like crying. I went straight to Joanna's room to discuss what we could do, obviously she was behaving abnormally. Joanna advised that we should observe more of such behaviour first, otherwise we may rush into doing things that might work against her. I went to my room. Joanna came knocking almost immediately saying that Ade was shouting and crying in the library and had driven all the other students out. I asked 'What other proof do you need? Obviously she needs our help!' We thought we should get her cousin's telephone number in London but she was in no condition to give it to us. I suggested we inform Nigeria House, so we telephoned them. They told us they did not have her on their record - she was a private student and she had to take responsibility for herself. She was not in a position to do that, I told them. I felt so bad. The only option left was to inform the college authority. Joanna and I went to see Miss Huggler, our overseas students' tutor. I explained 'Miss Huggler, we have noticed some strange behaviour in Ade, so we have come to ask if you can help her'. We told her about the episodes in the dining hall and in the library. 'Oh' she said, 'I have heard students say that she was shouting, disturbing people everywhere, and that she does not attend the right lectures and goes to those not meant for her, but does this mean she is sick?' At this point I was losing my temper. 'How could you not know that such behaviour is peculiar? At least when she first came she did not behave like that!' I remonstrated.

Miss Huggler went looking for Ade then and found that she was disturbing the nurses in the college clinic, asking them to call a doctor because she was sick. When the college doctor came, she said it was an emergency case. She telephoned for an ambulance and Ade was taken to a mental hospital. I wept that night. I wept because I felt like an orphan, who could fall a victim of negligence for being an African. I wept for Ade, for rejecting a strong weapon, the Bible, thereby falling into the hands of the devil. But I knew nothing was impossible. God could cure her and start her afresh. After some days, we visited Ade in the hospital. She could not recognise us, she could not talk to us. She kept silent in spite of all our efforts to talk with her. We asked if she could give us the address of her mother or a relation in the UK, so we could make contact with them. But Ade snatched the piece of paper and pencil from us and was angrily scribbling on the paper with meaningless scratchings. After much effort, we left for college. The next visiting day she was reviving. She recognised us, came up to us and asked how college was. She wanted to go with us to college but we told her as soon as she was discharged we would take her with us. She asked us why she had been taken there - she had not known it was a hospital until we told her. Our final visit to her was quite a happy moment. She had completely come back to her normal self and pleaded with us to take her back to college. When we came back to college we went straight to Miss Huggler and informed her of Ade's progress. She said she knew, because she had been visiting Ade too. She smiled at our joy and we left her. The next thing we heard was that Ade had been sent back to Nigeria.

After about a month Ade rang us from Lagos. She was safely home. The college had not allowed her back and had sent her home. She told us her mother was upset. We encouraged her to find a college in Nigeria. I did not hear from Ade for a long time after that but after my graduation, I joined my husband in Lagos, where he was the junior Minister of Establishment, and Ade telephoned me and welcomed me back to Nigeria. She was such a sociable girl but she could have coped better with Christ in her.

Leaving the UK

It was incredible but three years had passed and our examinations were over. The Lord saw me through all my subjects, including arts and crafts, which I had never tried before. Solomon came from Nigeria to help us pack and leave. It was such a joy to be together again. We took our daughter from her foster parents and stayed together at a hotel for three days before we flew back to Nigeria. In June 1965 we left England. It was nice to get back home amongst my own people. I felt secure, happy and accepted. I thought to myself 'This is where I belong'.

The memory of those who were nice to me in England

lingered on for so long and is still with me. I have realised that there is nothing impossible with the Lord, for in Christ, we are more than conquerors. If I had been alone in the UK, I would not have been able to succeed in my studies.

It was good-bye to a land where I had felt a foreigner, except among those children of God in that land who were guided by the injunction in Hebrews 13:2, which says 'Do not forget to entertain strangers, for by so doing, some people have entertained angels without knowing it'. These children of God, who were able to make me happy, knew they were doing that for the Lord. I pray to the Lord to bless each one of them according to His word.

Britain as one of the more privileged countries in Europe should think more seriously on how to show compassion to the less privileged. The less developed countries see the British as the Good Samaritans. As a nation Britain should not neglect this responsibility.

There are many oppressed, neglected and hurt people all around us in our homes, our offices, schools, hospitals and in society. David Watson in 1975 said 'Christians have a great responsibility in the world in which we live - God's world. Every area of our lives matters to Him. Our attitudes of inequality and injustice are of vital concern to a God who is pure, loving and just'. He would love to see His children in the world showing concern for all whom He has created. The Christians in Britain accepted me. They knew that as a Christian I needed the fellowship of God's people, where I could share my burdens. I thank God for them.

Chapter 6

LIFE IN NIGERIA 1965-1970

My training abroad had a great impact on me. I came back a more mature person having been exposed to a world where the initiative had to come from me. I became more thoughtful and creative and in my discussion I sounded more responsible.

Solomon, as a Junior Minister, was given an apartment at Lawrence Road, Ikoyi and I applied to teach in a school in Lagos. The Local Government hesitated to give me a job, as I was a Northerner, whose husband might leave at any time. I started teaching in Auntie Ayo Preparatory School, a private school at Obalende, in July. That used to be the school where teachers who were non-Lagos-indigents were sent to teach. Chalya began attending a private nursery school in Ikoyi but during the first two weeks, both Chalya and I had malaria.

I was given class seven to teach, the highest primary school class. Some parents thought that they noticed a change in their children and that they would like to meet this new teacher. Some of them asked me to give their children extra lessons and they were prepared to pay an extra £3 to £6 a month, but I did not have the time. At an Open Day I did most of the creative work for the exhibition, my arts lessons in the UK coming in very useful. And when Auntie Ayo was giving the report of her school, she mentioned that most of her teachers were trained overseas and there was big applause. I remembered all the suffering in the UK and I rejoiced that now it was receiving commendation.

That year there was an inter-school competition of teachers' creativity for the whole of Lagos State, organised by the British Council. I received the first prize, and the proprietress Auntie Ayo was proud of me for putting her school in the limelight.

In December we were preparing to go to our village for a family Christmas. I was looking forward to seeing every one. It was the first visit and the first Christmas after my graduation from college in England. We flew to Jos and passed on to Langtang. It was all a new experience for Chalya. We all expressed gratitude to God for a happy reunion with relations and friends, and our parents were delighted to see us.

Talking About the UK

That Christmas the late Revd Damina Bawado, our father in the Lord, who officiated at our wedding, asked me to give a report in church to the congregation of my experiences in the UK. I spoke about the high standards of honesty I had noticed there. They put newspapers in the streets and people who needed them picked them up and dropped the exact money in a box. The money was not stolen even when there was nobody to take care of it. 'Were there no thieves there?' they asked me after the service. 'It must be a wonderful place!'

I told them of the orderliness on the roads, where pedestrians were given priority, especially where there was a crossing. This was not the case in Nigeria, where motorists got angry with people on the road and would crush them and then blame them. I told them that the people in England were very considerate.

I spoke about neatness and the absence of flies. I spoke about the missionaries I had visited, including those who had been in Langtang, Mr and Mrs Crow, Mr and Mrs Potter and the Revd and Mrs Cooper. They clapped and showed delight, and I realised that the Tarok people loved and cherished these people. I spoke about the Christians and how they had kept me happy; and of my observation of people and time. 'Everyone seemed to be running - walking seemed a waste of time for their business, everything seemed to move so fast! There were hardly any slow and lazy people. No one was late for anything. Their timekeeping was very strict.'

I told them about my experience with the baby at the airport and how my countrymen did not think of helping me and only the whites rushed to help me. I spoke about the cold in winter - the worst winter for a century. Old people died, sheep and goats got buried in the snow. I told them more about snow, which most of them had never seen. It is hard to imagine the whiteness of snow in Isaiah 1:18 and Psalm 51:7. I told them there was nothing to compare with it in our Nigerian experience.

At the end I told them that God's world is big, advanced and wonderful. Some came to ask me if they had chickens and eggs in England as we have in Nigeria. I told them they had more. They thought that I had achieved much in my life and I thought so too. I continued to give God the honour and the glory for it all.

A Warning Word

Solomon usually derives great joy from giving out gifts at Christmas. He brought money, clothes, food etc for sharing. He would also encourage me to buy salt, sugar, and milk etc to share with the women. When we had used up all our resources, we left for Lagos. We arranged that my mother should visit us in Lagos in January 1966. At the time Solomon was a Director of the Tennessee Fishing Company and they would bring fish and fill our refrigerators with them. Mother had a nice time with all these fish!

We had three visitors from a church in Lagos. We had never met them before, but they saw a vision about us in their church and had come to pray with us. They informed us that people would be arriving from a long distance with plenty of fruit for us, but they warned us that we should not take any of the fruit because it would mean doom for us.

Two days later some friends from a far distance arrived in Lagos. We were delighted to see them but to our embarrassment they brought us many fruits, oranges, grapefruits, bananas, pineapples and tangerines. We were speechless! We did not tell them our feelings but received the gifts with much gratitude. It did not occur to us that the visitors we had been warned about would be our friends! I asked Solomon what it all meant. He said that these are our friends and we should enjoy the gifts that they had brought. We prayed and had peace about it. I took an orange and a banana and ate it in faith. Nothing happened to us. How the devil tries to confuse us with false prophecy!

The First Coup

Two days after our friends left, early in January 1966, we had a frightening experience. There was a coup. The Prime Minister, Sir Abubakar Tafawa Balewa was killed as was the Premier of Northern Nigeria, Sir Ahmadu Bello the Sardauna of Sokoto and were other top political leaders in the West and Mid-West state. It was the first experience of a coup d'etat in Nigeria. For days the world seemed suddenly changed for the worse. There were soldiers surrounding all the Government Officials' houses. Our apartment was also surrounded. I took Chalya away to sister Margaret Olowu's, where several Northern wives of officials took refuge and comfort. After the new Head of State was announced, Major General J T U Aguyi Ironsi, we were all given two weeks to pack and leave the government quarters.

We wondered if this was the vision of the church that visited us about two weeks earlier. But would the coup not have taken place, if we had refused the fruits? It was such a confusing issue that we just prayed to the Lord to perfect everything concerning our lives. After all, what could refusing to eat fruit do in the Lord's perfect will? He provided the good things of this world! I believe that when He has a special need to talk with us, he prepares us too. But we had disobeyed over the eating of the fruits.

We had nowhere to go after the coup. Solomon decided to go ahead of us to Jos, to see what he could find. Chalya and I had to stay behind in the house of our townsman, the late Mr Solomon Wuyep, who was a veterinary worker in Obalande. This enabled me to fulfil my contract with the school, which required me to give three months notice. These three months were not easy. Our driver left, Chalya and I fell sick and Chalya could not carry on with her private school. I got her into Auntie Ayo nursery school class, so it would be easier for me.

We left Mr Wuyep's house and moved into Ikeja where Captain Paul Thahal offered us a nice and comfortable house, but going from Ikeja to a school in Obalande was not easy. Sometimes I went by train, sometimes by these *kabu kabu* buses. I would leave home at 4.00 am yet, because of the changes of buses before I got to Obalande, the journey would take about four hours. Whenever I got to school late, the head mistress and the proprietress would hurl insults at me, threatening to reduce my salary. Out of sympathy for me Auntie Ayo paid my salary and waved the ten days remaining notice. I left the school and joined my husband at the Terminus Hotel in Jos.

It was from there that I attended an interview to work with the former Northern Nigeria Ministry of Education. I was posted to the Government Girls Secondary School in Bauchi, where I worked under a British lady, Miss Shier.

In May 1966, I was in Bauchi when the second disturbance, known as *A'raba'*, a call for secession of the country by the North from the South, took place. It was like a retaliation for the Igbo's action in the 1966 coup d'etat, which appeared partial because only the political leaders from the North, West and Mid-West were killed but not those from the East. The Igbo girls in the school were hidden in a toilet until the most dangerous days were over. Then they were sent to Jos. They arrived home safely although it was a terrible experience for them.

My Own School

By the December of 1966, a letter was sent to the Principal and to me from the Ministry of Education Headquarters in Kaduna, saying that I should move to Shendam and open a new Government Girls Secondary School there. I was to be the acting Principal of the school. What a challenge; a wonderful opportunity had come for me to run a school in the way I had been taught. As we travelled down to Shendam, the vehicle that conveyed my belongings dropped one of my suitcases without our knowing it. At the police station I was asked what was in the suitcase. I said 'among other things my Teachers' Certificate issued by the University of London, Institute of Education.' On identifying the suitcase, they insisted that I open it and show them the certificate, then they were quite content.

It was then a sincere and honest Nigeria. I took my suitcase and went to the house which had been given me in the Government Reservation Area, where only the District Officer, the Co-operative Officer and the New Principal of a Government Girls' Secondary School were allowed to live. I felt highly elevated and zealous about the whole work.

Meanwhile, after the coup of January 1966, Solomon enrolled for GCE 'O' levels, sat the examination and passed all his papers within six months. He also gained admission to study for a Diploma in Law. He took some days off to study and sat the 'A' levels examination. Being successful he transferred from a diploma to a degree course.

I then had time to devote to my work. At Shendam, prisoners were assigned to fetch water for the Government Officials and to sweep their compounds. I overheard the prisoners speaking in my own language but they were condemning 'educated' women saying they could not be good wives to their husbands, so I did not reply. But my husband's nephew arrived from Bauchi and greeted them in Tarok, our own language. They realised that I must have heard what they said, so they said 'Well done, we are proud of you!'

The list of girls for the school was sent from Kaduna and it included the names of some girls that I had recommended.

Kaduna sent me an assistant teacher and together we started the school. In February 1967, I planned educational programmes for them based on my Gindiri experience. The Chief Education Officer Miss J S Attah, now Nigerian Ambassador to Rome, visited the school and gave high commendations. I enjoyed my work with the girls and things went smoothly. The then Permanent Secretary, Mr Darlong, insisted that I should be loaned a car since until then no vehicle had been assigned to the school.

It was my first vehicle and I forgot it was for my personal use. I used it devotedly for the school eg conveying students to the hospital, driving to Jos to buy school materials eg gas lamps, home economics materials, receiving pay for staff and labourers from Kaduna. Virtually the car was assigned to the school and I was made to pay for it! But to me it was enough joy that I had a car to do all the running around.

Chalya was nearly seven years old and the problem of her schooling was a big burden. She attended the two schools in Shendam but quickly picked up bad habits with a preference for torn clothes, rather than neat ones. She was also picking up bad language. I wrote to the ministry that I would like a transfer to Kaduna so that I could get a good school for my daughter and also could be near my husband in Ahmadu Bello University (ABU), Zaria. They replied that I could not be transferred so quickly.

A Second Baby

By then I was expecting my second baby, so I went on maternity leave in Jos. My baby arrived on 8 December 1967, and I reported for work again in March 1968. Sister Rosary, a very charming lady, had been appointed to run the school in my absence. I taught under her for about four months before I was granted my request to be posted to Kaduna.

By then Plateau State had been carved into a State of its own out of Northern Nigeria and I wanted to cancel my request but Mr Durlong insisted that I must report to Kaduna, so I went there with my two children, Chalya and Beni. I was put in charge of the Annexe of Kaduna Capital

School. I enjoyed teaching the children who were the cream of society. Their parents were either Permanent Secretaries, Ministers or top Government Officials.

I met Sussanah Alheri at this school, who was now Mrs Sussanah Tense, who was teaching the higher classes. Soon after this I received a letter from the then Permanent Secretary, Mallam Haruna Soba that I had been transferred to the Womens' Teachers College in Katsina as the Vice Principal. I did not appreciate being transferred so often, so quickly.

One day as the Permanent Secretary, Mallam Haruna Soba, attended a party organised by the then government of North Central State, he met with the Secretary to the Military Governor, who started to talk to him about my transfer case. He said that his son had informed him that Mrs Lar had been transferred to Katsina. He asked why Capital School did not have steady teachers. He had noticed a difference in his son and wanted him to continue with Mrs Lar. The Permanent Secretary had to promise not to transfer me again for at least one year. The Lord used my job to give me some rest. He knew I needed it.

A New Girl's Secondary School

Towards the end of the year, I was invited to the Ministry and informed that the North Central State intended to open a new Government Girls Secondary School in Soba and, having heard of the good performance I had had in Shendam, would like me to open that school,. My husband was delighted that I would be nearer to him again.

In Soba, we started with the renovations of the house that was to be the school; painting and repairs were inevitable. We renovated an old Primary School building for classes and erected a dormitory. The students' hostels and classes were ready. I had an assistant teacher, a clerk, a messenger, a matron and some labourers.

The girls reported in January 1969 and the school was started in earnest. The difference between this school and the one in Shendam was mainly in the girls' attitude towards school. The girls in Shendam were eager to work and to receive education. They would come round with their parents and seek admission. Some of the parents, out of anxiety, would bring things like chickens or eggs to entice the principal to give their daughters admission, but I told them to take the things back, and if there was any vacancy, I would still remember them. Some of these girls became nurses, teachers, high court judges, lawyers, administrators etc.

But in Soba, the girls had a less positive attitude towards schooling. Some of them came crying and resented being sent to school. One of them was told she was going to visit her grand-mother in order to get her into the school bus! When she found herself in school, she screamed and resisted vehemently. She upset the whole school for days. One grandmother had warned the girls that if they found themselves in the school by force (as the local government had threatened) they should behave badly and refuse to work, so that the school authority would send them home again.

I told the problem girls about a girl I had been at school with - she was a daughter of a highly influential chief, who was sent to school like them. She complained about the school - that the food was bad and the beds hard. In her father's house she would have had tea and bread in the mornings but in school there was nothing like that. She would cry and disturb everyone in class. As her friend and prefect, the teacher used to ask me to take her out and talk to her, which made me angry because I wanted to learn and this girl was wasting my time. Eventually the holidays came and this girl refused to come back to school after the holidays. She married a very rich businessman and lived like a queen for a while. After a time, however, the husband wanted someone competent to help him with his business. He married an educated girl and turned the first wife out of the house. When I was Principal, I visited Jos, and this girl was trying to establish a market. 'You were the wise girls' she said, when she saw me in my car. At the end of the story, I asked the girls if they wished to be wise girls and learn something at school. I thought that they would not come back after the holidays but they all did and they later admitted to enjoying school. After this the girls in Shendam and Soba had something in common - they were very obedient and obeyed school rules. There were no disciplinary problems of any kind.

During one of my consultations in Kaduna, I met a friend of Solomon's who asked me to assist him secure places for his children in my school. He said he had heard people speak highly of the discipline and teaching, whereas the secondary school in Kaduna they were attending had lost its reputation. It was not possible for that year and I had to ask him to wait for the next academic year.

There was a very challenging period when I had two religious groups, which I had to care for equally. There was a very cordial relationship between the Christians and the Muslims in the school. The Head Girl was a Muslim, who had such a quality of love for everyone that one hardly knew that there were two religious groups in the school. The Shendam school had mostly Christians girls but here in Soba they were about equal in number with the Muslims. We all worked hard to make sure that there were equal opportunities for all the girls in all activities.

A Third Child

It was in Soba that I was blessed in expecting my third child in 1969. I went on maternity leave for three months. During my absence Sister Rosary, who took over from me in Shendam, was posted to Soba. She said it looked like she was pursuing me wherever I went! After my maternity leave, I was posted to Women's Teachers' College, Zaria, where I taught for six months before I left the Civil Service of North Central State.

During the four years I served the Northern Nigerian Ministry of Education and the North Central State Ministry of Education, not a single promotion was given to me, while some of my friends were promoted twice. I wrote to protest but each time the reply was negative. I was told that they did not promote staff on contract, yet I had not asked for a contract appointment, it had been forced on me as a married woman. They said I could not be given a permanent appointment because I was married, as though marriage was an offence! They were basing their standards on the British system where at that time, if a teacher married, she had to leave her post. I started to wonder if there were any prospects for me at all as a teacher (In 1976 the Civil Service repealed this rule - the repeal was recommended by a committee headed by my husband!). They said I could only be promoted in my own state, but that I could not be transferred to my own state because I was a contract teacher. Also I could not be principal of a school after Form Two because I was a holder of a certificate equivalent to the National Certificate of Education, and that was why I had been moved on after two years.

Because of all this, I decided to enrol in the University to get a degree but it was disturbing for this to happen while I was enjoying a school so much. The decision was endorsed by my husband, so I did not renew my contract. I went back to Plateau State and applied to Ahmadu Bello University, Zaria. I was determined to read Education, History and English and so I bought some books and started studying on my own.

When I had my letter of admission, some of Solomon's friends tried to discourage me from going. They said my place was with my husband and family and that I would be responsible for whatever may result from the separation. However, my husband insisted that I should go and that it would be good for the family. We prayed about it and we were both satisfied that I should accept the admission. My mother was readily available to look after my children.

Looking back over my life, I realised that if I had been allowed to go to school in Jos, that would have been the end of my education after primary school. Most of my friends seemed to end their education at that level because there were no higher institutions at that time and there were very few who were able to go to other places like Ibadan or Lagos. I would not have been privileged to go to Gindiri and achieve the Higher Elementary Certificate, which made it possible for me to go to the United Kingdom, which qualified me to enter a university.

Chapter 7

UNIVERSITY 1971-1974

Iattended my husband's very impressive graduation ceremony. It set an urge in me also to wear that flowing academic gown. When I looked at the financial situation, I was contributing actively towards the upkeep of the family, and decided that I could not join the academic life immediately. I had to wait for my husband to finish at Law School before I could go to Ahmadu Bello University in Zaria. In September 1971 I obtained an admission to read Education and English, even though I applied to read Education and History. The Dean of Education insisted they needed English teachers and not History teachers. He said that I would find English easier since I had been in the UK for three years. Failure to accept English would result in the admission not being granted. With such a strong threat, I had no choice but to take English. This gave me a very tough time at University, because having been in the UK did not really qualify me to study English.

The First Year
The first year I read Education, Sociology and English. I found the subjects too many and there were many sub-subjects to cope with. English in particular was sub-divided into Literature, Grammar, Drama, Poetry and Phonology. Even within these clear divisions, there were other clear units - eg in Literature there were units like Shakespeare and 16th, 17th, 18th, 19th and 20th Century Literature. Not less than two books were treated a week per sub-unit.

African Literature also formed a subject under a unit. In fact, English alone was enough to keep me at my desk 24 hours a day. As the work came in, I was getting more and more worried and I found that I had no time for anything else. I busied myself from morning till night and still was not satisfied with my progress. I started to dislike my lectures and tutorials because it was during such lectures that assignments were given. I started well, scoring 'A's and 'B's, but as time went on I became exhausted and was not able to do as well. I started to score 'C's and 'D's and even an 'E' once. I used to sit for long hours in the library without food, so I found it difficult to absorb much.

One day as I sat down in the library reading hard for an assignment, I heard the Fellowship of Christian Students singing - it was their usual evening fellowship. It struck me that my voice should have been amongst these voices praising God. I tried to dispel such a thought because I felt my study was such an important one. 'How could I have time for fellowship when there was so much to cover?' I asked myself. I was not going to spare my time on anything other than my studies. I had to succeed, otherwise it would be a bad testimony for a child of God to come for a degree course and fail. I could not stand that thought, so I decided that I would say my prayers and attend church services and that that would be enough for my spiritual well-being. I forgot the blessings of such a fellowship in the UK but I was able to pass all my exams by the grace of God.

My Second Year

I started my second year with a big problem, for it was the period I had my fourth baby - Deborah. The first semester went well until the Christmas holidays. I became too heavy with this pregnancy and had to wait at home until the Easter break for the coming of the baby. During that time I made arrangements with a capable colleague to send me regularly his hand-outs and copies of his lecture notes. I studied them and carried out my assignments, when I would post them back to him to hand to the lecturers. During this time, attendance at lectures was not compulsory. In this way I got over another semester. Some assignments were shelved to await the use of the library.

I joined my colleagues in the last semester of my second year. I had to take my baby with me, plus a nanny and a helper in the house, and had to look for accommodation in Samaru village. I attended lectures daily but assignments seemed to be tripled. The baby's demands seemed to be increasing. I worried about fetching water when the taps dried, I worried about the market. I had to go to the market to buy enough food to last the week in order to save time.

The first accommodation I had was next to a toilet. Children would mess the area and the place would be full of flies, like bees buzzing all round. I spent a lot of money on insecticide. I had diarrhoea several times and it was such a release when, after a leave, I was able to move to new accommodation in Samaru, owned by a friend of Mrs S Tense. I would not like to forget the sweet memory of this compound. It was occupied by four respectable Christian families. We saw ourselves as members of one body, with similar goals, as we belonged to the University community, kept the compound clean and cared for each other. People used to say that the higher you climbed academically, the less the work became, but to my great surprise, it was as if the workload was increasing every day. As it increased, I also increased my hours of work. I ate less, saying I had not got time to eat, and so one day my fragile body broke down.

I suffered from malaria attacks, had diarrhoea, and vomited several times. I was given librium capsules - I protested. It was assumed that students' problems usually resulted from hard brain work, so when students went to the clinic, before they described their complaints, the medicine had been prescribed for them - either librium or valium. This time I refused to go until my complaint was heard by the doctor. I told him I had diarrhoea, vomiting and high fever - he ordered that my temperature be taken and I was given some high dose of nivaquine, which I took on an empty stomach. Towards evening, I collapsed. I had terrible irritation all over me. I was given hot coffee. After the coffee and nivaquine, I had three sleepless nights and had to go back to the clinic to be given some sleeping tablets. This marked the beginning of my sleeping problem. I spent the whole day scratching my body. Without sleep, and with the hard scratching at night, I became tense. Vomiting and diarrhoea had left me, but I felt rough both inside and outside. With sleeping pills for three days, I started to be calm and sleepy.

News reached home that I was sick and my mother came all the way from Langtang to see me. I was very happy. I told her there was too much work in the University, so she suggested that I concentrate on my work and send my baby back to her father - she would help to look after them. So I looked for hostel accommodation and, during the holidays, I took my daughter Debbie, and Naomi her nurse, back to Jos. There they stayed with my mother, and their daddy was available to take care of their needs. This arrangement was a great relief to me. It enabled me to devote more time to my work. I was able to carry out my assignments on time, but I was missing the joy of having my children with me.

The sleeplessness continued. I used to enjoy a bottle of cold coke before I went to bed, and it tasted good. I did not know that coke contained so much caffeine and that it was adding to my sleeplessness. It was when my health deteriorated so badly and I had to return home to my family, and went to the Evangel Hospital in Jos, that the doctor took time to examine me and found out that I had a trace of diabetes, so I was placed on a diet of mainly protein and vegetables, and a tablet. During the next three months I still complained of sleeplessness and was told not to take coke, coffee or tea for a while, then I started sleeping well but I still had no appetite for food.

I continued to suffer ill-health for a while, which affected my results at the end of the session. For the first time in my life, I experienced failure. I was given a re-sit in English Language. Although I performed well in Literature, my performance was poor in Grammar. That was hard for me to take. I did not want my name in the newspaper published as a failure. Although I passed all my other subjects, I started to ask God why He allowed me to fail that one paper. It was then that I realised that I had pushed him so far out of my life and so I was bound to fail. Realising this, I accepted my plight and started reading thankfully and prayerfully for the paper. I began to fellowship with the Christian students and moved closer to the Lord and I felt the difference. My life was more organised and my health improved. I went back for my re-sit in Zaria and confidently left the result in God's hand, and I passed the paper very well.

Meanwhile, my diabetes was tested and I was told by my doctor to stop taking the pills, but to stick to the diet. I followed this rule closely and after sixteen more years there is still no trace of diabetes.

My Third Year

My third year in the University passed quickly and successfully. Everything seemed easier when I learned to spend my time well and follow a strict time-table. We were not encouraged to participate in any sporting activities. Occasionally, the times specified for 'relaxing with friends' was used for trekking from one hostel to the other. Since I was a fortunate student with a car, I did not arrive late at lectures. This car was usually full of student passengers who wanted to use it.

The Sunday visitation was something I used to look forward to. It afforded me the opportunity to follow up people who gave themselves to the Lord during Christian Students' yearly Crusades. We would listen to their problems and pray together. Having fellowship with new converts was wonderful. Sundays seemed to be the only day I could give such clear and joyful service. The Lord taught me many things that lectures could not teach. I learned self-discipline. I came closer to my Lord at the University and experienced more of a child/father relationship. I thank God for my many sisters and brothers with whom I shared a wonderful Christian life at ABU. I learned to love people, other than from my own area, by meeting them at the University, working with them and understanding them better.

I was told that any student who re-sits a paper could

never be passed higher than lower second class. My good lecturer friend, the Revd Dr Sister Halligan, believed that I had a gift for teaching, so she took a keen interest in me as her student. She told me it pained her that I missed an upper second class by just one mark. This she said was deliberately done because I had to re-sit a paper. But I was overjoyed to receive my degree. When I remembered all the hard times I had, I could not but join David in singing the Psalms 98 - 'Sing to the Lord a new song, for He has done marvellous things . . . ' To me the Lord has done marvellous things by restoring my health and crowning me with success. My husband joined me in praising the Lord and he bought a beautiful brown lace material to congratulate me for this performance. I cherished this material and kept it safe for remembrance of what the Lord has done for me. He has wiped away my tears, shed during my University days.

Chapter 8

LAUSANNE 1974 AND AFTER

During my last year at the University, the Revd Alan Chilver from the Theological College of Northern Nigeria, Bukuru, visited me. He said the college was in need of a teacher to teach education to the Diploma students and, at their board meeting, my name was brought up as someone they could ask to do this. My heart went straight to the Lord and I had a little dialogue with Him. I thanked Mr Chilver and said I would give it some thought, after consulting with Solomon.

Meanwhile, I joined a Theological Education by Extension group which used to meet at the ECWA Conference Centre, Jos. I worked closely with Alan in one of the groups. It was during this period that I found time to teach Sunday School in my church, at COCIN Sarkin Mangu.

The holiday periods at home afforded me the opportunity to meet with Christians in the Jos area, and as I worked quietly trusting the Lord during the 1973 summer holiday, I received a letter from Lausanne inviting me to attend a World Congress on Evangelism in Lausanne, Switzerland, to be held in July 1974. The offer included a free ticket, food and accommodation for ten days in Switzerland. I quickly fell on my knees and said 'Lord, do I deserve this call?' I was overjoyed. I showed Solomon the letter and he was equally excited. 'That's how God works in a miraculous way' he commented. I accepted the offer, then I went back to finish my last year at the University.

All arrangements for the world congress were decided by the time I completed my degree and left ABU at the end of June. I got home just in time to get ready, and leave for Switzerland. This journey was necessary for my new life.

I left Jos on the 11 July 1974 and stopped at Lagos to meet up with the rest of the Nigerian party, several pastors I knew from Jos. They included the Revd Isaac Bello, now a teacher at the school of Preliminary Studies, Keffi, but working with ECWA, the Revd Victor Musa, now pastor-in-charge of ECWA churches in Kano, Mr Bitrus Pam who was then the General Secretary of COCIN and many others from North and South Nigeria. It was the first time I had met the late Revd Dr Samuel Odunaike of the Four Square Gospel Church in Lagos. The late Revd Moses Ariye from Kwara state, the Revd Alan Chilver, Emmanuel Oladipo, of the Fellowship of Christian Students from Jos, and Dr Isaac Madugu, whom I had met earlier at one of the Fellowship of Christian Students conferences in Gindiri, were also with us. There were three females, Beatrice, Halima and myself from Nigeria.

Everyone seemed to be connected with the church or a para-church organisation, with the exception of myself. I started asking the Lord could it be because I was going to teach at TCNN that He had chosen me too. Anyway, I followed the path He was leading me quietly and confidently.

We took off in Lagos in an Alitalia aeroplane to Rome, where we waited for over six hours to change planes for Geneva. The annoying part was the restriction not to leave the airport. We were hungry and bored. When we arrived in Geneva, we were taken to the conference area by buses. We slept at a boarding secondary school, which was as good as the best hotel in Jos.

I Learn to Praise in All Circumstances

That night a sister, Aureola Jones from Sierra Leone, arrived on a different airline, without her luggage. She was joyful and said 'Sisters, come and help me praise the Lord for my missing suitcase'. I was surprised that someone should praise the Lord when things went wrong. She said 'Yes, what if I had not arrived here?' I said 'Yes, praise the Lord for bringing you here safely and ask Him to help you retrieve your suitcase'. But Aureola shook her head and insisted 'I have no request but praise'. She praised the Lord in her prayers - other sisters prayed the same. I listened but I was a bit baffled. Prior to this time, my attitude towards the Lord was for my self fulfilment, asking for this and that. I knew little about the doctrine of praise. I used to thank the Lord for anything good He did for me, and ask for more, but I certainly did not praise when things went wrong. This was my first spiritual lesson in Lausanne. I remembered that the Bible tells us to give thanks in all circumstances - I Thessalonians 5:18. This brought a dramatic change to my attitude to praise. Two days after Aureola's arrival, Aureola Jones was asked to report to the lost and found property counter. It was her missing suitcase which had arrived.

Solomon gave me some money which I used to purchase some travellers cheques in dollars. I bought things for my children. I could not explain how it happened but I left the things in the shop. As soon as I stepped into the hostel I realised that I had left my shopping behind. First, the shopping had been done collectively and I could not find my way back to the shop. Secondly, the people in Lausanne speak French and I could not communicate or explain things. Thirdly, I had only a few days left and the programme looked full. Would there be another opportunity for shopping? Would the people be honest and give me the goods then? All this went through my mind. I could not stand the thought of going back empty handed with nothing to present to my children. Aureola who I was close to in Lausanne said to me, 'Sister, remember just praise the Lord'. This checked my mounting anxiety. She then prayed, praising the Lord for my forgotten items and she said 'I'll accompany you to the shop'. She speaks French so that made it easy. On arrival at the shop, the cashier who received my money was relieved that we had come back. She did not know where to find me.

For most of us it is easier to praise the Lord when the going is smooth, but not when something has gone wrong. He is always giving us good things, even our very existence is by His goodness, so we should be praising such a God. Habbakuk 3:17-19 is a good example.

We spent ten days in Lausanne. I was strongly motivated, not only by the speeches at the plenary sessions where I listened to people like Billy Graham and Corrie Ten Boom, whose lives I have admired through their books, but the continental and national meetings were equally inspiring. I became interested in youth work, work among women, secondary school students and Sunday School work. At one of the continental meetings, the African people met to discuss Strategies of Evangelism on their continent. Revd Dr Byang Kato spoke. It was really challenging. He knew that reaching Africans through their culture could make the Gospel meaningful to them.

He spoke about the African concept of God - they believe in the all powerful and mighty God, but feel inadequate themselves to approach Him, so they make idols through which they can worship. It could be equated to the situation in Athens Paul faced in Acts 17:22-34. They believed there was a God but they did not know Him. They addressed Him as 'the unknown God'. Dr Kato recommended Paul's approach - that human beings are God's offspring. So how can the divine being now be seen as a silver, gold or a stone image made by man's design and skill?

He talked about syncretism - some African people mix up Christianity with culture. The Yoruba have a concept of many gods, so for them the Christian God is one of many who can be added to their own. Father and mother may be strong church members, yet back at home they may have sacred buckets under their beds that they consult in sickness or as security against the enemy. The Christian does not need to combine the power of God and that of the devil. We cannot serve two masters - Matthew 6:24. I gained so much from Dr Kato's message to equip me for evangelistic work among my own ethnic group.

I had earlier read Corrie Ten Boom's book *The Hiding*

Place. She spoke on the Holy Spirit. She said, some Christians struggle to possess the Holy Spirit instead of allowing the Holy Spirit to fill and direct them.

Lausanne was full of messages for me, which prepared me for the task ahead. I talked closely with Yemi Ladapo about the work he was doing in Jos with Campus Crusade for Christ. They had a little pamphlet to introduce the Gospel to unbelievers through 'The Four Spiritual Laws' which I saw it as an answer to my inability to introduce people to Christ. When I was at home in Langtang as a Grade III teacher, occasionally we would go out preaching and most times they expected me to do the speaking. Sometimes we spent a little time arguing about who should speak. The pamphlet is self-explanatory and speaks for itself. I asked Yemi if I could translate that into my own language. Happily he gave his consent. I did not know how I was going to do it, but I expressed a desire to do it. First, I had no clear orthography of my language and secondly, people criticised my knowledge of our language as being polluted by Hausa and English. Still I was determined to carry out this assignment.

After the conference we flew back to Nigeria - it was as though we were refilled and equipped for a task. We could not wait till we got home. We started witnessing for Christ in Rome, while we were waiting for the connecting flight - we could not keep our mouths shut. From Rome we sang Christian songs on the plane half-way to Lagos. We were full of joy.

When we arrived in Lagos, the customs men wanted to make life difficult for us. Luckily, that evening my cousin, Group Captain Banfa who was the airport commandant in 1974, was there to meet me. He made it easier for us to pass through in the normal way.

When we arrived home, Mr Bitrus Pam and I shared our experiences at our COCIN church. From this I received invitations from countless other churches and para-churches to share the Lausanne spirit with them, including the following: The Summer Institute of Linguistics - now Nigerian Bible Translation Trust, Students of the Theological

College of Northern Nigeria, Bukuru, the graduate fellowship, my church in Langtang, and some women's fellowship groups. Sharing Lausanne went on for a couple of years.

It was while we were in Lausanne that Dr (Mrs) Mary Ogebe and I prayed together for the Lord to lead us when we got home. He had already prepared the way for us. Yemi Ladapo's wife Susan was ready with a home fellowship study material entitled 'Christian Maturity' prepared by the Campus Crusade for Christ. Mary and I went to see her to explore how to start a home Bible discussion group for ladies. We decided we would go through the training ourselves together with Mrs Kure wife of Brigadier Y Y Kure (now a General) and Mrs D Cole. Then we had our first tea/squash party in my house, to which a large number of women came. After sharing matters affecting women in general such as children, marketing, dressing etc we shared the four spiritual laws, and people who prayed to receive Christ for the first time were followed up. We received the addresses of the ladies and generally invited them to a Bible Discussion Group. Our aim was to reach the 'elites' - ie the professional women. I believe that this study group formed in 1974 after Lausanne, helped many professional women to revive their lukewarm Christian faith and it is a real joy to see that many are today active in their various churches.

The Home-to-Home Bible discussion group was blessed by the Lord with the ladies meeting every Friday at 5.00 pm. I know of two women who were blessed with children after praying by members of this group. We shared attacks by the devil on our families or children, and the Lord gave peace to many in their trying times or solved their problems for them. There were many who received the Lord Jesus for the first time. This avenue was a wonderful opening which provided women with the opportunity to fellowship with other women of God. This group for ladies still functions in Jos to date and I praise the Lord for those who are still keeping it going.

Sister Mary Ogebe had to move to Benue after the creation of Benue State out of Benue/Plateau State. She also started a very active group in Benue where she is a medical doctor and her husband Justice James Ogebe, is a Justice of the Court of Appeal Benin, Nigeria. In short, Lausanne revolutionized my Christian life and made me more active and productive. Praise the Lord!

The Theological College of Northern Nigeria (TCNN)

I taught History and Philosophy of Education to the Diploma students at the Theological College of Northern Nigeria, which I enjoyed very much. I believe the students enjoyed it too. My little problem was getting to the college every day. The road to the college after Bukuru was untarred and could get very muddy. Many mornings I got stuck and had to trek to the college to get the students to help the car out of the mud, when there were no passers-by to assist but today the road has been tarred because the Lord touched the heart of the Governor, then Colonel Lawrence Onoja (now Major General).

I taught at TCNN for one academic year only. During that year I had a nasty experience. We used to supervise students on teaching practice in Kuru Secondary School. One day, before I left for Kuru, I asked one of the staff to help pick up my son Mark Mandam Lar from the Corona School, together with his own son, who was at the same school. He agreed to do that. I was confident my son was waiting for me at his house, but when I got there, he was not there, and the staff had gone to Jos. Nobody in the house knew about my son. I drove to the school, but he was not there. The watchman told me he saw a little boy anxiously waiting, but that the child had now gone. I went back to TCNN to find out if the staff had come back, but they had not. I did not remember to give thanks in this circumstance. Then the lesson I learnt from Aureola in Lausanne came to me, and I said 'Lord, I thank you for my missing child'. I decided to move farther in the direction I was shown, but I doubted because I could not see how a child of four years old could move that fast. Just as I started the search afresh, I spotted him coming directly in front of me on a bicycle. He said he was crying and walking about helplessly, when someone on a bicycle stopped and asked him where he was going. He told the man he was going to his mother at ATMN (Amalgamated Tin Mine of Nigeria), instead of TCNN. The man took him to ATMN quarters, but he did not recognise anybody there and nobody knew him either. So the man thought he would try TCNN and he was just cycling in when I caught sight of them. I shouted 'Is that you Mandam?'. He was overjoyed and I shed tears of joy. 'What happened to you?' I asked. He said he did not see me when school closed. After a long wait he was the only person left in school, so he decided to come to me. 'Where did you meet this man?' I asked. He said, the man just saw him and stopped to pick him up. 'He smoked cigarettes on my head and I did not like it.' I held him tight and cuddled him. I thanked this man sincerely, feeling that he had been a good Samaritan, and he cycled off. May the Lord reveal Himself to this kind hearted man.

When we got home to Jos, everyone was shocked at the news. During our evening devotion, we all praised the Lord for His goodness to us and believed the Lord loves Mark so much and certainly has a lot to accomplish with him in this world. It is my prayer that Mark will respond to this great love of God for him.

The man at TCNN later came back and heard the news of Mrs Lar's lost and found child. He had completely forgotten about my request. He felt bad about it and so rushed to Jos to apologise to me at home. 'All is well that ends well' say the English people. We asked him not to worry, God had taken care of our mistake.

TV Presenter

I had been asked to give a report of Lausanne on the television one Sunday evening in 1974. The TV programme co-ordinator asked if I would be interested in television presentations or even to be a newscaster. I told him I was interested but not as a permanent job, for I cannot compromise my teaching profession for anything else. So they invited me to present children's programmes which I gladly did for some years.

The military government of General Yakubu Gowon embarked on a compulsory education for Nigerian children. The programme was called Universal Primary Education (UPE). The programme was meant to cater for all Nigerian children of school age to receive free primary education. There were not enough teachers for this. A large number of secondary school drop-outs were recruited for a crash teacher training programme. The media wanted to make a contribution to the programme, so they approached the Ministry of Education to give them a teacher who would serve as an example to the other teachers. This was to be shown on a weekly TV education programme. The Ministry of Education suggested my name. I became the TV presenter of micro-teaching programmes, making a national contribution.

The Summer Institute of Linguistics, Jos

When I was in Lausanne, I had asked The Revd Yemi Ladipo for permission to translate 'The Four Spiritual Rules' into my language. The Lord in honouring this desire caused the Wycliff Bible Translators in Nigeria, popularly known in Nigeria as the 'Summer Institute of Linguistics' in Jos, to invite me to share the spirit of Lausanne with them. The whole mainly ex-patriate staff gathered together. 'What language do you speak?' they asked. I told them Tarok. 'Has anybody written your language before?' they asked. I remembered the Coopers in the twenties and said, 'Yes, some early missionaries had done that'. They asked if I could get copies of the work already done, either the New Testament or a hymn book or anything in the language. I promised I would. They asked if I would be interested in helping to write my language properly. At this point I got very excited and willingly accepted.

Mrs Pam Bendor-Samuel, wife of the then director Dr John Bendor-Samuel, invited me to her house the following week and we discussed how to go about the Tarok work. She expressed great interest in the project and we met every day both during and after my teaching at TCNN. It took us several months to come up with a suggested orthography for the Tarok language, which we took to a meeting of Tarok leaders on the 1 January 1976, to be corrected and adapted by Tarok people. Revd D Bawado chaired the occasion, and the meeting was well attended with the *Ponzhi Tarok,* Mr Edward Cirdap Zhattau, the Chief of Tarok, Mr S D Lar, Mr Ali Ndam, Mr Kazi Ndam, Mr J J Lakkai, Mr Kumbo Vyapban, the late Mr Josiah Lanyi Sanda, and many others. One thing they emphasised was that whatever Tarok we were going to write must be in line with the one written by the Revd and Mrs Cooper, the early missionaries in Langtang. I was delighted to hear them expressing their preference for Mr Cooper's Tarok writing system. But we had to organise more meetings to enable them to see a need for some alterations.

The *Ponzhi Tarok,* Mr Edward Zhattau and the late Revd D Bawado, the chairman of the Langtang Regional Church Council of the COCIN, the chairman of the Local Government Council, the late Mr Tonga Rimbut, and later Mr E K Gagara, all gave us their full support. With time each one of them understood and accepted most of our suggestions. They could see why the old orthography did not reflect the language - eg *ibal* - goat, reflected the right vowel, which used to be written as *ibil*. This showed that an outside reader would stumble and pronounce the word wrongly. The sure vowel was accepted and adapted. At the end of the exercise, we came up with the accepted Tarok orthography title *'Re i nyi i Tarok'* - 'Let's know Tarok'. This was distributed to all Tarok elites.

After the orthography was adapted, Pam and I prayed over the next step which was to write primers that would teach the Tarok people how to read their language. By the Grace of the Lord, we embarked on the literacy aspect of the language. We came up with the 'Nkun ki i Tarok' Books I and II, and we were ready with this by April 1978. The books were launched in Langtang by the then Commissioner for Education, Mr Samuel Mafuyai. More than half of the books were sold out on that day. We worked on Book III which was meant to cover all Tarok words, and when people could read Book III, it meant they could read anything in the language.

Selbut Longtau joined as staff and together we got Book III ready. Pam and I worked on the teachers' copy introducing how to teach the pages. Before then, a Tarok language committee was formed. I was made President, the Revd Damina Bawado the Vice-President, and Mr J J Lakkai was the secretary. Mr Kumbo Vyapban gave a lot of help too. Members were thrilled and they worked with all their zeal to enhance Tarok literacy.

At the end of the literacy work, Pam and I prayed for the next step to take. She suggested we embark on translating some Christian pamphlets so that the Tarok people would have some material to read. My first one was 'The Four Spiritual Laws' discussed in Lausanne. It took such a long time but eventually 'The Four Spiritual Laws' in Tarok was ready.

Meanwhile, Mr Nanlyen Dassah had invited some of us to share his vision to form a Gospel team involving the youth in Langtang. Mr Danjuma Gambo, the late Julie Zhembin and myself attended the meeting in our house. Nanlyen in faith started the group, known as the Crusaders, which is still functioning today. We all gave our support. When 'The Four Spiritual Laws' was ready in Tarok, the group took many copies out and shared them in their preaching.

Danjuma Gambo joined the Nigerian Bible Translation Trust before Selbut. Seeing the need to have reading material in Tarok, he was inspired to embark on the translation of all the parables in the Bible. It came out beautifully. We started to organise Tarok classes, not only in Langtang, but in all the villages, so they would be inspired to read and write their own language. Through their ability to read and write, they would be able to read useful material that would build them up socially, economically and, above all, spiritually. So we formed 'The Tarok Cultural Development Association' involving all the *Ponzhi Mbin* (the heads of the traditional religious practices). They got the Tarok people to be interested in learning their language. At one of the meetings, a decision was taken that eighty adult classes be established for Tarok lessons. Mallam Tali became the supervisor of such schools.

The New Testament in Tarok

It got to a point that CUSO (Canadian Universities Service Overseas) became interested in the programme. They expressed a willingness to assist our project financially, so we set ourselves a target that by the year 1990, all Tarok people should be able to read and write. We were seriously working towards that, when a coup d'etat took place in December 1983. A lot of our effort was wasted and CUSO did not come in again. People withdrew their interest and, as I was affected by the coup, I shifted my attention to the care of my family. I believed the Lord would raise up this work again so that the Tarok people would be able to read the New Testament that was translated by a group of us. Selbut Longtau was the main translator. I translated the books of John and James; Lakai and Bali Kassam translated other portions of the Bible. The New Testament in Tarok was launched in March, 1993.

Pam Bendor-Samuel and her husband, Dr John Bendor-Samuel, the Executive Vice-President of Wycliffe Bible Translators, and the Summer Institute of Linguistics, then stationed in USA, attended the launching. Dr John Adive, the present Director of the Nigerian Bible Translation Trust, gave great support for this project and was at the launching. I pray that the Lord will also make it possible for the Old Testament to be translated, so that the whole Bible will be available for Tarok people, in their own language, in the near future. I believe that all these achievements and the inspirations owed their origins to the Lausanne conference in Switzerland which I was privileged to attend.

A Vision for Cooper School

While working on the Tarok language, the names of the Coopers kept coming up. Tarok people expressed a lot of admiration for them. As I listened to their very favourable comments on these two missionaries, the Lord gave me an urge to speak with the church at Langtang to open a school that would teach the ideals of the Coopers, especially as the Church schools which used to teach those ideals were already taken over by the government.

I approached the Revd Damina Bawado; he in turn invited me to the elders' meeting in Langtang to put across my vision. I told them how Tarok people cherished the work of the Coopers and I was convinced that our appreciation should go beyond words. Since the Coopers had no children, those of us who accepted their ideals are their children, and should use those ideals and Christian principles in our schools. It would be a school founded on Jesus Christ whose servants the Revd and Mrs Cooper were. It should be a school where the discipline would be based on Christian principles. After I told them my vision of the school, they questioned where the money would come from. I insisted that it would be a school built to extend the Kingdom of Christ amongst Tarok children and should be carried out in faith, for the Lord would provide for His work. With this they did not argue anymore. They asked how we could go about it. I suggested a fund raising for a proposed Cooper school in Langtang. One single individual, the chief launcher Mr Danladi Shemu who was at one time a Permanent Secretary in the Civil Service of Benue Plateau state, donated 200 bags of cement and N6,000.00 (Six thousand naira). A total of about N12,000.00 (Twelve thousand naira) was collected. Soon the foundation stone was laid and the school was built.

Solomon gave much support for this school. He said that since I was named after Mary Cooper, I am their rightful daughter to take this decision on behalf of my parents the Coopers. I saw this as having a genesis from Lausanne. Today, many children have passed through the school. The church is thinking of establishing a further secondary school.

After about two years in existence, the church decided to have the school officially opened - Solomon had then become the Governor of Plateau State (1979). In April 1981 he officially opened the school and more funds were raised. The school is growing from strength to strength and caters for elites in the local government. Already the pupils of this school have passed to many secondary schools all over Nigeria.

Government Teacher's College, Jos.

I had left the Theological College of Northern Nigeria in August 1975 after one year of service there. I went back to the Government of Benue/Plateau State and I was given an appointment to teach at the Government Teachers' College, Jos, where I met with Mrs Angela Rogers, the Principal of the college, a very hard worker who was a disciplinarian. She would question the teachers and expect nothing less than their best for the students. Some teachers did not like this meticulous check, but it was good and necessary for the college. When Mrs Rogers left, Mrs W Shonekan, who was her Vice-Principal, took over.

In January, 1977, I had been transferred from the Government Teachers' College to assist at a new Advanced Teachers' College in Akwanga which started at a temporary site in Jos. I taught Educational Philosophy and English. After one year, the Sardauna Memorial College in Jos was handed over to the state government. They called on me to help bring the school up to standard. At that time it had become the Government Secondary School, Jos. I accepted the challenge working as Principal of the College from 1978 to July 1979, when I left for further studies at the University of Jos. During my stay in the school, I was handicapped by finance in many ways. I supervised the building of the administrative block which I initiated, the construction of a sports field, and a classroom block. Since I discovered that the college was handicapped by finance, I took upon myself to do some of the purchases for the school directly, rather than giving out contracts or local purchase orders to contractors who might inflate the prices of these goods that were much needed for the upkeep and the maintenance of the college. Of course, as it will be expected, some contractors did not like it because it prevented them from getting huge profits, so they petitioned against me to the Ministry of Education. But it was a delight to me to hear an honourable member, the minority leader of the House of Assembly in Plateau State, commend me personally, on the floor of the House for the improvement I had brought to the school.

University of Jos

I applied to go into the University of Jos to enable me to gain more experience in the administration of education. I went in for a Masters Degree in Educational Administration and Planning and gained admission in July 1979. I applied for study leave and went on this one-year course.

While on the course, the military government of Gen Olusegun Obasanjo was about to hand over power to the civilians in October, 1979. There were five political parties, Nigerian People's Party (NPP), The National Party of Nigeria (NPN), The Unity Party of Nigeria (UPN), People's Redemption Party (PRP), and the Great Nigeria People's Party (GNPP). Elections were held in August, starting with the State's House of Assembly, Federal House of Assembly, The Senate, Governorship and finally the Presidential. September was for hearing petitions on the floor of the House, and final judgement, 1 October, the national independence day, for swearing in all elected candidates.

Solomon was elected on the platform of the Nigerian People's Party (NPP) as Governor of Plateau State. We moved to the Government House four days later. It was a completely new experience to me because when the former Governor, now retired, Air Commodore Dan Suleiman (then Group Captain), was Governor of Plateau State, his wife Mrs Marie Dan Suleiman had invited me once and had shown me the inside of the Government House, with the exception of her husband's room. I did not know that I would one day occupy the house.

Chapter 9

LIFE AT GOVERNMENT HOUSE 1979-1983

When the result of the election was announced, we started to receive many visitors - individuals, groups, associations, Christian/Muslim organisations, Women's Fellowships, party representatives - from all the local governments and from all over the country. The house was like a market. Letters of support and solidarity poured in from all over the world. Most of these groups came with songs, music and dances. From morning till night the house was full.

They presented us with symbolic weapons like shields, swords, Bibles, and words of encouragement, and above all, prayed for us. I felt like a newly wedded bride and all the advice I received during my wedding days came back to my mind again. This prepared us for the task ahead.

We felt like the people's possession, who had been mandated to carry out a special assignment on their behalf. I felt inadequate and wished I was not involved. It was a mixed feeling of exultation and self examination. Will I meet the desire of the people? I felt the responsibility on me and I wondered how Solomon, the man who was directly involved, felt. He appeared undisturbed, unruffled, normal and with a tireless energy - happy all the time.

I remembered my heart's desire was to marry a pastor, but I found myself in this most busy and demanding position. Solomon to me was a prospective pastor. I thought we would eventually settle to it, but it seemed we were going farther away from my dreams. I was comforted by the fact that his Christian faith remained unchanged and that there is no position in which we cannot serve the Lord. So quietly and thankfully I kept to my husband's calling.

When I entered Government House, the first thing I did was to commit us all to the Lord, for the period He desired us to stay there. The people I had lived with daily were now cut off by protocol. It took some time before I realised that they were stopped from coming at the gate by the security men or Government officials who screened people before allowing them in. The policemen were on guard twenty-four hours a day. The thing to do was to send the name of the person coming to the gate for easy identification. Even with this, some policemen would choose to be difficult.

My first challenge was when some leaders of the Nigerian People's Party (NPP), ie the ruling party in the state, came to ask me to withdraw from the University course I was undergoing as it was humiliating for a Governor's wife to be a student. I told them I respected their feelings and would have loved to obey, but I chose to go in for this further training before we arrived at Government House. I was enjoying my training and had gone half way. If I dropped out, I felt I would be a loser, so I would rather finish the course. I said I would like to discuss the matter with Solomon. Solomon shared my view, so I carried on and completed my master's degree in June 1980.

Education for the Nomads

I was not certain what Solomon wanted me to do after that. For about a month I was idle, but later I had to find things to keep me busy. I told Solomon I'd like to go back to work at the Ministry of Education. He thought my presence could worry some people. I remembered one of the things he said during his campaigns was that if he was chosen into power, he would give nomads in the state a mobile education. I jokingly mentioned to him 'What about this nomadic education you mentioned? I would like to be involved with that, it would be a new area and could be quite challenging'.

He agreed to this suggestion, after consulting with the then Commissioner of Education, Mr Joshua Gamde, the Permanent Secretary, and another senior officer Dr Corbin, who was in charge of research at the then 'Teachers Resource Centre', now 'Educational Resource Centre'.

It was decided that I be posted to the Teachers Resource Centre (TRC) to conduct this educational project for the Ministry of Education. As soon as I was given an office, I started work, with the help of the head of unit, Mr P Mwoltu, and consultations with the then Dean of Education, University of Jos, Professor Cooper, Dr C Ezeomah, who had conducted research on nomads in Bauchi state, and Dr S Udoh. They came to Government House and briefed me.

At TRC we decided the project should be in phases.
Phase I   A survey of nomads and their attitude towards formal education should be conducted. The research would enable us to know whether the children would be available for the classes and whether their attitude would be receptive to education.
Phase II   Creating awareness of Government's intention to educate the nomads and analysing responses.
Phase III   Developing a suitable curriculum that would really cater for the needs of the nomads.
Phase IV   Training teachers towards the use of the curriculum.
Phase V   Implementing a pilot scheme for the project.

I requested the help of our National Youth Service Corp (NYSC). Two NYSC teachers were posted to me, Mr Isaiah Phar and Mr Dyikuk. They were as if specially chosen for a great national assignment. We came up with our research findings in less than two months. We organised special awareness symposiums and conferences. I travelled to places to meet with nomadic people's leaders in the State, ie Bassa and Vom Veterinary Institute in Vom, Mazat Ropp and Gashish in Barakin Social Government in Plateau State; I also met with them in Jos, where leaders from all over the States came for a meeting, where we took decisions together.

We held a workshop for curriculum development for nomads in Plateau State - it took one month. This involved some Ministry of Education veterinary workers and the Ministry of Agriculture officials, University lecturers and the Nomadic Education Unit of the Ministry of Education. We drew up the curriculum and sent copies to various Government establishments in the State for comments, including some legislative members - eg the speaker, and leaders of majority and minority groups. We organised an interview for teachers willing to participate in the project, then wrote to their various LGCs for their release.

We started a nine months' training course for the teachers who were mainly Grade II teachers. Some were secondary school leavers, but if they were teachers with nomadic background, we gave them priority. They went through the course which was based on Child Psychology, Mathematics and English, Social Studies, Animal Management, Health Education, Agriculture and Teaching Methodology. The students had practical farms in Riyom and at TRC where they learnt how to cultivate and produce relevant crops for nomads. They were taught how to make manure out of animal dung. There was an examination at the end and the students who passed were issued with certificates and then posted to a nomadic group to start pilot schools. The course started with thirty-three teachers, but only fifteen of them graduated. Some gave excuses and left because at that time there was difficulty in paying primary school teachers, as money was not forthcoming from Lagos, so many of them were not paid for months. This made life difficult for the teachers in training.

News of nomadic education spread around the country, so much so that the then Permanent Secretary directed the Assistant Director Primary/Adult Education in the Federal Ministry of Education, Mrs Sikuade, to come all the way from Lagos to find out more details about the new education. The discussion took place at the Ministry of Education Secretariat. The then Hon Commissioner, the Permanent Secretary, the Chief Inspector of Education and the Accountant were present at this meeting on 8 - 9 April

1981. Mrs Sikuade promised some Federal Government assistance which did not come because her superior in the Federal Ministry of Education did not consider education for nomads appropriate but I was not discouraged. Soon we were able to open three pilot schools in Mazat Ropp and Gashish both in Barakin Ladi Local Government and Zomo in Shendam Local Government. A school was started in Gidan Biri in Nassarawa LGC and there were proposals for Bassa, Keffi, Wase Kanam, Awe and Lafiya. Solomon launched the project at Mazat in April, 1981. There was a high Government representation at the launching since the Governor was personally involved and Fulani girls graced the occasion with music and dances.

Other duties in Government House included attending school speech and prize giving days, fund raising for charities, celebrations by organisations, ethnic groups, societies, funerals, marriages, naming ceremonies, visiting the sick and presenting them with gifts, especially at Christmas. As for schools in Plateau State, I visited more than three-quarters of them. I was guest of honour at games, visiting needy institutions, eg the Vocational School for the Blind, the orphanage etc. This was not only restricted to Plateau State, it extended to Kaduna and the then Gongola States, accompanying Solomon for some national and international functions which involved travel. I encouraged good initiatives - eg International Year of the Disabled, children, women, launching of women's centres, baby shows, cultural shows, etc. I was always busy performing the ceremonies. Press interviews were unavoidable with the newspapers, magazines, radio and television.

Receiving visitors was a frequent job, mainly inviting people to Government House to be served - eg Plateau State University female students, lady Commissioners and Permanent Secretaries, women's leaders of associations, political women's leaders, children's days and parties, important visitors from other states - eg first ladies of other states, and women's leaders from outside the country.

Joint Committee of Women's Societies.

The thought of enrolling the support of the women for greater achievement burdened my heart. So I invited some women leaders in the state, discussed it with them and we formed the 'Joint Committee of Women's Societies in Plateau State'. This committee embarked on fund raising and set up a house they named 'Alheri House For The Needy' at a cost of N80,000.00. It was commissioned by the Governor, Mr S D Lar, on the 28 May 1983. At this centre we share out food and materials with the very needy people like the aged, the lepers and beggars. We wanted this to be a house where grace is shown to the needy, so we bought materials like soap, grain and salt. We received donations of old clothes from people and distributed them to the needy. It was a full-time job, and Mrs Saratu Bature was employed to keep the service going, on behalf of the Joint Committee of Women's Societies. I thanked the Lord and rejoiced in seeing this initiative become a reality. Somehow, I prefer to cater for the needy in this way rather than distributing pennies to them on the roadside. It was my prayer that the needy will be served from this base.

Enrolling all the women's societies for common service became more than just an idea when the President of The National Council of Women's' Societies (NCWS) from New Zealand visited Nigeria in 1982. Plateau State was one of the states chosen. She was impressed with our efforts when she called on me at Government House, with some of her officers. She suggested that what we were doing should be the pattern for NCWS too and requested that the already established committee in Plateau State should become the NCWS Plateau State branch, a wing of NCWS. I had no personal interest but to encourage the women towards giving a service and I had no objection if the service would continue under a different name. So our joint committee became NCWS Plateau State branch. There were other programmes drawn up by the committee. The committee used to meet weekly, then fortnightly and later monthly at Government House. One of the programmes was to convert 'Alheri House for the Needy' to train some handicapped people, mainly the lame but the problem was gaining a trained staff who would carry out this project. The women were to advertise and get suitable people to train in craft work and some special needs of this particular group of disabled but we did not know where such a training would be available. We discussed embarking on large-scale farming, so there would be enough to sell at a subsidised rate to the needy. When the Joint Committee became NCWS, all was transferred to the President of NCWS Plateau State and I continued to give guidance and advice behind the scenes.

More Training for the Less Privileged

After the Joint Committee of Women's Associations was formed, I encouraged the women to assist our less privileged young girls to learn the type of home economics lessons we received during our days at school. The schools complained of lack of finance, so we started vocational classes for girls from 10 years and above. These classes usually started a week or two into their summer holidays and we brought them to an end a week before they resumed school so they had about seven to eight weeks teaching. At the end of such courses, we would invite a Governor's wife to present certificates to the participants which provided the girls with something to look forward to, and they learnt what they missed in schools or at home.

The most successful one was the 1983 programme which ushered in Her Excellency Hajiya Goni, wife of the Governor of Borno State as guest of honour. The girls displayed their skills and what they had learnt from these courses. It was quite impressive, seeing their knitting, crocheting and embroidery work so I suggested we had a permanent centre for this. We had negotiated for a place in Bukuru and hoped that it could even become an international centre, but the coup d'etat of 31 December 1983, halted all the effort. I begin to understand the effect of a country that has an unstable Government, even at a Governor's wife level. It was clear that a country needs a stable Government to facilitate development and progress. It can be frustrating to see laudable projects being thwarted by constant changes in the political situation.

The Tarok Cultural Development Association was very successful. Cultural days were big days for the Tarok people. We divided ourselves into several committees to take care of various cultural aspects and how to achieve them - eg language, attire, craft, dances, research into Tarok's archives, history, food, literacy, etc. I spent time visiting different parts of Tarok land to discuss the progress of our literacy project with the people. Translation work also progressed at Government House. Occasionally, I used to find time to help the language committee. My being in Government House provided some support for the Tarok project. I soon discovered that Government House, which people had given me the impression earlier was a relaxed place, where one does little but eat, became the busiest place for me. I hardly slept earlier than midnight. I was either planning visits or a programme, or writing, translating or reading and after a day's work I was very exhausted. But as a family we found time in the evening to praise the Lord for the day and we would commit our daddy to the Lord before the children retired to bed.

Visit of the Archbishop of Canterbury

In 1963, when in the UK pursuing my studies, I was invited to stay for two weeks with a Christian friend, Christine Grundy in Canterbury. She took me round the city and to the Cathedral and the Archbishop's court - it was beautiful! I could not imagine the sort of man who was living there.

It was a real joy for me to hear later that I was going to receive this great man into Government House. The Most Reverend Robert Runcie arrived in Jos accompanied by his special envoy Terry Waite. My daughter, Debbie, was asked to present him with a bouquet of flowers.

He was a humble man who looked relaxed and happy to visit Plateau State. In one of his addresses, he said that he had been told that the weather and other things would not be the same when he arrived at Jos, they would be better in Plateau State, so he was looking forward to his visit. Now he had arrived and felt at home. It was a small world. I had been outside his house in Canterbury, now he had come to mine. One never knows when one will be a host to important people.

The Political Situation

As for Solomon, Government House created a big gap between him and his family. He was away a great deal - we rarely had time together and I was feeling a bit lonely. I knew it was not deliberate, so I supported him in prayer. He was good at telephoning to let us know his schedule and that he cared for us, whether in the House or when he was travelling. His particular party, the Nigerian People's Party (NPP), formed a Government in three states of Nigeria. The National Party of Nigeria controlled the Federal Government and seven other states. The PRP controlled Kano state and narrowly controlled Kaduna. The UPN controlled five states, the GNPP controlled two states. Those members of the National Party of Nigeria felt strengthened by their control of the Federal Government. I knew they tried to make governing difficult for Solomon in Plateau State, being the only state in the North which was controlled by his party, but God really overruled all hostility, obstacles, evil intentions and countless hazards.

Solomon saw a lot of enmity from the opposition party. People attempted to burn down our personal house in Langtang, but God saved it as people noticed the havoc in time and put the fire out without much damage.

Hostility mounted in various forms as the second election date approached. We, the family, increased our prayers for him too. On one occasion when I came back from town, I heard that the NPN people were demonstrating against the Government but because of the tension of that period, the police were not supposed to grant permission for any group to demonstrate. One could not tell how these NPN people got permission to come so near to Government House without being checked. When the police at the gate threatened to fire at them, they turned back and decided to wait for me, because they knew that I was out at a function that day. Fortunately for me, when I came back, something went wrong with the car, so I was given a lift back in a car from our education office and they could not recognise me. The Lord allowed the car to break down for a good reason. The police at the gate expressed how they were worried about me. I had no idea what was going on.

I really did not know how Solomon remained unruffled and carried on with his work normally. Yet Solomon carried out a lot of development in the State - eg:

-   He enhanced the status of the chiefs.
-   He built many dams - eg in Pankshin, Langtang and Lafia, Toto, Shendam, Keana, Nassarawa Eggon, Doma, Nassarawa Keffi, Bokkos, Forom Du and others.
-   He established over 300 post-primary institutions in the states and the College of Education, Gindiri.
-   He introduced the shift system in our secondary schools, which were able to cater for more children.
-   He built many hospitals - eg in Mangu, Quanpan, Bassa, Obi, Nassarawa Eggon, Toto, Karu, Akwanga, Nassarawa Keffi and Wase.
-   He created more Local Government areas - eg the present Toto, Obi, Bokkos, Karu Nassarawa Eggon, Doma and Quanpan.
-   He set up Plateau State Television which was officially commissioned by the Right Honourable Nnamdi Azikiwe, the first President of the Federal Republic of Nigeria, and the Owelle of Onitsha on 21 June 1985. Many distinguished personalities were in attendance.
-   He established the Quiz Company in Jarawa Chiefdom to operate under the Jos International Breweries (JIB.). He went far with the establishment of BARC Farms, part of JIB. I accompanied him to Denmark in 1982 when he went on an official visit to negotiate for the setting up of BARC Farms. I saw a similar farm in Denmark, which has exactly the same features as the one in Jos.
-   He initiated and encouraged the natural spring water industry in Kerang, Mangu Local Government Area. Being influenced by the Evian water in Europe, he wanted a

similar thing in Plateau State, and on the 3 December 1983, SWAN natural spring water was commissioned by him. Today we all enjoy SWAN water in Nigeria.

- He established a State Bank, to which he gave the name Lion Bank (Mr I Shammah was the first Chairman) and an insurance company called Savannah Insurance Company (Chattalas was the Chairman), one of the most viable and popular underwriters company in the state. But unfortunately these economically viable companies were destroyed as soon as the military government took over in 1983. The cancellation was ordered by Vice Admiral Samuel Atukum Rtd, who was then the Military Governor of Plateau State. Paradoxically, Samuel Atukum is also from Plateau State.

Solomon had a vision to boost tourism in the state, and initiated the building of the Sheraton Hotel in Jos at the Liberty Dam. Even though the building is still not completed, it is hoped that money will be available in the near future, for it is of such economic significance, not only to Plateau State, but to the nation in general. This is another disadvantage of frequent changes of power. I believe that if Solomon had been able to complete his term he would have completed his vision of tourism in the state, having visited some of the key tourist countries like Kenya, United Kingdom and Switzerland. Solomon used to travel a lot for official assignments and I was able to accompany him on some of these journeys. He made friends with all the states whether they belonged to the same political party or not.

The first inter-state visit he undertook was to Kano State, which was governed by the People's Redemption Party (PRP), and he established a great friendship with them through their first civilian Governor, Alhaji Abubakar Rimi.

I accompanied him on his visit to Gongola State (governed by GNPP), which enabled me to visit the Government Girls' Secondary School, Yola, where I addressed the girls and encouraged them to work hard.

He visited Cross River State which was then NPN and I accompanied him. This brought me many surprises. Dr Clement Isong was the Governor and also of the Central Bank of Nigeria. I had earlier invited Mrs Isong as First

Lady of Cross River State to Plateau State for some women's function. She must have influenced her husband to invite both Solomon and me and she organised my itinerary. Together we visited a girls' secondary school, Ugep, in Obubra Local Government area. The people had gathered in their thousands to give us a rousing welcome and I was crowned with a chieftaincy title - the 'Ugbonji of Ugep'. It is a title given to a woman who has excelled in yam production; yam is the staple food of the people. She would then be crowned as an outstanding woman who had the power to cultivate more yam than anyone else. In my own case, I was not identified with yam production, but by my educational achievements. At that time, the papers made big headlines of the MEd degree I received from the University of Jos, and also my initiative in starting the Nomadic Education project. It was for this that they gave me the chieftaincy title. How wonderful! I recalled my childhood when I was deprived of education, and now I was being given a chieftaincy title for achievement in education; it was almost inconceivable.

I visited another school, The Union School, Ikot Ekpene, and spoke to the girls. The Ugep school was built by the women's united effort. I was privileged to visit a co-operative shop established by women and a town hall built by women and it was a very impressive economic effort. There was a workshop by the side of the shop that produced all the varieties of finished goods, and whatever was desired that was not in the shop could be ordered in the workshop. When I got back, I discussed with the women the possibility of a similar thing being started in Plateau State.

More Foreign Visits

Solomon went to Australia and Bulgaria and I accompanied him. The most exciting one was the Australian visit. The long journey took about two days by air. The largest city, Sydney, has a population of three million people and has streets with similar names to London streets - eg Oxford Square, Kings Cross, George Street etc. From Sydney we visited Canberra, the capital city. I was impressed by the recognition accorded to all the citizens of Australia, irrespective of their sex. They name their public places, or name boats and streets after personalities who have contributed to their societies, including wives of governors. Even their pictures were printed on the national currencies. I was surprised at this recognition accorded women in this way and found it encourages their daughters as well.

We have Australian missionaries in Nigeria like Revd and Mrs Keith Black and Mr and Mrs Graham Rule. The distance between Nigeria and Australia made me appreciate the missionaries from that country. Some of our people used to feel that the missionaries were people who went to Africa in search of chickens and eggs! It was nice to see Revd Keith Black and his wife at their church in Sydney.

We visited Adelaide - this is another state capital where I saw the air school - ie Correspondence School. I saw all the radio classes, the homework sent by students and the packages sent to the students. We also visited Perth, capital of Western Australia and then left for Singapore, where we spent the night at the Mandarin Hotel. From Mount Faber we saw the whole of Singapore. God's world is so beautiful and the people there are very warm hearted. I made two friends on this beautiful mountain and corresponded with them for a while until a *coup d'etat* which displaced us completely for a while.

Unforgettable Memories

When people elect leaders, it is good that they encourage them as the leaders need their support. I was glad that many people knew this and visited us, prayed with us and gave honest advice. Leaders of various communities came to see us. Government House was theirs, so we enjoyed them coming to it 24-hours a day. Some Christian leaders from other states also visited us and prayed with us. The Revd (now Archbishop) Benson Idahosa, his wife and other members of his ministry visited us twice, and Revd I Umaren of the Qua Iboe Church from Cross River State, now Akwa Ibom State. Their visits were of great encouragement to us. Revd Idahosa said, 'I have come to remove fears and doubts from you. God has called you for a mission for Him in Government House. The enemy will try to rob you, but you are going to be a new tool for the Lord'. He said Solomon should see himself as a servant of God. He came during the second elections in August at a time when we were going through great stress from pressure from the opposition who were creating stories of blackmail and making a great effort to take power. While he was talking to us, rain fell. He said, 'This rain is symbolic, rain washes dirt away'. So he said 'The Lord shall wipe away all your tears, this rain is not ordinary rain, God has sent it to wipe away all your suffering'. He asked us to promise that we would not worry about our detractors who are putting deliberate pressure on us. He said 'The Lord knows that you have passed through water and fire. He is your Saviour, fear not. When you walk through the fire you will not be burned, the flames will not set you ablaze. God will deal with all your enemies, so you should go to the office with a light heart'. These verses had been given us by another Christian group six weeks earlier, so we knew the Lord was speaking to us and preparing us for the tough time ahead.

During the first election in 1979 Solomon's eldest brother Mallam Ibi Nimak Lar, who brought him up and who proposed Solomon's family's desire to have me as a wife, died. It was a great shock to us all - it affected us emotionally and in our performance. But the Lord uplifted us. He died just before we got into Government House; this was the most painful part.

About two years later we had another shock, the death, in a motor accident, of his son Dr Sunday Lar, a medical doctor of whom we were all proud. It was a tragic sad memory. Solomon quoted Romans 8:38-39 at the graveside during the funeral, 'For I am convinced that neither death nor life, neither angels nor demons, neither the present nor the future, nor any powers, neither height nor depth, nor anything else in all creation will be able to separate us from the love of God that is in Christ Jesus our Lord.' This encouraged all of us.

We were just by His grace picking up again when news

came that my mother was dead. Early on the 1 September 1983, Solomon's ADC said that my mother was sick and needed a blood transfusion. Confused by everything around me, I helped to organise who would go for the blood donation. Soon after that, my mother's only surviving sister, Mama M Banfa, and her son the late Albert Banfa, came to tell me that my mother had died. I was greatly confused, I hated not seeing my mother again before it was too late. I started to develop high blood pressure. How could mother leave without my seeing her? It was too sudden. I was looking forward to visiting her as usual in the hospital, and to watching her get better. She seemed to know she was not going to live long. In April she called me and said to me, 'Mary, these days people pass away so fast. I want to tell all of you, my children, that I have a commitment to the Baptist Church in Langtang'. She had taken responsibility for an evangelist who worked with the Baptists. When she was gone we should try to keep that commitment going by paying the evangelist from the rent we might collect from her house. I said 'Mother, people do not die by age. I may be called before you'. I thank her for sharing with me. She was called to rest only four months after that.

Second Term Election

The Nigeria's People's Party (NPP) of which Solomon was a member, eventually elected Solomon for a second term in office. This did not please the opposition. They mounted more serious campaigns of blackmail against him. Some of them spent sleepless nights planning how to discredit him. In fact, one of them confessed this to me later. He said that they deliberately made up stories that they felt would bring him to an end. Great pressure mounted from the opposition but Solomon would say 'Pray for them. All is in God's hands. I have a calling and must keep on until the Lord Himself wants me to give up. He would know how to end it too'. There was never a time when I found him scared of any of these accusations which he called malicious. His spirit was high, he was full of confidence with tireless energy. Surely his strength was from the Lord.

NPN Plan to Rig the Election

Rumours went round that some aliens were brought into Plateau State to cast votes to increase NPN's numbers. It was said that during the registration, some NPP strong-hold areas were denied registration of voters in order to give advantage to NPN, the opponent. Names were deliberately mixed up on the voters list, or left out eg some people could not vote as they were far away from their voting centres. They said ballot papers were being hoarded and only released to NPN supporters and that there was a deliberate delay in distributing voting materials in NPP strong areas. Other accusations were that the Federal Electoral Commission (FEDECO) deliberately employed half literate people in Plateau State, so that they could twist them the way they liked. Many believed that FEDECO favoured NPN since they were set up by the NPN Federal Government. They said, all these grounds were carefully planned to make election rigging easy. With all these stories, Solomon remained unruffled.

Another Dream

About six weeks prior to the election, I had gone to Langtang to conduct a literacy class which I had earlier organised, helped by Mr J J Lakkai. The course lasted three weeks. After two weeks, the Lord revealed some coming events to me in a dream, which upset me so I took time to pray and fast about it. The dream was that some torment fell on the whole Nigerian nation, people were suffering, even those that appeared happy were suffering within. I met with the wives of two other Governors and they too could not stand the hardship. All over the whole country there was great suffering and misery. I found myself alone and tried to escape but there was no transport. As I stood there gazing, a lone taxi came by, stopped and picked me up. But when we got to a lonely dangerous bush part of the road, the taxi man robbed me. He took my bag and pushed me out of the car, then he drove off. I shouted for help, but there was no-one around. I stood there wondering what to do. Then suddenly I noticed my daughter Beni calling me on the opposite side of the road 'Mummy, come let me show you the way'. It was such a big relief. I ran to her and she held my hands and led me through a path. We arrived at a town called 'the town of the enemy'. I was afraid of the town, but Beni led me through it. People had fled from this town which was deserted; some left food cooking on the open fire. After going some distance, Beni turned round and said 'Mummy, the road is closed'. I woke up at this point. My body felt heavy, surely the dream meant something but I had no appetite for food. I told my mother when she visited me in the afternoon, and mother said 'Surely the dream was a bad one. Some calamity is going to befall the nation, but the aspect of the enemy running away was a good one. Let us leave everything in the hands of God'. By then I was praying about this revelation. I knew some hard times were coming, but I could not tell in which form. I fasted and prayed for four days and the Lord gave me peace about it all.

After three weeks of the Tarok course, the *Ponzhi Tarok*, Mr Edward Zhattau, and the then Chairman of the Local Government Area, the late Mr Tonga Rimbut, attended the closing ceremony and encouraged all participants to form literacy classes in all Tarok land as programmed by the Tarok Cultural Development Association. They emphasised that a literate society would enhance development.

I went back to Jos at the end of the literacy course in Langtang, and I noticed that the political campaigns had heated, because it was three weeks to the election. We intensified our prayers as we listened to allegations and counter allegations on the television or in the daily newspapers. It was to my greatest joy that my daughters Chalya and Beni gave us Psalm 12:1-8 at one of our devotions in the evening, taken from their daily notes. Beni said 'Do you ever feel as David feels in this Psalm? Wickedness seems to be everywhere, and the situation appears to be getting worse. Corrupt men are in power and the upright are being squeezed out of public life. Promotion goes to those who are prepared to bribe or who belong to the ruling political party. The notes urged us to remember that God knows all about what is happening and He will intervene at the right time'. I shared these verses with their father when he came in. I was encouraged by the faith of our children. Mark our son said, 'I am expecting a miracle from God about daddy's election'. It would appear that even the children felt the pressure.

The second term election of the Governor took place on the 13 August 1983. It was characterised by lots of rigging, varying from the disappearance of Federal Electoral Commission (FEDECO) officials and lack of voting materials in some NPP strongholds - eg ballot papers and boxes. It was also alleged by Paul Gindiri, an Evangelist, that some NPN stalwarts were arrested and that figures were altered, etc. Despite all these stories, Solomon won by a comfortable majority despite 69,000 votes from Doma LGC, a stronghold of NPP, being rejected by FEDECO, and NPN. It was really by the Lord's hand that victory came. FEDECO Plateau state did not want to announce the result or declare Solomon as the winner, even when the votes had been counted and collated. I sensed it was another of their efforts to twist the results, so I invited some women and paid their tickets to Lagos to lodge our complaints to the FEDECO Chief Executive. On hearing the complaints, he wondered what was happening in Plateau State. But they had made the point clear to the FEDECO Chairman.

There was an unusually long delay over the announcement of the result of the gubernatorial elections in Plateau State. The newsmen in Lagos got very curious - they organised an interview with the Chairman of FEDECO - Justice Ovie Whiskey. They said all the results of gubernatorial elections had been received from all over the Federation, except in one state. The public was interested in knowing the reason. The Chairman then responded by saying 'I do not know what is happening in Plateau State either. I do not know why they are delaying the result. From the results we have here, Mr Lar has won the election but they do not want to announce it'. As soon as the Chairman said this, the branch of the FEDECO in Plateau had no alternative but to declare Solomon the winner. We then knew that the miracle my son referred to had taken place.

Solomon was due to be sworn in for the second term in office on the 1 October 1983. The opposition delayed their complaints until the 29 September 1983 and then brought a petition against his election. A special police plane brought a summons from Lagos requiring him to be in Lagos on the 30 September 1983, for the hearing. The plane with the summons arrived in Jos at 11.30 pm but refused to wait and take Solomon back with it. The first flight at 9.00 am the next day, the day of the hearing, was delayed. Clearly some people planned to take advantage of his absence. But as God would have it, the matter was referred to Jos High Court. The letter explained that the case could be heard after the swearing in which went ahead as planned. The case which was filed by the NPN gubernatorial candidate in Plateau State, Mr John Jatau Kadiya, against the elected governor, was heard for the second time on the 25 October 1983 and rejected. I remembered in my dream that we did not go far after passing the town of the enemy, before my daughter told me the road had come to an end. The thought of that scared me. But whenever I prayed about it, my peace had always been restored.

In 1983, the family travelled to Langtang to spend Christmas as usual. General Yakubu Gowon's children visited us, obviously to show appreciation to the Governor for the way he had organised a rousing welcome back for General Yakubu Gowon, whom he saw as an illustrious son of Plateau State, having served the people so faithfully. He had raised funds to settle him well at home.

This Christmas happened to be our last Christmas at Government House after four years.

Exit from Government House

The police band accompanied the Governor to Langtang in 1983 to treat the guests to a Christmas Eve party. Many Tarok people attended and some generals from the area were at home for Christmas too. As usual, the Governor, Mr Solomon D Lar, invited all of them to lunch, and all came with the exception of General Joe Garba. There was a lot of discussion in the house. The next day, Solomon treated them to a lunch again. Air Commodore Dan Suleiman and General Hananiya went to stay with General Bali's family. They all attended the luncheon party with their families, after which they went to Yankari for the New Year. Solomon went back to Jos from Langtang on the 29 December 1983, and he presented the State's budget to the House of Assembly of Plateau State the following day.

Hostility increased. On our way back to Jos, a commercial bus from Mangu tried to hit the Governor's car and probably cause his death, but the car swerved around and it hit the spare car behind causing our son Mark, who was in the car, to be involved in an accident. Mark was injured and the driver was even more hurt. This happened at Yabit, after Kwanpe, in Langtang LGA, but the entourage advised that the injured be taken to Pankshin hospital because there may be too many people to greet in Langtang, and they may not have the desired rest. I felt sick within me. I hated our involvement in politics then. When I reached Pankshin, I rushed to where my son was taken and found that he had a cut on his mouth and had injured his arms and neck. After treatment, he was transferred to Plateau Hospital in Jos, and requested to be taken back to Government House. He was then asked to rest in bed as he was still in pain. That night I stayed a while with him, but went to bed late after giving him his pills. Because of the late night, I overslept. At about 6.00 am a steward came knocking at my door. I was annoyed that anybody should disturb me whilst sleeping late so I called back angrily, 'What is the matter?'. The steward answered 'I heard marshal music on the radio, that is why I came to inform you before the soldiers arrive. You may want to leave the house because they might maltreat you'. 'Where is my husband?', I asked. 'He was called out this morning'. I went to wake the children. 'Let us leave, the soldiers have taken the government'. We were all delighted at the news at first because after all, things were not moving well politically. There was dishonesty, fraudulent behaviour and hatred. I got my children in my personal car and drove to the town, leaving all our personal belongings, including Solomon's personal cars and all our property behind.

A week earlier a message came to me from an unknown army wife. She said she did not know me but she was full of admiration for me so if I had any belongings in the State House, I should remove them to our personal home. I thanked the messenger but I did not take any action. I did not think it was going to happen so suddenly.

Everything was left behind in the State House and we did not even have soap, toothpaste and brushes, shoes, clothes or bedding. We went to stay with brothers in the Lord at the Nigerian Bible Translation Centre, then with my brother, Barrister Stephen Lar, who was then occupying our personal home. I had a mixed feeling about the coup d'etat. It was a welcome event because it served as a relief from the task of governance which was becoming very unbearable because of the opposition's confrontational attitude towards the State Government. I was not sure whether the people who took power would behave better or not, especially as Solomon was detained by the Military Government. I worried about what they might do to him.

With this, the end of my dream came to a reality - now the path had come to an end. When I told a sister in Christ this, she said to me 'The Lord will open the path again, keep praying'. I comforted myself in the words of David expressed in Psalm 121. I believed that the Lord will keep his own from all harm.

We left Government House, Jos, on the 31 December 1983. A major chapter in our lives closed abruptly.

Chapter 10

THE COUP - SOLOMON IS DETAINED 1984-1987

After the coup, we expected the military government, headed by General Buhari, to be more understanding, because he was the General Officer in charge of the 3rd Armoured Division in Jos, and was a member of the security of Plateau State with Solomon as the head. He knew all the problems that Solomon faced, so we thought he had brought an answer to the endless difficulties posed by the opposition. But, all the governors, the ministers, commissioners and some public officers, including contractors, were arrested and thrown into detention. They were accused without being charged.

After some time, some of the public officers were released while others were specifically instructed to be kept in prison without charges or trial, and Solomon was one of them. He was left in detention in Jos for three weeks before being sent to Lagos. In Lagos he was thrown into the maximum security prison, together with some other Governors, ministers and the former Vice-President, Dr Alexander Ekweme.

After two weeks when Solomon had not returned, I started to enquire of his whereabouts from a General from Langtang. He told me my husband was well and that they were awaiting the setting up of a panel to hear their cases before a decision would be taken. I asked where he was. He told me, 'in police hands'. Nobody was allowed to see them.

I bought certain necessities and pleaded with him to send them on to my husband.

When the news came that we could visit our husbands on certain days, I undertook a flight to Lagos and tried to find Solomon's whereabouts. I was asked to go to the State Security Service (SSS) and ask permission before they would direct me to where he was. I looked for the SSS office and signed that I wanted to see my husband. I was shown a room and told to fill in papers and wait. Then I saw the wives of other politicians arriving to go through the same process, among them was the wife of the Vice-President, Mrs Beatrice Ekweme, whom we once invited to Plateau State to launch the women's 'Alheri House' project. All the Plateau State women had met her at Jos airport as she arrived in the Presidential jet, and received her with dances and merriment. We queued together to be allowed to see our husbands. She was called first. I was sent to another block to see the boss, who interviewed me and called an officer to lead me to where I could see Solomon. This officer was to go with me in my own vehicle if I had one. Luckily for me I had a car given to me by my cousin, who was an airforce officer. I was taken on a road that led to the maximum security prison. As soon as the man reached the prison, he handed my name to the prison officials and I was asked to wait outside. There were all the wives of politicians, standing lined up. The environment of the prison was deliberately polluted with some unusual dark greenish coloured dust that I could not identify. When a vehicle passed by, the dust would be all over us but there was nowhere to move to - we had to wait in the sun with no provision for seats. We waited for over three hours, then they started to call us in groups. I was among the second group that was called. When I entered the maximum security prison's office, I saw the miserable look of the officers. Some officers had prisoners brought in and they were being beaten. They were shouting but there was no help. My heart sank, I wondered if they were political prisoners, but I discovered that they were not.

Later they started to bring out the political detainees.

There was a seat arranged for each couple to sit and discuss for not more than ten minutes. After about twenty minutes of waiting, I saw Solomon come in - he had lost a lot of weight, but was very cheerful. We hugged each other and the officials shouted 'Ten minutes only please'. To start with, we could not even talk. We gazed at each other for some seconds. Then Solomon asked about everyone one by one. I told him we were all being looked after by his friends and that he should not worry. We had hardly said anything when the official said 'Time's up'. We held each others hands and prayed. Then I left. When I got home to my cousin's house, I was covered with the green dust. My sister-in-law took great care of me and comforted me.

The next day I went back to Jos and I told them my husband sent greetings to them all. Meanwhile, I stayed with my brother's family, Barrister Stephen Lar, in the house we used to live in. Their being in the house was God's special provision to care for us. My children went to boarding school and so I had only myself to look after. It was not easy separating from my family so suddenly.

The first week we left Government House, my son Mark developed pneumonia. I remembered our Government House doctor whom we used to call for all our health problems. He was specially chosen by the Governor and my mother spoke well of him. I rang him up and asked a special favour if he would please assist me because my son was sick. He promised he would come but he did not. After about two hours of waiting, I rang him again and pleaded with him to help my son. Again he promised he would come but he did not, and he did not bother to explain either. At this time, Mark lived with his auntie. Her husband was then the new Minister of Defence. My sister Lillian, a senior nursing sister, looked after Mark. He was so bad that she had to spend the night with him. The next day she suggested that he be taken to hospital. I went to the doctor in charge of Evangel Hospital, Dr Verbrugge, an American missionary doctor, to inform him of my son's illness, but he was not in. The wife spoke with another missionary doctor in the hospital and he came with me immediately to see my son. He commended the efforts of my sister Lillian and asked her to carry on the treatment she had started for a few days. With this assurance, we committed Mark to the Lord and we watched him get better and well after about two weeks. This happened in January, which is quite a cold season in Jos. Mark's accident and his illness made his resistance so low that he broke down completely.

I had confidence in Dr Verbrugge as he was a Christian. I knew his dedication and love for human beings, that was why I could confidently call on him. Mrs Verbrugge I had met at the Christian women's club to which we both belonged. I became the President of the club, so I worked closely with her as our patron. This acquaintance gave me the confidence to choose them to treat my son Mark. They proved to be friends in need.

Meanwhile, people from all over Nigeria expressed their concern for our family after the coup. They came to assure us of their support, morally, spiritually and financially. They visited us in the same way that they did when they elected us into office. The Christian groups sang, shared scripture verses and prayed with us. They gave us gifts of money, food and other materials. The Lame, Blind and Beggars Association in Jos came, greeted us and gave my children N30.00. In fact, they shared in our sufferings. Through this, I also knew that the Plateau people really loved Solomon. Chiefs were not left out; some chiefdoms that were created by Solomon and those chiefs that he elevated either to third, second or first-class chiefs, were quite appreciative; they too sent us their greetings, either personally or through their people. I used to spend the day receiving people. The Lord did not leave us comfortless. I used to send details of all these visits to Solomon to comfort him too.

After my first visit to Solomon, I had to wait to hear the next time I could visit. This time a tribunal, the Special Investigation Panel (SIP), had been set up to try politicians. I was directed to see the Chairman to obtain permission to see Solomon and waited the whole morning from 8.00 am to 12.30 pm. I was quite relieved when he came into the office, but he turned down any request for me to see him that day.

Nigeria

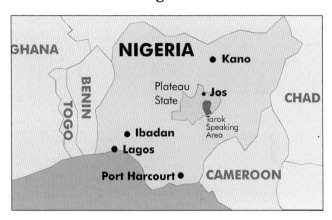

Tarok Tribe 1949 – Housing

Preparing the Roof, Langtang

Thatching, Langtang

Langtang 1949-50

Mary Lar and her
Girls Life Brigade Cadets

Missionaries' Residence,
Langtang

Girls Life Brigade Display
Christmas 1949

Bathtime

Early Days

An Anthill, Gerkama

Mary as a Teacher, 1957

Typical Tarok Compound

Miss J Maxwell, 1949

Family Portraits

Sisters: Mary with Lilian

Wedding Day 1960,
Solomon and Mary

Mary Lar with her father,
Nansep Lar

Mary's mother with her six children,
Mary, Lilian, Esther, Stephen,
Sunday, and Kefas on Mothers lap

Friends in London
Miss Evelyn
Goldstein, Mrs I K
Muchela Ekpe, Miss
Joyce Milverton and
Mary
1962-1963

Mary with Pamela
Bendor-Samuel
working on the
Tarok translation of
the New Testament
Jos, 1977

Baptismal
Service
1950

Education

National Day 1982
Mary presenting shield to
St Louis School

Graduation Day 1983
Mary presenting
certificates

Mary and Chalya
Graduating together 1986

Mary receives her PhD Jos,1986

Convalescing

Solomon convalescing
following his release
from detention
1988

Mary convalescing in
London with her family.
Nanna, Esther and her
three daughters,
Chalya, Beni and
Debbie

In Government

New Year Party in Government
House, Solomon in the centre
1982

Visiting dignatories to
Government House
Mary in the centre
1981

Solomon and Mary Lar with Clifford and Monica Hill at the Easter Monday
Open Air Service (see below) in Jos, Plateau State, 1991

He said I should see him the next day. That day I waited in the rain. There was a gutter between where we stood and the building so we had to stand near the road, endangering our lives to passing cars.

The next day I repeated the visit and requested that I be permitted to see the Chairman. He asked me to wait, that he was going out. When he came back, he refused to grant me any audience until about 2.00 pm. Then he said to me 'I am sorry a visit is not possible, you have to go back and come again next Wednesday'. Then he walked out on me! I went home and wrote him a rather sarcastic letter.

There was no reply to this, but when I reported the following week, I was given permission without seeing the Chairman. The Black Maria vehicle went to Kirikiri, Apapa, Lagos maximum security prison to bring Solomon to No 1 Ekotie Eboh Street, near Ribadu Road, Ikoyi. When I went into the room, I found Solomon had been there for a long time, anxiously waiting for whoever had come to see him. He was not told who it was. When I was ushered into the room, it was such a joy to see Solomon and Professor Ishaya Audu. He had to wait for Solomon to see his own visitor before they could leave together in the Black Maria to return to the maximum security prison. The national security man ordered us to speak in English and it had to be in his presence. We could not speak in English to each other as it appeared ridiculous. So the man said we should go ahead and speak in our own language, but whenever we saw anyone coming, we should switch quickly to English. Solomon was not allowed to take with him the provisions I brought for him, which included some few necessities like soap, toothpaste, brush etc. and two cartons of SWAN water. This water proved very helpful in view of the fact that in prison they had only well water to drink, and no means of boiling it. I gave a detailed list of the items to the office and they forwarded them to him within three days.

It was not long after that the date for the hearing of Solomon's case was fixed - May 1984 in Jos. News came that he would be arriving two days earlier. I got ready on this date, but he did not turn up. I was worried about whether he would be arriving by road or by air. There was nobody to ask for this information because everything about a military trial is kept secret, so I had to get ready for him whenever he turned up.

He arrived two days later. Some people who saw him at the airport came to tell me. When Solomon arrived at Jos airport, he was taken to the same prison where his officials were being kept. Mrs Esther Wazhi cried when she saw the way Solomon had lost weight. On hearing this, I ran to the prison yard. They were awaiting the chief prison's commandant to sign his detention warrant. I sat with him on the bench and I asked him what I could cook for him. He had gone through a lot during the journey.

He told me they left Lagos about four days ago. First he and his secretary to the Government, Mr S Gofwen, were taken to the airport, much against the wishes of his friends who pleaded with the authorities to allow him to have some medical attention because he was very ill. They got in touch with the military authority in Lagos, but they were told to carry him on a stretcher into the plane and so it was done. He was given no medical attention, yet he was forced out of his cell in that sickly condition. The pilot hinted that the plane was not in good condition, but the authorities insisted that the pilot should be able to manage it to Jos. Reluctantly he took off. As soon as the plane took off, it developed some technical problem when they were half way. The pilot announced their difficulty and told them they had to turn back and try to crash land in Lagos. The two National Security Service officers who were asked to accompany Solomon and his secretary confessed that they had been unkind to Solomon and asked him to forgive them. Solomon told them that he had no grudge or any ill feelings against any of them. He assured them the plane would land safely. The plane got to Lagos, but the pilot told them that they should be prepared to rush out as soon as the plane touched the ground. Poor Solomon, when the plane touched the ground, all the healthy people rushed out, but there was no way Solomon could run. So he sat there helplessly, trusting in the Lord to save him. The others ran half way and when they turned back to look at the fire which had broken out, they found Solomon was cheerfully looking at them. They came back to him and apologised. They helped him out but they had to wait for three or four days before they could find an alternative plane to convey them to Jos. They had left the prison early in the morning without food. Solomon had been unable to eat for some days and he had no appetite, so he lost a lot of weight. They had to wait for a vehicle to take them back to the prison. They arrived in the prison yard around midnight. There was nothing to eat once more, so they slept without food. The next day the authorities woke them up early in the morning for the journey, without food again. They left to go to the airport and waited a whole day for the plane to be repaired so they could be flown on to Jos. They were taken back to the prison in Lagos again that night because the plane was not ready. In this way, they had been without food for three days. Eventually, the military had to ask the police to convey them to Jos. Solomon certainly was affected by this ill-treatment.

I took leave of Solomon at the Jos prison and I went to get permission from the chief prison superintendent to allow me to cook something that would help to build up Solomon's strength for the trial. At first he did not give permission, but when I insisted, he asked me to bring pap only - ie something similar to corn custard. I put in everything I knew was good for Solomon, chicken broth, orange juice, eggs, groundnut and it looked like pap in a flask, but contained a lot of good nourishing food. The difference in him after this diet was seen within a few days.

Solomon Sentenced

Solomon appeared before the tribunal on 4 May 1984. The interesting thing was that all those who were called by the military to testify against Solomon turned out to give evidence that favoured him. Yet he was still sentenced to 22 years imprisonment. That year, Solomon asked me to send Christmas cards to each member of the tribunal to show that he was not bitter against any of them. After the sentence, they were more relaxed about visiting. We could visit him almost every day at the usual prison visiting time.

The Lord used Solomon mightily in prison. He was a source of comfort to many political detainees; some of them called him their chaplain. He used to uplift many of the detainees who could not take their plight. He made more friends in prison and brought many to the knowledge of our Lord Jesus Christ. Some of them came to inform me of how they were helped by him in detention. He led most of their prayer meetings and had words of comfort for their souls. They said his being with them was a blessing. On the day of the trial, Solomon told them 'The country belongs to all of us. Whether in prison or out of prison, we shall all continue to build our nation, wherever we may be'. Earlier during the interrogation, Solomon had told them to hold him responsible for anything that went wrong in the State, and that they should not blame his Commissioners for anything. With this strong statement from the head of Plateau State Government, no Commissioner was held or charged for anything specifically, but they were all bundled into prison.

We set up a prayer cell for Solomon and his commissioners and in fact for the whole nation, every Monday evening from 7.00 pm to 8.00 pm. Sometimes we went on until 10.00 pm. This went on for four years. My children wondered what sort of prayers we offered for such a long period and still did not give up. Some of them said 'God would be tired of you by now'. I told them I was strengthened through this fellowship with the Lord, and I believed He had answered our prayers. He would let us see it clearly in His own time. The Lord heard our prayers and the Commissioners were set free after twenty months. We continued to pray and rejoice, trusting in the power of the Lord. We believed all things were possible with Him.

About a year later the news came of the release of the Secretary to the Government, Mr S S Gofwen. His wife was the third member that formed the prayer cell with Mrs M M Ibvori and myself. Throughout this period of incarceration, the family was comforted by the love and caring attitude of the people of Plateau State. The fact that there were people who understood us and were sharing in our pains was very comforting. The people who cared came to advise, to pray, to give gifts too many to mention. People stood by so strongly that I did not have any need to buy food and other necessities. I equated them to the people who stood by Jesus during his trials. The family will forever appreciate them and pray the Lord to reward them all the days of their lives.

Solomon was not released for a long time. The agony of a lonely family mounted up. Occasionally, I got a member or two of the family to visit him in prison. We were, at the end, allowed to take in fruit to Solomon. In the fruit basket I would add meat or vegetables and no-one had bothered to check this, so I continued with the practice. We would send Christmas food to him too. He was in Jos and I used to see him every day.

Solomon used to make requests for his colleagues in detention. He was very disturbed about Dr C Isong's health (former Governor of Cross River State where I was given a chieftaincy title). He was later admitted into the Jos University Teaching Hospital (JUTH). Solomon told me to help Dr Isong as much as I could. When I went to the hospital to see him, I could not hold back my tears. All I could do was to assist with food, and medication. I wished I had been able to do more than this. Dr Isong's people heard of his ill health and came to Jos to look after him.

It was Atukum that took over the governing of Plateau State after the *coup d'etat* in December 1983. It seemed he had open hatred for Solomon and all he stood for. He started by dissolving some of the projects started by Solomon - eg The Lion Bank which was established in 1981, the Savannah Insurance Company Ltd, Quiz Company Limited, BARC Farms Limited, The Bottling Company Ltd in Barakin Ladi. He closed down some of the secondary schools and was about to sell out the hospitals which were established by Solomon and privatise some of the water dams. Anything that had to do with Solomon Lar was to be completely wiped out and forgotten. Someone told us that Atukum felt Solomon's presence in Jos was threatening his governing, as people still addressed Solomon 'Your

Excellency' and he still used the stick he held while he was Governor. They said the military were afraid that the stick may have some magic power. I could not understand why someone the authorities had locked up and people visited only with their permission should cause them such anxiety.

During this time, Makpa Lar, a five year old girl, fell sick and was admitted into Plateau hospital where she died. She was the daughter of the late Dr Sunday Lar, Solomon's nephew. Makpa died as a result of carelessness. The doctor we later learnt refused to answer an emergency call from the hospital. The nurses tried to get in touch with the doctor in charge, when she collapsed. Earlier, a suggestion was made by a female doctor on the right treatment for her, but he discarded the suggestion. Makpa died, needlessly. Her death left all of us very sad. We continued to look up to Jesus and tried to forget those trying times.

Visiting Solomon was a joyful experience; since we could not be together as a family, we rejoiced in the fact that he was well and it gave us hope that one day we should be reunited. This was more assured by the series of revelations I had in my sleep. I dreamed twice in one month that Solomon was released. I kept it all to myself and just gave God the honour and glory.

We woke up one morning at about 7.30 am and a neighbour's watchman came to inform us that there had been another coup d'etat. The children rejoiced that there was a change of government and that daddy would be back home soon. I was not sure whether to rejoice or not. Things had by then become confused in my mind. It seemed there was so much hatred and love at the same time. Obviously, from the military there was hatred, but from the people, there was much love and care. We all prayed for the country and carried on normally. The children were excited and hopeful, while I was unmoved.

By now we had moved up to a three bedroomed bungalow I was able to erect at the old airport road. My sister Lillian lived in one section of it. We chose to move there so we could have more rooms. My sister Lillian and I found great comfort in each other. One day, Debbie came back from school (she was then in Grade 8 at Hill Crest School), happy over the election for the Presidency of the middle grade classes that she had won by 32 votes. Debbie, our youngest daughter, was a girl blessed with many gifts. Many called her 'university girl'. She had remained steady in her progress, by the grace of the Lord.

We developed an enormous appetite for food at this time; mine was worse than any of the children. It was as if the people knew it, that they brought us so much food to eat. I used to take a flask of food with me wherever I went. I had to eat almost every two hours else my body shivered and I would feel weak. I would run to Solomon to consult him on issues affecting the family when there was a need to do so. Then suddenly one Sunday evening the prison officials telephoned me and informed me that my husband was to be transferred to some unknown prison; he was to leave the next morning. He needed some necessities. This news upset me. I could hardly wait until the morning. Next day I was at the prison gate as early as 7.00 am, but I was not allowed in until about 8.00 am. They called Solomon to me and he told me almost all the Governors were transferred but not the Commissioners. Solomon hinted it could be Lagos, or Ibadan or Kaduna but nobody knew where the detainees were being taken to, except the military and the prison officials. Those who came to know where they were going, later told Solomon, and asked him to inform their families. I rang up their families. I ran back home to bring Solomon's needs. We both knelt and prayed in the prison office that Solomon should not be taken to the maximum security prison again, then I waited to see them off. About 11.00 am they were all taken into the Black Maria (criminals' vehicle). They bade me goodbye one by one. By then the news had reached the people around, so quite a crowd gathered outside and they greeted them. Some cried and some prayed for them loudly, 'God be with you'. I stood outside the prison yard and watched the vehicle drive off out of sight. We had no idea where they were going. That night I spent on my knees.

It was some weeks before news came that Solomon was

back in Kirikiri maximum security prison. That was how the Lord answered our prayers - we gave Him praise! Others were at Ikoyi, which is a better prison. I could not understand why Solomon alone out of all the Governors was taken to this horrible place again. I comforted myself with the fact that the Lord knows it all. On 22 November, 1984, a message reached me that I should hurry and find my way to Lagos because Solomon was seriously sick. Chalya, my eldest daughter, accompanied me to Lagos the same day. Kefas, my youngest brother, met us at the airport and took us to Lagos University Teaching Hospital, where we found Solomon had been admitted the day before. I was worried about his health for cancer was suspected - oh, how I wept! But Solomon said we should give thanks to the Lord and to remember Ephesians 5:20. I had no right to ask God why this illness should befall him. He was taken to Creek Military Hospital for a very tiring intensive test. I went with him and a sister from the ward. The Lord gave him the strength to stand it all. I stayed with Solomon for two weeks before I returned to the children in Jos. I had to go back home to look for means of meeting his hospital bills and medication. While in hospital, we were helped by many visitors, but it was not enough to pay all the expenses. The charge for food was over N500.00 a week, and they had given Solomon a private room and a prison warder who guarded him from outside twenty-four hours. The warder had to give permission for people to go in to greet Solomon.

Mobility Problems

The Lord continued to be good to us. Stephen Lar visited Solomon in hospital. He told him his family were well but suffered from a lack of mobility. Our car had broken down and was giving us a lot of problems. I was quite angry with my brother for telling Solomon such news that might disturb him because there was nothing he could do about it. He asked his colleagues that day to remember his family in prayers because they had mobility problems. The car I had was over four years old. Amongst those who listened to Solomon's prayer request was a German who was detained at the same time with all the politicians. Solomon met this German for the first time at the maximum security prison in Kirikiri, Lagos. He appreciated Solomon's role in helping him to survive by the type of advice he received from him. This man was released earlier than many of them. He went back to his home in Germany and remembered Solomon and his prayer request while in detention. He flew all the way from Germany with some German money equivalent to N10,000.00, which he took to the Minister of Defence whose wife he had heard was my sister. He gave her the money to send to Mr Lar's family in Jos. My sister rang me and I travelled to Lagos and received it thankfully. Solomon reminded me to take the tithe of this money to Cooper School, Langtang. We used N7,000.00 to purchase a new Volkswagen to help us. The man left without leaving his address so I could not write to thank him. After about two months he came back again and left N20,000.00 for us in the same manner as he did the first time. This miraculous provision was beyond words. This time I was able to buy a new car for myself at the cost of N19,000.00. I used to refer to the car as 'the miracle car'. This is the same one that I am using to date. I apologised to my brother for being angry with him when he told Solomon about our mobility problem.

Solomon at one point got very sick in hospital and one of the Langtang army leaders, Brigadier General John Shagaya, then in Lagos, out of concern for him, sent to Revd Kumuyi of the 'Deeper Life Ministry' in Lagos to pray for Solomon. This man prayed a simple prayer of faith, and after a few days his health was restored by that strong power that keeps all God's children victorious over their bodies. When other Christians heard about this, they also visited him at the hospital and prayed with him; people like Mr Samuel Mafuyai, one of his Commissioners, Archbishop Okogie, the Catholic Bishop of Nigeria, and President of the Christian Association of Nigeria, Revd Damina Bawado and the church elders in Langtang - our Local Government Area. Also, President and leaders of the Church of Christ in Nigeria (COCIN), Dr (Mrs) Mary Olutimayi of the Federal

Ministry of Education, Lagos, Mr Austin Ukachi of the National Petroleum (NNPC), Archbishop Idahosa, and many other individuals and groups. Those who could not visit Lagos came to the house and prayed with us and encouraged us. How we cherished them all!

My Career at This Time

With the Lord's help I was able to carry on with my usual office work at the Teacher Resource Centre, and also had time for church activities, especially Sunday School and my study programme at the university. I had started a PhD programme in the University of Jos in 1982 while in the Government House. This study was prompted by a friend, Mrs Katherine Hauwa Hoomkwap who encouraged me to enrol for it after my Master's Degree, and I was studying as well as working and looking after the family. It became too much, so I asked for study leave. I had full-time for study then to complete the PhD programme.

Professor Peter Lassa and Dr C Ezeomah were my supervisors in Curriculum Studies. The special group which I took for this study were the nomadic Fulani cattle rearers. I defended my thesis successfully on the 10 January 1985. Professor Samuel Aleideno from Ahmadu Bello University, Zaria, was the external examiner. I graduated and was awarded the PhD degree in 1985.

At the end of the study programme, I reported to the Ministry of Education at the Teacher Resource Centre. I was asked to carry on with my Nomadic Education project. A journalist from the Vanguard newspaper was waiting for me in the office one day. It was this interview that was read by some Nigerians who were interested in development to involve me in a conference organised by seven world organisations, the main ones being the Aga Khan, World Bank and Ford Foundations. The conference entitled 'The Enabling Environment Conference on Economic Recovery in Sub-Saharan Countries' took place in 1986 in Nairobi, Kenya, to which I was privileged to go for the first time.

The Lord sustained my interest in the Tarok Cultural Development project, although by now some Tarok people started to lose interest probably because the Government House support was no longer there. I got busy with other activities like National Congress on Evangelism, Nigerian Bible Translation Trust, COCIN Education Board, Gindiri Resource Centre for the Disabled, Child Evangelism Ministry, Nigerian Evangelical Fellowship, women's associations, my church and numerous invitations to fund raising activities, weddings, etc.

After my PhD degree, I applied to teach in the University of Jos, seeing the slow promotion prospects of the Ministry of Education. I had been promoted once more by 1985 to an assistant Chief Education Officer. I attended an interview at the University in 1985 and I was given an appointment as a Lecturer. I hesitated because the promotion to my next rank was due. At that time my colleagues at the NCE level had achieved higher ranks, some were Permanent Secretaries, others Chief Education Officers or highly placed officers in other offices. I felt a bit under-used and asked myself so many questions. Was it due to my inability to measure up or lack of recognition or other reasons, but then friends had assured me that God's achievement for me was not in the civil service. My sister said my success lay in my public involvement, so I would not have time to do all the other things I was doing in society, if I were promoted to a higher rank. At the same time, I was informed at one time that my promotion was delayed because a Permanent Secretary felt I was more interested in publicity than in my work. I hated idleness. I would always find something to do. I thought this should be commended, but it was the opposite. My involvement in different societal needs caused a bit of uneasiness in some people. I was deprived of things that would enhance my status in the civil service. But God had provided me with many other venues of service among my ethnic group, church, etc that were satisfying to me in their own way.

The Lord continued to give me His strength, His peace and His grace to keep me going. When I was invited to the Nairobi Conference of Enabling Environment for Economic Recovery in Sub-Saharan Countries as someone recognised to be involved in activities that might promote economic development, I went to Nairobi with great joy. After the conference which lasted ten days, I came back to Nigeria feeling encouraged, but on arrival, my family told me I was retired from the civil service of Plateau State. I knew the military were at it again after they could not go any further with Solomon. It was surprising that my work was recognised by the outside world, but my State was retiring me just to render me redundant. They said it was on the basis of age, yet I was blooming with energy. The pension age I signed at the beginning of my contract agreement was sixty years - I was only fifty. It puzzled me. The Government forgot that I had earlier given them a letter informing them that I would like my services transferred to the University of Jos, and this was effected two weeks earlier than their retiring panel exercise came into being.

I delayed my going to the University because I knew my promotion was on the way. As soon as I had the promotion as Assistant Chief Education Officer, I wrote to the University accepting my appointment. I was to resume on the 1 September 1986, and also wrote to the Ministry to transfer my service to the University. I was surprised at the way the Ministry was tossing me about. The man who brought the news home heard that I had already left the Ministry of Education. He reacted sadly to the news because he knew that I was the only source of income for the family. I learned my name was not among those retired initially, but some members of the panel were interested in seeing that I was affected, so they sent for my file and involved me.

Anyway, many Christian groups called to pray with me when they heard of the retirement and were delighted to know that I was not affected. The group that comforted me most was the Christian Women's club. They understood I needed to be encouraged.

A New Tribunal

One day, I went to visit Solomon at the Kirikiri maximum security prison in Lagos. I felt in despair and could not sleep afterwards. I recalled how he looked and my suffering at the gate of the prison. I was upset by all the memories of that visit. I got up around 2.00 am and picked up my Bible for comfort. The Lord led my hands to open Psalm 69:33 'The Lord listens to those in need and does not forget his people in prison'. I was delighted with this assurance. The Lord saw my desperate heart and could not leave me comfortless all night, so He spoke with me in this miraculous way. It was like pouring some water to quench a fire. I knelt down and thanked my Lord and was then able to sleep .

Sometime later, the coup d'etat which was announced by the then Brigadier Joshua Dogonyaro, ushered Major General Ibrahim Gbadamosi Babangida into the highest seat of the land - ie the President of the Federal Republic of Nigeria. When he came into power, he announced that a special review tribunal would be set up to review the cases of the politicians. By then, they had spent over two years in prison. Solomon's case came up on the 14 January 1986. I travelled from Jos to Lagos to hear the case. Mr D B Zang, one time Chairman of the party NPP Plateau State, was in attendance; likewise Mrs K Hoomkwap who was the Commissioner of Health during Solomon's regime. Stephen and Kefas, my brother, were also there. A judge of the Supreme Court, Mohammed Bello, was the Chairman of the panel. A lawyer spoke for the government and Solomon's lawyer, Chief G O K Ajayi, defended him. The prosecuting lawyer said that he was ashamed of the situation which led to the jailing of the former Governor of Plateau State - Mr Solomon D Lar - during the Buhari regime. When he was asked to spell out the difference between Mr Lar's case and other Governors who equally used security votes but were not jailed for it, he did not give any answer. The case was clear that Solomon was not treated fairly. We knew that the new head of state was out to do something about it. However, they were taking their time to review all the cases. Meantime, Solomon remained in hospital and in detention.

Chapter 11

SOLOMON IS RELEASED 1987-1991

One day the Lord manifested his love to us clearly. A message came that a very senior officer in the army wanted to see me and he told me that my husband was going to be released on 1 October, the National Day, so I should prepare for his home coming. It was a lovely surprise. The Lord was going to bring our hard-felt separation to an end. When I left this officer, I sang all the way home, a distance of about 400 kilometres. I got people to re-paint the house and bought a new set of chairs with the help of my brother Stephen. Then I travelled to Lagos with my cousin, Mrs Cecilia Sheni, to meet Solomon and to bring him back.

We received a letter notifying us of his release from detention a day before the nation's independence celebrations. By then many people in Lagos had heard that Solomon might be released, so by the evening, friends started to come to the hospital. A singing group was formed where Solomon had stayed for over ten months, receiving one treatment after the other. While my cousin Cecilia and the rest rejoiced by singing and praising the Lord; I sat on a chair behind them and wept. I wept throughout that night. I could not hold my tears back. I tried to sing and praise the Lord, but whenever I opened my mouth to sing, I ended up crying. One could not understand whether these tears were tears of joy or sorrow. It was at this point that I was able to release all my emotions pent up for three years and nine months. I had earlier sung and praised the Lord on hearing the news of his release, but when it actually happened, I could only weep.

We accompanied Solomon from the hospital to Kirikiri maximum security prison the next day to collect his few belongings. The hardest part was when we met with Sa'adatu Rimi and daughter who had gone to see their husband and father, Alhaji Abubakar Rimi, the first civilian Governor of Kano State, who happened to be Solomon's very good friend. It was not easy leaving him behind. When we were about to leave the prison, both Sa'adatu and I burst into tears, but the man Rimi, for whom we were crying was so happy that his friend had been released that he forgot that he would have to stay behind. Showing courage, manliness and love, he helped to get Solomon's things together. God is wonderful in the way He sustained these special people.

We found a place for Solomon in Lagos to rest while I went ahead to prepare to receive him in Jos. There was a lot of cooking to do to serve the visitors on the night of his home coming. Relatives, friends and well-wishers called to see us. Then finally the day came when Solomon flew into Jos - that was on the 6 October 1987. There was such a mammoth crowd at the airport to receive him that it looked like a Governor or Head of State was being received. People from far and near came, mostly from Plateau State. As soon as the plane touched the ground, the people became uncontrollable. The whole thing was turning out to be very dangerous. There was no order, everyone was trying to shake hands with Solomon or touch him. When he emerged from the plane, he appeared fragile, smart and handsome. I went up the stairs of the plane to accompany him to the people, but the disorganised crowd almost tore us to pieces. I was pushed away and Solomon was very wisely and quickly whisked into a car and driven off. This proves that even joy needs to be controlled. I was concerned about Solomon's weak condition and did my best to help him overcome it. He responded beautifully and fast. Within a week or two he turned into a healthy strong man again. We thought he needed a thorough check-up on his health, but where would the money come from? We trusted the Lord and he provided. Some of his quiet admirers offered to pay for the two of us to travel abroad to have his health checked properly. I took leave from my work to accompany him. We went first to Germany and then to London, so he could be properly examined.

The next thing we organised was a special thanksgiving to the Lord. A committee of friends got together, planned and implemented it. The occasion took place sometime in March 1988 and was graced by relations, friends and well-wishers from all over the country. There were representatives from all over Nigeria, representatives of political colleagues, church groups, etc It was a big day. People brought cows, rams, chickens, rice or grain for the occasion. A lot of dances and merriment took place after the service at our house that day. We all realised that the Lord had wiped away all our tears. I asked some of my children who had earlier expressed doubt, as to whether the Lord ever answers people's prayer. 'Yes' they answered, but they felt He took too long to answer us! They forgot that 'With the Lord, a thousand years is like a day' - Psalm 90:4, 2 Peter 3:8. I told them 'I have had occasions when the Lord answered my prayers instantly and occasions when He had asked me to wait. This does not mean that He had not answered that prayer', and they knew from that day that a delay in answering prayers is not necessarily a denial. In this particular case, we waited nearly four years before the answer came. The Lord had a purpose in this. It could have taken even longer. Praise Him for He knows best.

I would always remember Mr D B Zang, General J T Useni, Mr Bala Angbazo the Aren Eggon, the late Reverend Damina Bawado, the various women fellowships of COCIN and ECWA churches, and my brother Kefas who sent us a book from America entitled *Tough Times Never Last But Tough People Do*. His friend, Ephraim Nimak, also gave us a word picture which encouraged me. It read 'This Too Shall

Pass Away'. The Lord really brought everything to pass. We give Him all the honour and glory.

Chairman of Lion Bank

All this time the Lord kept me faithful to my mother's commitment to the evangelist, who worked with the Baptist Church in Langtang. Mother took it upon herself to be his partner - she was paying him a certain amount of money every month. Then came a time the Lord knew I needed extra help to ensure the continuity of this mission. One day as I walked to my car two gentlemen moved towards me and said 'Congratulations Madam!', 'For what?' I asked. 'You mean you have not heard? You have been made the Chairman of Lion Bank.' This was the bank Solomon established while in Government. I quickly responded 'Sorry, you are congratulating the wrong person!' 'Are you not Dr Mrs Lar?' they asked. 'Yes I am' I answered. 'Go and listen to the radio, you will hear the news about you'. I drove home and called my son Mark and asked if he had heard the news of my appointment as Chairman of Lion Bank. He answered 'No'.

The Lord gave Solomon the vision to emancipate the people politically, economically, socially and educationally, so he embarked on many projects, including the Lion Bank. When the military regime of General Buhari overthrew the civilian government of Alhaji Shehu Shagari, they scrapped the Lion Bank project and many others. General Buhari was overthrown by General Ibrahim Bodamasi Babangida, so new officers appeared on the government scene. These people reviewed the decisions of the earlier military government and re-established many of these institutions initiated by Solomon. A new Governor was posted to Plateau State in 1987. He was Colonel Lawrence Onoja; he identified truly with the yearnings of the people of Plateau State. One of the many things he did was to restore the Lion Bank initiative. The person he chose to be Chairman of the bank was myself, probably in appreciation of my husband's work. Other developmental projects that he was known for in the state were the construction of roads and the beautifying of cities. We thank God for Colonel Lawrence Onoja (now Major General Lawrence Onoja) and for his good works. That he had been promoted to the rank of a Major General soon after was a deserving promotion.

After I had served the bank for two and a half years, a new Governor was posted to the State in the person of Colonel Joshua Madaki. He dissolved the boards in the State, including the Lion Bank. The three Government Board members of Lion Bank, including myself, were replaced.

The Lord knew Solomon was then in a position to take over all the financial needs of the family. And I needed to be eased of some responsibilities, so I could carry on with some of my other duties like the writing of this book.

Jos University

I continued to enjoy my work, lecturing and researching. I was recognised in the University as a specialist in Nomadic Education, having studied nomads at PhD level and led the education group in a research project for UNESCO/UNDP. The research took place in Plateau, Bauchi and Gongola States. When I was co-ordinating Nomadic Education at the Ministry of Education, Plateau State, I wrote a proposal seeking for the sponsorship of the project from UNESCO. I sent the papers to Paris, then followed personally. I was commended by their high official in Paris and found that UNESCO actually budgeted the sum of $50,000.00 for the project. I came back feeling contented and waited to hear officially from them, but nothing came through. I enquired from someone in Lagos; he told me that all world aid must come through the Federal Government. So when the then Civilian Government saw this amount sent for Nomadic Education in Plateau State, they asked that it be diverted to the University of Jos. This showed a dislike for the then Plateau State Government which was formed by a different political party from theirs. They did not consider that it was Plateau State's initiative. Anyway, since the money was still going to be used for the same purpose, there was no need to quarrel over it.

When I joined the University, I automatically joined the

UNESCO/UNDP research team. I was made the leader of the education group. The group was requested to tour some African countries, so they would benefit from their nomadic experiences. Three African countries were chosen, Kenya, Somalia and Mauritania. A research tour to these countries was planned, but the tour to Somalia was cancelled by Dr C Ezeomah, the leader of the project, because there was a famine in the country at that time. It made the Government of Somalia afraid of entertaining visitors. They wrote that they were not ready for us due to the hard condition of their country.

I had earlier visited Kenya and taken the opportunity to visit their nomadic areas. For this reason, I participated only in the Mauritanian visit. We left Nigeria for the Islamic Republic of Mauritania in 1988/89.

Mauritania

I had not had the opportunity of visiting a purely Islamic country before. We arrived on Sunday and were taken straight to the offices, where they settled us into a hotel. The Ambassador of Nigeria, His Excellency Mr Ameh and his wife, came round to the hotel to greet us. Seeing I was one woman among four, they offered for me to stay in their house and I accepted. In the first place it was better than the hotel. Secondly, I was going to be with my own people. People in Mauritania speak French, so I had my first difficulty of communication. The Nigerian Ambassador's house was a Godsend for me, and for all of us. It was the Nigerian Embassy that provided us with a guide, without whom our visit would have been a wasted effort. I marvelled that the desert looked very hostile, but that human beings were happy and working normally in this wonderful strange land. There was no farmland, no water, no industries; where the people's food came from seemed a mystery. We were told their food comes mainly from abroad, reaching them by air or by sea. The only thing that I saw them do for a living was either working as civil servants, fishermen or sellers in the market. However, we saw some cattle rearers, who lived in plank houses. They were the nomads who have migrated into the outskirts of Mauritania.

Somebody asked me why I did not go to school. I told her I did go to school. So she asked why I could not speak French. To her, everyone that went to school must speak French. I also asked if she went to school. 'Yes' she said. So I asked her why she could not speak English. She smiled at me and we ended the discussion.

There is only one church in the whole of Mauritania. It is a Catholic church built by their French Colonial masters for themselves. All the people who attended the church were either ex-patriates or people from the Embassies. As far as I can remember, there was not a single Mauritanee that was a Christian. The church was usually opened for only one hour from 7.00 until 8.00 pm. They kept to time and it was all in French. The Catholic Sisters still help to run the Mauritanee's hospitals but they were forbidden any form of preaching. After the service, people could not stay in the church to talk. As soon as the service was over, people dispersed quickly to their own homes. A Sister, who I wanted to speak to because she was the only one who could speak English, dodged me after the service. She said if she stayed a minute longer, people would come round and send her away. She urged me to go home too. I told her I could not see anybody around. She assured me that people were hiding in nearby places ready to descend on the Christians if they violated the orders given to them.

One cannot reconcile this situation when Christians were the people helping the Mauritanees with food, medicine etc and yet these Christians are not allowed to practise and worship their God as they wished to in Mauritania. I felt bad inside me. No wonder the land looks cursed, with dry sand stretching from north to south and from east to west with no trees and punitive sand storms. When a storm arose the sand got into my nose, eyes, ears and mouth. I thought I would die. I watched in fear and trembling. Sometimes this went on for days.

We were to travel to a nearby town to see more of the nomadic life of the people, but the sand storm had covered all the tar and the roads were invisible. Everything in the market was dusty, and in this sand storm, some people were drinking *'shayi'* black tea and even eating. How they survived I do not know. In the second week I became ill. My host, His Excellency the Ambassador, advised me to buy some antibiotics. He knew that the sand storm must have got some bacteria into my system. At the pharmacy I did not know the name of the medicine I needed in French. I said in English that I wanted to buy nivaquine and some antibiotic. Nobody could guess what I was saying. It was the biggest chemist in Mauritania, so I was reluctant to go elsewhere. Luckily a Frenchman came in. I asked if he spoke English. 'Yes' he answered. I told him the nature of my illness, fever, diarrhoea and cough. He explained it to them and I was given the medicine I needed. The Lord is good. He had sent me help in time.

What baffled me most in Mauritania was the fact that all the indigenous population were Moslems, both black and white, but the blacks were being discriminated against. There is a clear feudal system being practised in Mauritania. In fact, one can say that there is a semblance of slavery in that country - eg A black girl of the Wolof ethnic group (who had asked me why I went to school but could not speak French) was assigned by her office, the UNDP, to accompany me to the town for the day. On getting to places where they were white, she would behave as if she were insecure, and would speak with a quieter voice. In some shops when she asked for the price of goods, they could not even answer her. Some would ask her to leave their stall. After the marketing was over, she took me to her house in a predominantly black area. The blacks had no freedom at all, not even to play any loud music. And in the markets they were acting as servants to their white masters.

The wife of an ambassador told me that the blacks are treated as slaves in the real sense. They work for the white Mauritanees and their wives serve the wives of their masters. Where the wife of a slave and the wife of a master had babies at the same time, then the wife of the slave had to feed her own child on camel's milk while she fed her mistress's baby with her own breast milk, so that the mother could be freed of the burden. What an idea! Did they not know that feeding one's baby is a means of imparting the mother's personality, love and emotions to the baby and that this is a time of bonding between mother and child?

I was shown a shop which a black man used to own, but he was pulled out of the shop and killed in front of all the market people. Nobody came to his rescue. His shop was taken over by a white Mauritanee. Black people cannot own shops.

I compared these whites and the Christian whites I met in England, who gave me so much comfort. It was among the Christian whites that I found love and joy. They knew I was the same as they were but only different in colour. Discrimination amongst the whites in England I noticed was more pronounced amongst the non-Christian communities. Why cannot the blacks and whites of Mauritania, who are both Moslems share the same spirit of oneness?

This was not a very pleasant trip. There was such a big difference when I got back to Nigeria. Nigeria is indeed a free country. People mix freely, irrespective of their religions and ethnic differences.

When I was in the Mauritanees' market, I discovered that they cherished 'Made in Nigeria' clothes, which made me proud of being Nigerian. They sell them at a higher price than others. Yet back in Nigeria some Nigerians are not proud of their 'Made in Nigeria' goods. Nigeria is looked upon here as superior, especially when Nigeria sent Mauritania two boats full of Nigerian goods as a gift to aid them. It was televised while we were there and the people showed a lot of admiration for the fact that the ships' captains were Nigerians. They did not know that blacks could be ships' captains.

The Lord has certainly blessed Nigeria with many good things, with plenty of arable land and natural resources, including minerals, as well as human resources. If only Nigerians would demonstrate a mighty flood of justice - a torrent of doing good, then God would surely bless us even more. With righteous people to harness these resources, Nigeria could become a world power within the next decade!

The Philippines

It was by His grace that the Lord brought over 4,000 of His children from 191 different countries of the world to a World Congress on Evangelisation in the Philippines. I was amongst those who attended. There the Lord met with us in a new way.

There were two groups that travelled to Manila from Nigeria. Half went via Amsterdam and direct to the Philippines, but the rest of us went via New York. I had never had a journey that took 36 hours of hanging in the air before. The journey itself took two days. We took off in Lagos, flew to the Republic of Benin, then had further stops at Togo, Abidjan and Dakar. From there we flew into New York but because we did not have visas, we had a harsh time. Paradoxically, before we left Nigeria we were told by the American Embassy that we did not require a visa to pass through New York. After a long delay at the airport, we were eventually whisked into a bus and taken to a hotel where we were guarded by the security for the night. The next day we were whisked back to the airport as if we were criminals and put straight on to the plane for Seattle, where we spent a similar night to the one in New York. We were taken to a hotel near the airport, where we ordered various food. I ordered a hamburger. The man came back to me with something as big as the size of a birthday cake. I was speechless. I invited the rest of the group to join me in a birthday party, even though it was not my birthday. All who ordered food were given two or three times the size of what we could eat. This was an American wonder. They said, Americans act big, everything of theirs must be big. The next day we left Seattle and went straight to Manila. We met brethren from all over the world at the congress which started the day after we arrived.

The most striking experience was the wonderful testimonies from brethren who came from communist countries. They had been under communism for over 70 years since the Russian Revolution of 1917, when the Russians had the dream of a new society with no oppression or exploitation of people, no darkness, ignorance or backwardness. This liberating message set the Russians' hearts on fire and so the victimisation of Christians started. The story of *Animal Farm* is known to all of us. We know how the communists drove out the Czars, in the name of freedom, then they turned round to categorise freedom for different people, and the dictatorship of the state started in earnest. In carrying out their objectives, they banned Christianity because they blamed the bad situation on Christians. But they did not succeed in wiping out Christianity in Russia. Why did communist Russia not succeed? Because the church is Christ - no matter what the persecution; Christians are more than conquerors, because He is with the church.

After the congress, those of us who were routed via New York were not allowed to return home because we did not have American visas. We rushed back to the congress hall and luckily the travel agent was still around. They had to book a hotel for us for three days, after which all the money they had would be exhausted. They gave us only enough money for snacks twice a day. We went to the Nigerian Embassy to help us speak with the Americans. Despite our Embassy's intervention, the Americans still would not listen. In that hotel, our breakfast, lunch and supper was prayer. We would gather for encouragment at our brother Bishop Gbonigi's room, which we used to call the energy room. We saw ourselves stranded with no accommodation and no food.

While we were waiting to receive instructions from our travel agent in New York, some of our members who had earlier exchanged complimentary cards and addresses, phoned the brethren in Manila informing them of our plight, and immediately the brethren came to our help. They sent buses to convey us to their church. There we had fellowship together and thereafter we were well fed. They tried to cheer us up by taking us around Manila. We ended up with an evening service which was led by the Nigerian delegates. We were richly blessed as many people went forward to the altar.

The Lord heard our prayers and on the last day of the

three days, early in the morning, one of us had a telephone call from America. We were informed that arrangements had been made for us to pass on immediately we arrived in New York. We all praised the Lord and left Manila immediately. We went via Tokyo, straight to New York, where it was announced that all passengers should remain on board until all the Nigerians had disembarked. We were then shown to a Lufthansa from New York to Amsterdam, then on to London, and from London we got on Nigerian Airways to Lagos. When the plane touched the ground in Lagos, we all clapped, rejoiced and praised the Lord that we were back in our own country.

Pan-African Christian Women Alliance (PACWA)

After the coup of December 1983 I had plenty of time to give to church work. The Church of Christ in Nigeria (COCIN) Women's Fellowship had to attend the Nigerian Evangelical Fellowship (NEF) Women's Wing Conference in Ilorin, Nigeria. I was asked to be part of COCIN Women's Fellowship participants at the seminar. Apart from that, I was asked to give a paper on the 'Role of Women in Evangelism' in 1985. The conference lasted for three days. At this seminar, I met with some of our brethren whom I had once travelled with to Lausanne I, in Switzerland, and had met them at national congress meetings - the Revd S Akangbe, the General Secretary of NEF, was one of them. He organised all these women's fellowship seminars at which we were richly blessed.

In 1986, 1987 and 1988, the seminars were repeated and I presented papers at each of them. After the 1988 seminar, Revd S Akangbe informed me that there was some new thinking on the Women's Fellowship of NEF Women's Wing. I got very interested and he said he would inform me as soon as the final decision was made. He expressed that he wanted me to participate fully in the new development.

After the seminar of NEF Women's Wing of 1987, I received a letter from Nairobi, Kenya, inviting me and five others from Nigeria to a Pan-African Christian Women's Assembly in Ghana. While in Ghana, I met with great

Christian women including Sister Judy Mbugua from Kenya. She was a pioneer of PACWA. Her name was mentioned several times as someone being used by the Lord to fulfil the great commission to the women of Africa.

Judy one day invited me for a discussion; she asked me what I was doing back in Nigeria. She insisted that she wanted to know in detail, so I told her I was a Sunday School teacher, a Bank Chairman, a Chairman of a School Board, involved with the Women's Fellowship of my church, a University Lecturer, Patron to the Children Evangelism Ministry, executive member of the Nigerian Bible Translation Trust and the prayer secretary of the National Congress on Evangelisation. I was also involved with the National Council of Women's Societies, Plateau State branch, etc. I thought Judy would rebuke me for doing so many things. Instead, to my amazement, she said 'You are the type of person I am looking for. It is the busy people like you that I want to involve in this task'. She said 'People who are busy indicate ability, and they are the ones that can cause things to happen'. This was a new philosophy to me. With mixed feelings, I re-stated all these to her to make sure she meant what she was saying. She said to me 'Truly Mary you can use your ability to promote PACWA in Nigeria'. She could see me being used for this. I kept quiet, so she asked me to think about it very seriously.

At the end of the conference in Ghana, the Nigerian delegates gathered in my room and asked me to take the lead in promoting PACWA in Nigeria. They said they would give their maximum co-operation. Their decision was based on the fact that I was already a NEF member. I took up the challenge and I wrote a report of the Ghana conference and sent it to several churches as well as to NEF.

Judy informed me of the PACWA launching in Nairobi, Kenya, in August 1989, so when I got to Nigeria, I sent invitations to many churches. Some women responded and these women and those who received direct invitations from Nairobi joined hands and travelled together to Nairobi where the big conference took place. Indeed, it was a movement for the Lord Jesus Christ; there were about 2,500 women from 36 different African countries. The theme of the conference was 'Our Time Has Come'. This conference challenged African Christian women to rise and affect Africa with the light of Jesus Christ. Africa for a long time was known as the dark continent, but the evangelical Christian women of Africa were saying that the time had come for Africa to change from its dark state to the light of Jesus Christ. In Africa today, there is so much poverty, unstable governments, hunger, refugee problems, ignorance and disease. The Christian women of Africa are saying that they have to be on their feet to fight against these calamities that have befallen the continent. Surely if the continent knew Christ, all these depressed states of affair would disappear. We believe strongly that our continent needs Jesus Christ in order to change.

The challenge was great. We, the fourteen women who were privileged to attend Nairobi, came back full of zeal for the Lord. Our brother and sister, Revd Dr Tokumboh Adeyemo, the General Secretary of the Associations of Evangelicals in Africa and Madagascar, and his wife Mrs Ireti Adeyamo, invited us, the Nigerian contingent, to their house in Nairobi. There again they threw the challenge to us to be in action.

We picked some protem officers who would take the lead back in Nigeria. I was asked to serve as the Nigerian co-ordinator, Dr (Mrs) Deborah Turaki as the Secretary, Mrs Na'omi Famonure as the Assistant Secretary and Dr (Mrs) Mary Ogebe as the treasurer. The Lord gave us the spirit to push on in Nigeria. The fact that the majority of participants were from Plateau State was responsible for giving the Plateau State women the opportunity to serve and promote PACWA in Nigeria.

Back in Nigeria, we formed prayer groups to pray for vision and a sense of direction. We wrote a report of PACWA, Nairobi, to many churches, and Christian women responded to our invitations. They attended PACWA activities such as the prayer day, seminars and meetings.

In November 1990, Nigeria launched its own Chapter. Sister Judy Mbugua, Sister Lewanika Inonger and Sister

Florence Yeboah, continental officers, attended the Nigerian Chapter launching in Jos, Plateau State, with about 3,000 Christian women from nine states. The women were equally challenged to carry the same light of Jesus Christ to their own states. Since then the Lord has picked on His rightful women from these States and they too are working as co-ordinators to create awareness and to move the women into action for the Lord.

The candles that were gallantly lit on the day of the launching of the Nigerian Chapter will certainly brighten all the corners of Nigeria. God will do the work He has started in Africa. PACWA is very dear to African Evangelical Christian women. It is a vehicle of change presenting Africa with the best alternative. The Lord meant Africans to enjoy the land which He has given them. This cannot be possible with a society that does not enjoy peace and tranquillity, where there is so much uprising, hatred, laziness and injustice. May all PACWA women be endowed to be effective in carrying out this great assignment. Jesus Christ is the only answer to Africa's problem and so unitedly we shall move forward with the only solution. The Lord Himself will go ahead of us all.

Chapter 12

WORLD TRAVEL

I see clearly how God is fulfilling His purpose for my life as I travel step by step with Him through this life. Through these journeys I have seen some of His great and wonderful works in the air, sea, mountains and land. The African countries I have visited, or seen from the airport, are Cameroon, Republic of Benin, Togo, Ghana, Cote d'Ivoire, Senegal, Republic of Guinea, Liberia, Mauritania, Congo Brazzaville, Ethiopia and Kenya. I saw many similarities but also differences in the physical features. Some are thickly forested, some are arid deserts, some mountainous, others flat.

Despite many African similarities, the people differ in the colour of their skin, hair texture and size. Coming closer one would observe their cultural differences, mainly in the language, food and dress. God found a way of uniting the people of Africa by providing a more common language like English or French to influence the regions. I found I could communicate with women from Northern Ghana and Niger in Hausa, but we had to keep separate during the real business of meetings. The ones from Niger have to sit on the French speaking side, being a Francophone country, while those from Northern Ghana and Nigeria, have to sit on the English speaking side, having come from the Anglophone countries. Somebody from the French speaking Africa once teased me in Paris that we, the Anglophone countries, do not have any link with our British colonial masters. 'You have no benefit of anything. I come to Paris and I am accepted and given equal rights with the French, but you are strangers in Britain'. I did not know how to react to that, but the whole idea created some conflict in me.

The Lord showed me a bit of western Europe too. I have been privileged to visit Great Britain, Denmark, France, Germany, Holland, Portugal, Switzerland, Bulgaria, Italy and Yugoslavia.

Yugoslavia

I was in Zagreb, Yugoslavia, to deliver a paper at the International Congress on Anthropological and Sociological Sciences, which was held at the University of Zagreb in 1988. My paper was on 'Nomadic Education in Nigeria'. While we were in Yugoslavia, tension was already high amongst its citizens. It was clear to us that the country was moving towards disintegration. It was sad listening to the claims of the various groups, Croats, Serbs and Muslims. But there was nothing we could do about it.

I joined a group of Christian participants to attend a church service on Sunday while in Zagreb. There was no Protestant church, we were told, so we were taken to a Catholic church. All I longed for at that time was a worship atmosphere, so that I could worship my Lord. The service was in their language, so I could not follow anything, but I worshipped the Lord in my heart. During the service, the collection plate was passed round. Before it came to me, I had a battle in my heart as to how much to put in. I was told on the way to church that I needed to have some money for the airport tax. This worried me a bit because I had already spent nearly all my money, believing I was leaving Zagreb early on Monday. I would not need any Yugoslavian money apart from what I needed to pay for my taxi. The new information caused me a little anxiety knowing that I did not know anyone in Zagreb to turn to for help, so I wanted to give the smallest unit of their currency to the Lord. Even with that, I did not have enough to pay for the airport tax. A voice urged me not to worry but to go ahead and put whatever I had wanted to give the Lord. I obeyed this voice and I am thankful I did because the Lord acted in my favour later. On our way back from church I asked some of the participants, who were leaving at the same time with me to join together in a taxi, so we could share the cost. This was special wisdom from God. I did not tell them why I needed to share the payment for the taxi, but they willingly agreed. To my joyous surprise, without any explanation, one of them offered to pay for the taxi and, as if that were not enough, he also paid for our airport taxes. The money I was trying to save for a purpose became useless, it had no function. I took it home as a souvenir. The voice which spoke to me in church was right, I wish I had given more to the church.

We were in Zagreb for ten days. It was not long after the congress that I received a letter from a congress participant from Zagreb informing me of the outbreak of the civil war, and in it I was requested to approach my country's government for support. Obviously, the letter was a circular sent to all congress participants. I thought the most effective solution to their problem was to put the whole country of Yugoslavia and its people before the Lord. So I took the letter to church during our mid-week prayers and we all prayed for them.

I had a stop-over in Bahrain, Saudi Arabia. The experience was so different from that of Israel, which I had visited several years later. The miles of desert land and the sand dunes, which I observed from the air, were a wonderful sight. Everywhere looks so spotlessly clean that one wonders who has been sweeping all those thousands of miles of sands. I wished they had some of the abundant trees we have on the West Coast of Africa, at least for the shade.

I saw Singapore, Australia, South Korea, Japan and the Philippines. I saw their level of development and I thank God for each of their advancements.

America

The latest of God's world I saw was America. I caught sight of it on my way to Manila in the Philippines. We entered America the second time through New York and from there we flew into Washington DC. I recall in my childhood how we used to sing about American wonders! The song goes 'If you want American wonders, come and see American wonders'. Usually, we sing it when we feel there has been an achievement. I remembered the song as I was being driven in and out of American streets. The skyscrapers were indeed a wonder! Not to mention the trained dogs that sniffed into people's luggage looking for drugs.

The roads in America reminded me of the Bible story of the wide and narrow ways. I was worried and hoped that the six-lane roads would not lead to destruction. The speed on these high roads was scary. The shops were full of lovely things, considerably cheap too - American wonders indeed.

When I became ill in America, I was admitted into hospital and a physiotherapist was assigned to me. His name was John. One day, he took me out to practise walking on the walker. He was telling me some nice places to visit, when I could do so. In the course of our discussion, I asked if he were a Christian. He said 'No'. 'Where did you get the name John from then?' I enquired. He told me from his parents. I asked further if his parents were Christians. 'Yes, they go to church, so I guess they are Christians'.

I explained that being a Christian does not only come from going to church. It had to come from the heart first, then going to church will manifest itself naturally. Going to church is the desire to be with God's children and worship Him together. The true Christian is the one who has accepted Jesus Christ as his Saviour and has established a relationship with him. I explained, 'John, I hope you are not carried away by the American wonders of high science and technology, with everything in abundance at the expense of your life, because it is eternal death for those who reject Jesus in their lives'. I see the Americans as speeding on a very wide, high road and I hope their choice and advancement will not lead them to eternal death. I told him I preferred our narrow way back at home.

My daughter once said to me she has a belief that in the end, more Africans might enter the Kingdom of God than the people from the advanced world she saw. 'Why? They brought us the Gospel!'. Someone replied 'Yes, they did, but many of them have thrown it away. Sunday, a day of worship, they use for businesses and car washing etc. If they really love God, why do they remain so distant from Him?' She further asked 'Yes, it is true that we know them by their fruit and it appears that their hearts are more on the things they see such as houses, cars, science and technology, forgetting that the things that are unseen are the ones we should seek, because they are eternal. The buildings that we live in here on earth are hand made and can be destroyed, but our eternal home in heaven is everlasting.'

Pilgrimage to the Holy Land

After the Lord had shown me so much of His world, He decided to show me where my Lord and Saviour was born and bred. When Solomon was a Governor he was the first to establish a Christian Pilgrim Board in the country of Nigeria. Prior to his time there had been the Muslim Pilgrim Board nationally established, but no-one had thought of giving the Christians a National Pilgrim Board. The establishment of a Christian Pilgrim Board in Plateau State in April 1980 really created an awareness of the need to cater for the Christian community in Nigeria. It was a joy to see that his bold step has been taken by other State's Governors in the country. It is our prayer that a National Pilgrim Board will in the near future be established to serve the Christians in Nigeria.

It was as a result of Solomon's initiative in establishing the Christian Pilgrim Board that I was recognised by the board in 1992 as someone the Government of Plateau State could sponsor to go on a pilgrimage. I had earlier wanted Solomon to put me on the list of Government sponsored pilgrims when he was there, but Solomon felt the people might feel that the board was established for his own gain.

And now, ten years later, a favourable Government came into power and they remembered me. This was the Civilian Government of the Social Democratic Party under the leadership of Sir Fidelis Tapgun (KSM). I remember with great joy when the Executive Secretary of the Board came round to me and said 'You are our mother and this is the least we can do for you'. Yes, I agreed with Solomon, it was more honouring and happier for others to recognise our worth. I would not have had this happy experience if Solomon had sent me during his time. Many people could not believe that Solomon deprived himself and his wife of these earlier privileges. Many Plateau State citizens have benefited spiritually from the yearly pilgrimage. Many said they were blessed spiritually as their faith became strengthened seeing things for themselves.

The year 1992 witnessed the highest number of pilgrims from Plateau State. Two hundred and fifty left Jos to go to the Holy Land. First we assembled at the COCIN HQ Compound Church, where we were informed about travel arrangements. Then the Governor addressed us the next day at the Good News Church in Jos. We finally left late in August for Kano and on to Rome. The Nigerian Ambassador to Rome, Her Excellency, Judith S Attah, came to the hotel where we were staying and addressed us. Judith Attah happened to be the Chief Education Officer who supervised me when I was made Principal of the Government Girls' Secondary School, Shendam. She was delighted to see me. She invited some of us to lunch at her residence. At the end of it she gave me a beautiful bag, which I still cherish today. She gave us the VIP treatment in Rome.

After a visit to the Pope we left the next day for Jerusalem, a city we used to feel was in heaven. That I was physically in Israel was thrilling to me. I discovered my suitcase was torn and some of my personal belongings were hanging out but it did not bother me. I was too happy to worry about that, but as I was carrying the suitcase to the bus waiting for us, someone observed the torn suitcase and asked whether it had happened during the journey or before the journey. I told him it was during the journey, so he showed me where to go and lodge a complaint, so that I could be given a new suitcase, similar to mine. This was a new experience for me. What open kindness! They gave me a note and the address of the shop to acquire a new one without costing me anything. Because our programme was too tight, I could not get round to it, but the wife of our guide sent me a similar suitcase from her house. It was wonderful that everybody was concerned. Praise the Lord for this attitude.

In Israel the houses are built with white limestone. This struck me because it is so different from the type of stones found in Nigeria, which are either grey, brown or black. In the Holy Land one sees the Bible coming alive; the stories became clearer and meaningful as we visited Bethlehem where Jesus was born, Mount Carmel, the City of David, the Mount of Olives, Mount Zion, the Garden of Gethsemane (the place where Jesus was crucified), and Mount Tabor (the Mountain of Transfiguration), Bethpage (where Jesus took off for the journey of the Triumphant Entry), and the land of Hananiya and Bethany. We were told that Bethany means the land of the poor and afflicted. We also saw the Paternoster Chapel, near Bethany, where Jesus taught His disciples 'The Lord's Prayer'. All the main languages of the world have this prayer interpreted into their language and it is written on the walls of the Chapel.

On Mount Zion we saw St Peter's Church from where we were shown the valley where the Canaanites and the Jebusites used to sacrifice their children. We saw the home of Jeremiah - Anatoth. We were taken round the dome of the rock where Abraham was about to sacrifice Isaac, his son. Other places visited were the Good Samaritan Inn. In Jericho we saw the sycamore tree which is said to be the one that Zaccheus climbed to see Jesus.

There is a Greek Orthodox church in the area which is known for fruits and perfume products from the Dead Sea. The Dead Sea has 32% salt, while other open seas only have 3%. The Dead Sea is so salty that no living creature can be found in it. We went through Zoar, the land Lot went to when he was taken out of Sodom and Gomorrah. In fact, we were actually in Sodom and Gomorrah. Although no-one lives in the area, it is well identified. We saw an area where John the Baptist ministered along the River Jordan. We saw the Yabak River where the angel had struggled with Jacob, the place that Jacob's name was changed to Israel. We saw where Saul fought with the Philistines and where Saul's body was buried. We saw the beautiful green town of the Shunamite woman in the Bible story.

We went on to Nazareth, a town built up on the

mountain. We were told that there are 50 churches scattered all over Nazareth. During the time of Our Lord Jesus Christ, there were only 50 families in Nazareth, but now there are about 60,000 people in the town. The guide informed us 50% are Moslems and 50% are Christians. In Nazareth we were shown the carpenter's workshop. We saw Jonah's home in Gathaphra. We visited Cana of Galilee and saw the wedding house. We saw Deborah's town and the Mediterranean Sea.

We arrived at Tiberias in the evening. It was a beautiful city with very nice hotels and we spent the night there. It was a very joyous night where we fellowshipped in the open at the Jordan Hotel. The following day we crossed the Sea of Galilee. After we had had the traditional Peter's fish for lunch, we almost broke the boat with our voices and our excitement was uncontrollable.

Throughout the period of pilgrimage, we sang in the buses, the hotels and even when walking in the streets. We started each day with prayers and ended with prayers. We enjoyed the food, the people and the land. We joined them at the Wailing Wall and prayed in our own manner and style. I inserted my prayer for my family and my country into the wall. We also went to the River Jordan. Some of the pilgrims bathed in the river - all of us entered it. Some of us drank the water out of love for what took place in the river - ie the Baptism of Our Lord Jesus Christ by John the Baptist. It was all a wonderful experience. We took the water from the river back home where many usually come to sip from Jerusalem Pilgrims. Most of the places where important events took place had a church built on the spot. We held services in many of these churches.

After two weeks of vigorous visits to many places in Israel which are mentioned in the Bible, we finally assembled in one of the hotels where certificates qualifying us to be pilgrims were bestowed upon each participant. This ceremony marked the end of our pilgrimage and we returned to Nigeria through Rome. (We recognise that there is no merit for salvation attached to a pilgrimage to the Holy Land, unlike the Muslims who by Islamic law have to make the pilgrimage to Mecca at least once in a lifetime.) Before our plane touched the ground at Aminu Kano airport, Kano, we sang in the air for about 30 minutes. Everybody was overjoyed. We sang, thumping our feet, and forgot that we were in the air. It was surprising that the plane was not forced down by the kind of pressure we used. We were refreshed in body and soul, it was 'Shalom! Shalom!!' all over us. Praise the Lord.

From Kano I left the pilgrims and travelled to deliver a paper in Kaduna to a group of Nigerian journalists who were holding a seminar at the Hamdala Hotel. My paper was entitled 'Women in Politics'.

The Lord needed to enrich my experience and equip me for greater service. When I travelled to the West African Coast it was for either PACWA meetings, or it was a Bank meeting. All were adding more to my experiences and improving my services in these areas.

It was as a result of my travel to Mauritania and Yugoslavia that my position was elevated in the University. I was given an added responsibility as a Director of the Centre for Research and Evaluation in Nomadic Education in Nigeria. I believe my being privileged to attend a conference on 'An Enabling Environment for Economic Recovery in the sub-Saharan Countries' in Kenya was a contributing factor in causing the State Government to place me in the position of Chairman of Lion Bank. Also a member of The Enabling Environment for Economic Recovery in Nigeria. This was quite demanding back at home after the conference in Nairobi, Kenya.

That I attended Lausanne 1 & 2 naturally gave me the membership of The National Congress on Evangelisation in Nigeria. Going to Kenya the second time prepared me for PACWA responsibility. Before the end of the conference in Zagreb, the African female members formed an association of the female branch of Anthropological and Sociological Sciences in Africa. I was selected the Secretary. I found my work at home as a lecturer, researcher, writer and other social responsibilities did not allow me to carry on with this lauded position, so I let this responsibility go. Each time I travel away for conferences or meetings within and outside

Nigeria, I know it will add to my work load. I really thank the Lord for this provision. The expenses of each trip were born either by the organisations or governments in Nigeria with the exception of one or two PACWA journeys.

My visit to Australia yielded much fruit because the Australian High Commissioner in Lagos, through one of their staff, Judith, who acted as a guide to us while we were there, offered me a scholarship to send a teacher to Australia, to learn from their education and agricultural extension programmes, for one year. So the blessing of the visit was passed on to another teacher who benefited from the programme. All these journeys enriched my experience and gave me a wider vision and inspiration.

It was as a result of my visit to Denmark that I got to know that a small percentage of a nation's population - eg 6% - could feed a nation with the proper use of technology. I then took it upon myself that the Joint Committee of Women's Societies, which I initiated in Plateau State, would be involved in mass farming production, and they could feed the nation.

I also planned some sporting activities for both young and old women to enable them to keep fit for the farm services I had in mind for them. I was quite overwhelmed with the way the old and the young in Denmark ride bicycles about and they look healthy and get on with their work without any problem. I wished the same health for my people back in Nigeria, but Nigerian society has yet to understand why the elderly, who own cars, may choose to trek rather than ride their cars all the time.

Unfortunately, the December 1983 coup which took place not long after we came back, put an end to all the visions and inspirations that I had come back with from Denmark. Nonetheless, I was able to make this suggestion to PACWA. It is my prayer that they will take the lead in this mass production of food for the sustenance of the nation. It is even right that Christian women should be the ones in a position to mass produce food to feed their nation.

Chapter 13

TOGETHER AGAIN

The family had a period of togetherness once more for about four years (October 1987 - November 1991), although it was not totally free of interference from the Military Government. The Military Government of General Babangida freed all politicians in 1987 from detention, but banned most of the front liners from further participation in any form of politics, or from holding any public office. This included Solomon and his friend Alhaji Abubakar Rimi, the former Governor of Kano State. But Solomon and his colleagues, undaunted in their political ideology, continued to push forward. The Military Government on the other hand re-doubled its effort in thwarting them from making their impact felt in society. The family therefore continued to experience arrests and molestations by the State Security Agents from time to time. Sometimes, these arrests took place at airports and at other times in hotels as well as at home. For instance, Solomon was arrested in Kaduna at the Hamdala Hotel and in Abuja in the Nicon Nuga, Hilton Hotel.

Summoned to Lagos
On 30 November 1991 when Solomon had returned from Langtang, the Plateau State Commissioner of Police telephoned to deliver a message from Lagos to summon Solomon to meet with the Inspector-General of Police in Lagos at 10.00 am the following morning. Solomon therefore had to leave at once for Lagos to be able to make the

appointment. He was at the Inspector-General of Police's office by 9.45 am the next morning. He was asked to sit and wait. As he was waiting, his colleagues started to arrive. They had all received similar letters summoning them to a meeting with the Inspector-General of Police. These were Alhaji Abubakar Rimi of Kano State, Alhaji Lateef Jakande of Lagos State, Chief Bola Ige of Oyo State, Chief Jim Nwobodo of former Anambra State, Dr Olusola Soraki of Kwara State and the former Senate Majority Leader, Chief Arthur Nzeribe. They were all kept waiting until about 10.45 am when General Shehu Musa Yar' Addu'a arrived, then the Police Commissioner went in to address them. As Solomon later informed us, he did this in few words saying 'Gentlemen, we called you here because we heard that you have been participating in politics and therefore we are taking you all to the 'Transition to Civil Rule Tribunal'.'

House Arrest

On the evening of 2 December 1991 as I was watching the 9 o'clock news on television, I heard them report that some banned politicians had been arrested and their names, including Solomon's, were listed. Naturally, I was disturbed by the news and I was worried because Solomon was due for a medical check-up abroad. However, the news further informed us that his case was pending a doctor's report. Solomon telephoned us that evening to confirm the news of their detention and of his being subject to a doctor's report. However, the next day it was broadcast that Solomon had been fully detained along with his other colleagues. He was then charged with the following offence that 'between January and October 1991 at Jos, Mr S D Lar sponsored a candidate to wit, Fidelis Tapgun, for the purpose of the governorship election in Plateau State under the platform of the Social Democratic Party (SDP) and you hereby committed an offence under Section 1 sub-section 4 . . . and punishable under Section 1, sub-section 5 of the same act'. For this offence he and others with similar charges were driven to the Lagos State House to be placed under house arrest. It all seemed well for the first day, with reasonable comforts, for people in such conditions.

This was not to last as the next night they were taken to Epe, a town about one hour's drive from Lagos - Epe Government Guest House. At first their families were not allowed to visit them. However, this changed, but visits were restricted to family members only. Our daughter Beni was the first to visit her father as she was studying at the Nigerian Law School in Lagos. She telephoned to tell me on her return that Daddy was well. I was delighted with the news. Soon after this, Chalya and I set out to visit Solomon in Epe. At the gate of the Government Guest House where he was being held, we noticed the blatant corrupt nature of the soldiers who had been deployed to watch the gate. They looked like hungry lions waiting to consume any prey in sight. Being so numerous, it seemed they had no other job than to while away the time guarding an isolated location. There were more than ten armed soldiers at the main entrance gate, more seated on the lawn inside, with each bungalow still guarded by six other soldiers, all idling away. This all seemed unnecessary. After searching us thoroughly and finding nothing, one of the men asked us to give them something to give to the soldiers to allow us to go in. I stood bewildered and exclaimed in exasperation 'You mean after all this trouble you still expect me to give you something more?' This I had said in Tarok. There was a Tarok man amongst them who heard this and moved closer with interest. He greeted us enthusiastically when he realised we were members of Solomon's family. He then pleaded with his colleagues to allow us to go in. This meant that we did not have to give 'something', which we realised later meant money.

Visiting the Prisoners

We were pleased to see Solomon and his colleagues looking well in their detention camp. Solomon was staying with Chief Jim Nwobodo and Dr Olusola Saraki in one bungalow. They were denied access to the outside world - no means of communication was allowed. However, there was a spirit of comradeship and solidarity amongst them.

We exchanged the normal pleasantries and asked after each other's health and well-being. We then unwrapped the small parcel we had brought along for him which included toothpaste, chicken meat and carrots, which he had specifically requested. After we had spent more time with him, he insisted we go round to the other detainees and greet them also. Obviously, the confinement had brought them all closer together. This was irrespective of religious, political and ethnic differences amongst them. Here I noted was one place people lived together as brothers. How I wished this were translated to the larger society - one free of religious, political and ethnic differences. This kind of a society is surely a desirable one for progress. By contrast, where leaders show discrimination or favouring of one religion or ethnic group above another, citizens are bound to lose their sense of belonging and start to cause problems to the society. Leaders showing favouritism will certainly result in oppressing the unfavoured group. And God detests oppression and injustice (Jeremiah 7:5-6).

After seeing Solomon, we later returned to Lagos where we spent the night in order to catch the first flight back to Jos the following day. Again, I had a sleepless night which I used to communicate with the Lord. I kept asking why we had to suffer so much political harassment. I reflected on the politics of the nation and wondered if any good was going to come of it. I kept asking the Lord if Solomon should not quit politics. The last thing I asked of the Lord that night was that he should show me the reason for all this harassment and for how long it would last. I did not know why I asked, or what I wanted to do with the knowledge if told. However, after asking these questions, I fell asleep. I was asleep for not more than fifteen minutes. In this short sleep, the Lord revealed to me that there was no reason for this political harassment, it was for no cause, and it would soon end. I believe the Lord allowed me this short sleep so that I could receive answers to my questions. I did not sleep again after that until daybreak. I spent the night thanking God. The next day we left in the morning for Jos.

Release Again

Just as the Lord had revealed to me in the dream, about a week later, the detained politicians were released from detention, but it happened after the elections for governor had taken place on the 14 December 1991. That night, Solomon got someone to telephone us to find out the election results. When he was told his candidate had won, they celebrated the news of victory in detention. They were released on 19 December 1991, which made it possible for us to spend Christmas in Langtang, our home town, as we normally did.

I praised God for his safe arrival. Throughout this period, the Lord stood by me and assured me that all would be well. My salvation was because I have the Lord and I speak with Him as clearly as I would with any other friend. The Lord speaks to His children all the time in many different ways (John 16:13). Sometimes He speaks through other humans, but sometimes it is through our involvement with His work. The way we understand God depends on the depth of our relationship with Him. I thank God for uplifting me in the midst of all these trials and tribulations. There were pressures from my work place, friends, family and children alike. There were people who thought my devotion to God's work was just a way of trying to gain popularity, but we cannot deceive the Lord. His eyes see and he knows us all from above.

Chapter 14

PAN AFRICAN CHRISTIAN WOMEN'S ALLIANCE

As National Co-ordinator of Pan-African Christian Association, later known as Pan African Christian Women Alliance (PACWA), my responsibility included organising conferences, seminars and meetings. I had just completed organising a national two-day conference in May, 1993 on the theme 'Christian Women and Politics', and was thoroughly exhausted. It was such a successful conference, with participants drawn from several states in the country. The Plateau State First Lady, Roselyn Tapgun, delivered the key note address while a prominent female politician, Mrs Sarah Jibril, gave a passionate challenge to fellow women, and so did Mrs Hannatu Ibrahim from Bauchi State.

While savouring the joy of the success of the conference, I did not appreciate how fatigued I was. My daughter checked my blood pressure and noted that it was high at 150/100. I took medication for two days. but women from PACWA kept coming in and out to make sure of travel arrangements to represent Nigeria at the launching of the American chapter. On the 21 May, at 11.00 am, I locked up the room and slept. God blessed me with a sound sleep for two hours. I tried to get out of bed, but found that I could not move. Only my head could move. I tried again and again. By the fourth time I tried with such great force that my whole body shook on the bed, but still did not move. It was then that I realised something was seriously wrong with me. I was thankful that my voice was not affected. I shouted and called on the Lord 'Lord, where are you? Your daughter has been attacked by the enemy, but I know you are here in this room; come and help me. I don't know by what disease, but all I know is that I need your help'.

Taken to Hospital

I then called out to the children, who had kept their distance to allow me to get some rest. They were outside enjoying a game. I had to pray to the Lord to make them hear when I called again. Suddenly, one of them, Nansak, heard this time and ran to me. He came to the door and said 'Momi, open the door', but I said I could not. He then had to force the door open before calling the others. They took me to Jos University Teaching Hospital, where I was taken to the emergency out-patients department, where a young doctor with hands in his pocket came in staring at me and said 'What is the matter with you?' I prayed to God that this was not the doctor who was going to treat me.

Immediately Professor Bello, a brother in the Lord and the Chairman of the Medical Advisory Committee of the hospital saw me and called out 'What's the matter with you, Auntie?'. He then instructed the doctor and all the other paramedics to leave what they were doing to attend to me promptly. This surely changed the junior doctor's attitude. He took down my story and proceeded to examine me. He asked me to raise my arms and legs - the right side did not move. After checking my blood pressure he said half of me was not working, that blood was not circulating on the left side of me. I told him Jesus will cause the blood to circulate. He then gave instructions for me to be given an injection. I was left to rest there for almost two hours, after which he returned and asked me to wriggle my toes and fingers, which I did. We were both happy to realise that all were functioning again. Praise the Lord. Yet they told me they would need to admit me for some observation. The whole admission process took another hour, including x-rays. I was then wheeled to the Amenity Ward.

As soon as people heard about my admission to hospital,

they trooped into the hospital in such large numbers that it became difficult to control them. Almost every person or group of persons that called to see me said prayers. Prayers I was told were said in churches, homes and various Christian groups. There were so many prayers being said that a patient's relative was forced to ask 'Who is the patient in this hospital?' because he has heard prayers said everywhere. He was told that it was Mrs Lar that was sick. Their sister is sick - no wonder!

I remained in the hospital for eleven days and I was told I had had a mild stroke. I did not see it as mild. I felt horrible. My body did not feel like mine. It felt as if it had been replaced by some bodily earthquake. I was told that if I rested well I would get over it, but there was no rest in that hospital. Day and night, visitors trooped in to see me. I had to be placed on a strict visitors' regulation but still many resorted to going round the back to greet me through the window. I was extremely grateful for the concern of the many visitors. I appreciated the doctors and nurses who were so good to me. My sister Lillian and Bonkat, my niece-in-law, nursed me with all the love they had within them, for which I will be forever grateful.

Left at Home

During all this, the day came for the PACWA women to leave for Lagos, en route to America for the American launching. They came to bid me farewell in hospital. They prayed with me and left me with one of the most reassuring verses on healing in Isaiah 53:5 - '. . . by His stripes we are healed'. Their visit was quite cheering, but when they left, I cried, as I was full of self pity that I could not go with them. In an assurance of God's healing miracle, I told them that God had healed me and that I would meet them in America; they should wait for me the next day. I was told the next morning that they had telephoned to say that they had arrived safely in America, and I gave thanks to God and I looked forward to meeting them. I asked the doctor if I could travel. He initially said no, it was too soon after the stroke to travel as it could happen again. I refused such a statement in faith, claiming the power of Jesus. I told him I would go and that Jesus was going with me so there would be no problem. He gave in and said since the blood pressure had been controlled, he felt I could go, but to be strict with medication and to look after myself. The next day I was discharged from the hospital to prepare to leave for America. People were praying with me during all this time which I found very encouraging. On the morning of the journey, a pastor, a dear brother in the Lord, came round and prayed for me for so long that we missed the flight!

Preparing to Travel

However, it turned out to be a blessing in disguise as I was really too exhausted for the journey that day. I enjoyed another day for rest and I was able to find some of the remaining travel documents. My family, including all my children, sisters and brothers, saw me off at Jos Airport. My husband and Chalya accompanied me to Lagos. My sister-in-law, Abigail, had waited with me in Jos to accompany me to the States - what a show of faith - as she believed so much that the Lord would heal me and enable me to travel with her. At the airport we waited for about three hours for the plane; Lilian and Manko left to prepare lunch for us, but by the time they returned the plane had arrived ready for take-off. This lunch was then packed luggage and became dinner for the four of us who had left Jos for Lagos.

I was so strained from the journey, I ended up crawling to get to the protocol lounge. The food we brought with us from Jos became very handy indeed. It was comforting to have Solomon by my side and Chalya assisting in everything. They encouraged me all through, exhorting me to continue to claim God's healing. This situation would have been avoided, if there had been a wheelchair readily available. I felt God's presence, especially when I had been settled into a first-class seat on the aircraft. Solomon and Chalya then said farewell to me and we took off at about 1.00am. God had prepared one of the air hostesses to take special care of me on the flight. As far as I was concerned, she was the best air hostess I had ever come across. I was surprised to see a fine Christian girl aboard as a hostess on Nigerian Airways. After the take-off she moved nearer to ask what was my problem. I told her I had just had a stroke. She took a keen interest in discussing healing from the Christian point of view and said 'You are a Christian madam, I want to pronounce God's healing on you'. She prayed for me. She shared the verse 'by His stripes - you are healed' and brought me a booklet on healing. She laid hands on me and prayed healing into my body. I felt the Lord had come in that form to comfort and assure me of His presence. It was surely His personal love and care for me at that time.

America

We landed in New York at about 8.00 am. Immediately on arrival, the five PACWA women and the air hostess who cared so much for me, held hands and gave praise to the Lord for a safe arrival. I was amazed at the level of care at John Kennedy International Airport, New York, when I realised that a wheelchair was waiting for me. I went through customs in this wheelchair and on coming out, my nephew Timothy Sheni was there to receive us. We were transferred to the US shuttle to board a flight for Washington DC. We arrived in Washington around 2.00pm where my niece, Zainab Sheni, came to take us to her house in Rockville, Maryland. It was such a lovely welcome to see my cousins Mrs C Sheni and Mrs D Aliyu, and a friend Joyce, who were around to receive us into Zainab's home. We were so thrilled at seeing each other that we did not go to bed on time that day. I woke up early, instructed everybody to get ready on time, so as not to be late for the PACWA convention at 9.00 am. By 6.00 am I was so weak I could not get myself up from the bed. I could hardly speak. My sisters were so terrified, thinking I was passing away. They all cried and prayed. My niece, Zainab, who is a nurse tried to feel my pulse, it was very faint, so she phoned for an ambulance. On the way to hospital they placed me on an immediate intravenous drip and I was given oxygen to inhale. I was taken to Montgomery Hospital in Maryland, where I was examined and admitted for seven days.

Another Hospital

The nurses and doctor were kind, giving me immediate attention. After all the tests, the neurologist, Dr London, was surprised that I was still maintaining my speech, my legs and sight. By the damage he saw of my brain, I was not supposed to have all these so he said. 'You are a lucky woman, go and be happy'. I was impressed by the number of different specialists that attended to me, such as the cardiologist, three different neurologists with separate areas of concern, and the physiotherapist. There were two patients to a room, a curtain partitioning the room. Each patient had a telephone by the bedside, a colour television and basic necessities such as towels, toothbrush, toothpaste, soap, water jugs and bed-pans. These the patient could either take away with him or let it be destroyed by the hospital. No such things are shared amongst patients. I did not know the telephone was meant for my use. The bed was made in a way that one could adjust it oneself by pressing a button either to sit up or to lie down. The whole hospital was set up in a way that one could take care of oneself, even without relatives around to help as is the practice at home. I wish Nigeria was able to offer such a level of care to its sick sometime not too far from now. As I was in hospital, my heart was full of the joy of the Lord and I was claiming his promises.

I went to America for PACWA but ended up in the hospital. I did not even see where the convention was held. At the end of the convention, PACWA members came to visit me in hospital and I was greatly encouraged. Both the African and American Co-ordinators of PACWA, Mrs Judy Mbugwa and Mrs Arnette Taylor respectively, were among the women that visited me. On seeing them I was full of self pity. I then asked Judy how the Lord could use me in this situation. I had been told that stroke patients hardly ever make a full recovery. She replied 'Mary, it is not for you to decide but the Lord will decide that for you.' This reminded me of the word of Jeremiah 10:23 'I know, O Lord, that a man's life is not his own; it is not for man to direct his steps'. This I found quite reassuring so I handed over everything to

Jesus waiting for Him to decide. I continued to improve in health. I stayed an extra two weeks in America to recover after the other women had left. My cousin Mrs Cecilia Sheni, stayed to look after me for these two weeks. Meanwhile, news had reached my husband in Nigeria that I had had another relapse in the United States. He was so upset and telephoned me in the hospital that he was going to take the next available flight to New York from Nigeria, and he arrived in the United States the following week. When I saw him I shed tears of joy.

I received my American blessing during the two weeks that followed the convention. The co-ordinator, Mrs A Taylor, invited Solomon and me to lunch. She took time to show me the PACWA video for about 2-3 hours. I felt part of it and was thankful to God for all that had taken place at the PACWA convention. I also had a wonderful Christian fellowship with Mrs Dele Abafarin, a PACWA member in America and a sister in the Lord. She gave me several Christian books and other literature including a book entitled 'How to Heal the Sick' written by Charles and Frances Hunter - a book which I found most useful. Dele also introduced me to her church, Bethel World Outreach Ministries, in Maryland, where I was prayed for and my healing claimed in faith. After the two weeks' rest and recovery, we left to go to the United Kingdom to see our doctor and physiotherapist. Earlier, the doctor in America had said to me 'Eat well, drink a lot of water, exercise, rest and take your medication daily.' These were my special prescriptions. I thought to myself, he has forgotten two other very important things to add to the list, which I did. Pray and give thanks.

Chapter 15

CONVALESCING IN THE UK

Whilst in London, Solomon made all arrangements for a doctor and a physiotherapist to take care of me. My coming to London allowed me to practise the doctor's prescription of eating, drinking, resting, etc which would have been quite difficult to follow back home in Nigeria. There would have been regular 'welcome home' visits with many concerned visitors, which might have been a bit too burdensome for my then fragile health. I also would not have had enough time to relax and eat as desired. I found this period of rest quite significant, reminding me of how Jesus Himself when he was on earth, needed to find a place to rest.

When Solomon had made sure I was settled down, he had to return to Nigeria to attend to other home and political responsibilities. Two of my daughters were with me and this offered us a precious opportunity to be together. Chalya, my other daughter, by now a medical doctor in the Ministry of Health, also visited me in London.

I also enjoyed visits from Christian friends such as Clifford and Monica Hill, Joyce Milverton, Maureen Parry, Pam Bendor-Samuel, K Maxwell, and Dorothy Richards. Such brotherly and sisterly visits encouraged me in the faith and were always a great joy to me. Some brought me Christian literature to read. My children and I shared them. They kept our spirits happy in the Lord.

Joanna Ibiwoye's Visit

One day I had the privilege of seeing Joanna Ibimidum, now Mrs Joanna Ibiwoye, who was on a sabbatical. She said 'I did not understand the teachings within Christianity'. She recalled the time she had wanted to join the Christian Union of All Saints' College, where we both trained as teachers. The CU officials told her she could not be a member because of doctrinal differences. She was very angry with them. She visited a Baptist pastor who took time to explain the difference. She was still convinced that her belief was right until one day she sat alone in the room with the Lord and her Bible, and the Lord convinced her. It was then that she was certain she had believed amiss. At that point she had found peace and changed her church. She found the true children of God and fellowshipped with them. She now felt she had brethren. The loneliness was no more. Her sabbatical was joyous, not as strenuous as when we were at college. She said she realised she had lived under fear all her life. So she knelt down and cast all fear out, and now she is a very happy person. She encouraged us all. My two girls, Beni and Deborah, were thankful to God for meeting her.

While my daughter Beni forsook her National Youth Service Corps to look after me in London, a friend of hers rang her from Lagos to tell her about the death of a colleague. Naturally, it shook her that a young boy who was so popular at school, just graduated as a young lawyer, full of a bright future, should just suddenly die in a minor dispute with the police. We both hoped that he found the Lord before his death.

British Television

In between their visits I found myself preoccupied with watching television. This was very unlike me; I used to scold the children for watching television all day, calling it a waste of time. However, I found new and revealing experiences from the television programmes. It is up to the viewers to decide which programmes will be of benefit to them. I was highly selective as to what to watch, such as the Christian programmes on Sundays, documentaries, the Open

University programmes, the news, wild life and athletics. It was disheartening to see from the news that there was so much war, and suffering in many parts of the world.

I watched a BBC programme on 26 August 1993, showing the Nigerian Military President, General Ibrahim Babangida, relinquishing power after eight years. The send-off parade was very colourful with a lot of pomp and gallantry. However, the reporter's remarks underlined the general feelings of the Nigerian population by saying 'General Babangida has left the country poorer, more divided and less confident than when he took over power in August 1985.'

Documentaries

The documentary programmes on television were my favourites because they showed God's creation both great and small; many countries were covered, ranging from Mexico to Japan, Australia to Sudan, Greece to India; with such diverse cultures it was very interesting. I noticed human beings have the same basic behaviour all over the world, such as being sympathetic towards the sick and needy. Though there were many similarities, each country was unique and satisfied in their environment. It was amazing the way the documentaries stirred up different reactions within me. Sometimes I was so pleased after watching and at times I would be so sad. The life of the aborigines in Australia, Red Indians in America, and the Sudanese in North Africa as depicted in the documentaries, revealed such a seemingly primitive way of life like many had lived thousands of years ago. They seem to need help from the more advanced people who have been enjoying civilisation and plenty for more than a thousand years.

Were the films made as a way of appealing for help? or were they made to spite the people? or just to state the facts as they were? I wondered. The documentaries went on to show how these people were either being killed or becoming extinct and I pondered further on what right does any human being have to decide who should live or who should not live, all because someone thinks the other has not met some standards he has set up for himself, killing precious lives for whom Jesus died.

As I watched the documentaries, I could see the wonders of God's creation in the seas, on the land, and in the skies showing birds, forests, mountains and seals. One such documentary revealed a family in Norway who came across a baby seal and took it into their home. The girl took time to make friends with this baby seal going out together into deep water where she taught it how to catch and eat fish. I wondered why the advanced countries prefer to spend so much time with animals rather than with less privileged human beings in other parts of the world. Then again I reasoned that these creatures are also part of God's creation which need our love, protection and care. However, we must remember that God has placed man above all creation (Psalm 8).

Sports Programmes

I enjoyed watching athletics programmes and especially the World Championships in Stuttgart. I was impressed by the way the athletes started off together, but some slowed down before the finishing line which I found significant in terms of the Christian race. Significant was a Chinese athlete who kept glancing at her coach, who was giving her instructions. She went on to run exactly as she was told and, not surprisingly, she won the race. This is true of the Christian life, if we run according to the instructions given us in the Bible.

One athlete was Merlene Ottey, a girl from Jamaica. She was clearly one of the world's best athletes, but for some very odd reason, she never won a gold medal, although she clearly deserved it. She was said to have been jinxed for the bronze. Merlene had turned 33, which meant that this was her last chance. Her perseverance in trying to win a gold medal before she left the sports scene made her clearly everyone's favourite. The spectators cheered her so much, the applause from the stadium was unusually thunderous, even my daughters watching at home could not control their excitement. Sadly she came second in the 100 metres.

There are times we find ourselves in the same position as Merlene. We feel we have done our best, yet our best may not be good enough. In the 200 metres race everyone in the stadium was on their feet, applauding and encouraging her - she won by .02 seconds. I was fascinated by the fact that the whole stadium, man and woman alike, screamed and shouted for her to win. Then with her country's flag she ran a lap of honour.

After watching Uncle Tom's Cabin, an anti-slavery film, I was left crying and sobbing for some time.

Above all, I looked forward to the Christian programmes on Sundays. It made me feel part of the service because I could join in the worship, sing hymns, read the scriptures and pray. This usually lifted up my spirit and kept me joyful. The summer Sunday programmes made me think of heaven and a host of people praising God. Some of the prominent lessons I received on these programmes were on forgiveness and love.

My stay in London was peaceful, restful and refreshing. I attended physiotherapy sessions and when I started to feel better, I attended a church at Golders Green. All the rest of the days I stayed indoors. I am thankful to God for my three girls who were very patient and kind in looking after me. Each one of them played their part with concern and understanding.

Action Partners

There came a time when the Lord spoke to me about giving again. The Action Partners of the Church of Christ in Nigeria sent a circular seeking help for a Bawtry Hall project. I could not respond to that then, but while in England, the Lord wanted me to send something to them. I was a bit hesitant. The devil made me think I was not earning my income in England, and people in Europe do not easily give gifts in cash, which I needed in the foreign land. The Lord brought to my memory the experience I had in Yugoslavia when the Lord blessed me with much more than I gave Him as an offering in church. This made me obey quickly. I sent a gift to Action Partners. Again His words in

Malachi 3:10 'test me in this' says the Lord Almighty 'and see if I will not throw open the floodgates of heaven and pour out so much blessing that you will have not have room enough for it'; the foreign land did not stop this. The gift I sent to Action Partners multiplied in return one hundred times during my stay in UK Several people from Nigeria came to London and each gave some substantial amount to help me. I remembered my daughter saying 'The Lord is showing you so much love in your illness!' Oh! how I need an obedient heart - a heart to rejoice in carrying out His will.

The Lord was my strength during this period of illness. I learned a lot and realised that God works through me better when I am peaceful and not straining. God knows I need time to rest and pray so that I will be under His control. When I realised this, my healing was also experienced. Jesus came to bind up the broken hearted to proclaim freedom for the captives and release prisoners from darkness (Isaiah 61:1). I was broken hearted by this illness and I felt like a prisoner tied only to my bed, but God completely released me from the effects of the stroke.

Solomon's Visit

After five months in England, Solomon came from Nigeria and took me to Germany for a second opinion with the doctors at DKD Wiesbaden. I went through several tests and my health was generally good. One morning, as I was coming out of the breakfast hall in Wiesbaden, I saw Solomon comfortably chatting to a Nigerian. Solomon introduced him to me as 'A one-time Chief Security Officer in Nigeria'. I recognised him as the man who had once caused us so much difficulty. I gathered that a new Military Government detained him for thirty months without any charge. He was explaining to Solomon the people who were responsible for his detention and the treatment meted out to him.

My life as a child of God has not been free from troubles but each time I cried out to the Lord He has saved me (Psalm 107). I have had delays in answering my prayers, which were necessary for the purpose of testing my faith, to humble my pride, to break me from any self righteousness or to equip me for future service. It could even be to correct my relationship with my Lord and other people. I discovered that during such trying periods, the Lord has used it to do other works in my life which, under normal circumstances, with everything running smoothly would not have been possible.

During such times, one is more aware of the dark, silent pain one is going through. But when I have accepted in faith that in everything God works for good with those who love Him, and that nothing is outside His loving purposes for me, then I rejoice.

The most sustaining verses in my life are found in Jeremiah 29:11 'For I know the plans I have for you' declared the Lord 'plans to prosper you and not to harm you, plans to give you hope and a future. Then you will call upon me and pray to me, and I will listen to you.'

The second verse is in Nahum 1:7 'The Lord is good, a refuge in times of trouble. He cares for those who trust in him'. With these verses I rest my life in the hands of my Creator who knows everything and He has never failed me.

Solomon is Reinstated

On 25 November 1993, I picked up the telephone and someone said 'Congratulations!'. 'What for?' I said. 'For Solomon's appointment!' It was still a blur to me. 'Your husband has been appointed Minister for Police, and they will be sworn in on Saturday, 27 November.' I felt 'then this is no congratulations', because of the state of Nigeria.

Sometimes the television in England had mentioned Nigeria but only the bad aspects, never any good news. They reported a series of protests by the people. When Babangida left in August, 1993, he handed over the Government to a fragile body, set up by him. This transitional government was headed by Chief Ernest Shonekan, who rose up as Chairman of a big multi-national company in Nigeria - the UAC (United African Company) formerly owned by the British. He was about to retire from this company, when he was made Chairman of the

Transitional Government. But Nigerians were impatient for a democratically elected government. The value of the Naira continued to fall. Internal hardships increased, so the people increased their pressure on the Government. The Trade Unions were no longer interested in serving the nation. Indefinite strikes were the order of the day. Everything came to a standstill. With so much difficulty the Chairman of the Transitional Government resigned his post, leaving in November 1993.

Whilst reading Ezekiel, the Lord showed me that Israel and Judah had been destroyed because of their sin. The land had been full of bloodshed and the city full of injustice. I could equate this to my country. Both America and Nigeria were full of diversity but why was Nigeria's diversity so unharmonized? The main areas of diversity are religion and ethnicity. The natives of Nigeria would rather leave their own country to do slave labour in other countries, so we are losing the cream of our society (a brain drain) to other countries.

Looking at the Nigerian situation, I could see the dissatisfaction and the level of suffering of the people - the level of corruption. Why should my husband be placed there? He has already had such a hard life. It will be a hard task, almost impossible for him. 'No,no' he said. 'This time there is relative peace in the country and people have a high expectation of the people now placed in high positions'. 'Can a few people at the top stop all that goes on underneath? What if the people become dissatisfied again and start to rebel?' Then I remembered that Solomon had already sacrificed his life for his people. He fears nothing, including all forms of persecution. He is convinced that his calling is in politics and if the time has come for him to be released from redundancy or God to use him in any position, then who am I to feel miserable about it? All I can do is to support him and the nation in prayer. The suffering people of Nigeria were anxious to see what this group of politicians, who at one time were banned from holding public office, and were now brought back into Government, would do.

My prayer and the prayer of the nation was that they had come back with richer experiences to serve their country with all their strength, sincerity, fairness and justice. They could do this in their own strength. They needed time to seek God's face in all their decisions, for it is God who touches the hearts of people to behave in the right way. Nigeria desperately needs good leaders who will be free of corruption and who will govern righteously. Before his recall to Government, Solomon was renovating the family house for our return, and he had planned to spend a week with us in Britain before accompanying us home. Now everything had changed and I knew I must not stress him further with my demands on his time.

Prophecy Fulfilled

The news about Solomon coming to power again strengthened my faith in the Lord. When he was released from prison he went to a Christian convention in Port Harcourt in 1988. There he met the Revd Dr Clifford Hill and his wife Monica. At that convention Dr Hill prayed for Solomon and prophesied that he would be restored to Government. It is a miracle that this came true five years later. 'If God be for us, who can be against us?' Romans 8:31.

For five and a half months I had rested in England - the first rest I had had since leaving Government House ten years before. My body had to be broken for me to respond to its needs. I left the UK on 11 December 1993 to return to Nigeria.

Chapter 16

SOLOMON:
THE MOTIVATOR

Solomon Danshep Lar is a man God has specially given to me as a husband. He is indeed a husband of great repute. We got married on the 30 January 1960 with the understanding that he would later attend a theological college and be ordained a pastor. I was quite confident that this would happen because he possessed all the qualities of a pastor. Being a child of God, he has a good knowledge of the Bible and talks about Christ at the slightest opportunity. But just before the wedding, things took a different turn.

The Call to Politics
The nation was to become independent in October 1960. Christians wanted to have strong and committed people to represent them in Parliament. They pleaded with Solomon to be their voice in the Assembly. With a similar plea from our parents, we were convinced that this was God's agenda for Solomon. We then prayed and accepted the call, which marked the genesis of Solomon's involvement in politics.

Having been prayed for by the church leaders and sent forth in the name of the Lord, Solomon stood for election into the House of Parliament and God gave him the victory.

He became the people's first representative for Lowland Division, ie his constituency which consists of the present Langtang North and South, and Wase Local Government areas. He was given a car to help him attend meetings but as his car was the only one readily available to serve every needy person in the division - the sick, women in labour and people needing to attend to emergencies elsewhere - Solomon hardly ever had access to this vehicle as it was serving the whole community.

Since I married Solomon, I have love and meaning in my life. His activities motivate me to love others as he is a man of the people. He interacts freely and happily with everyone, calling everyone a friend or a relation of some sort. I wondered whether I would be able to meet his standards. For example, he would be quite upset if he discovered that I had turned people away who came to see him, on the grounds that he was resting or sleeping, but I was trying to protect his health to keep him from breaking down.

All through our married life he has wanted me to cook food in abundance and keep it ready to serve all who call at the house. He often forgets the hard labour of grinding, fetching water and cooking for a large number of people. He feels uncomfortable whenever visitors come to the house and leave without eating or drinking. He likes to be flanked by people all the time, so that I hardly have any personal time with him. And he can overstretch himself to make people comfortable, even to the extent of going into debt for them. When I was newly married, I occasionally returned to my mother's house just for fellowship.

1966 Coup - Solomon Becomes a Lawyer

Solomon became a Parliamentary Secretary or a Junior Minister in the Federal Ministry of the establishment. However, with the January 1966 *coup d'etat* in Nigeria, we had to leave Lagos and go back to our home town, Langtang. There, we learnt to live in poverty for a time - for there was no job, no politics, no means of livelihood. Solomon was busy paying off the debts he had incurred on behalf of the people.

With plenty of time at his disposal, Solomon decided to take some GCE papers. At the same time he went to read for his Diploma in Law at the Ahmadu Bello University, Zaria. He passed three papers at advanced level in his GCE, so he decided to go in for a Law degree. He excitedly and enthusiastically went through his LLB programme in Lagos, and was called to the Nigerian Bar.

By this time many who earlier seemed to have abandoned him, started to be friendly again. He never counted anything against them. People would advise him to beware of so-called friends who had deserted him in time of need, but Solomon insists on obeying the Word of God. Many see this as a weakness in his character. He always maintains that we should forgive others as a condition for receiving forgiveness for our own sins and shortcomings.

After his graduation as a lawyer, he established a very successful law firm in Jos. But this was only the beginning of the many good things God had planned for him. A chain of events was to occur to bring him into the limelight of Nigerian politics. This began with the military intervention in 1966. General J T U Aguiyi Ironsi took over the government and ruled for six months and was followed by General Yabuku Gowon.

Democracy Comes - Solomon is Called

When General Murtala Mohammed was in power for six months, he set up a timetable for a return to a democratically elected government. This was faithfully followed to the letter, even after his death, by his successor, General Olusegun Obasanjo.

Solomon was asked to run for the position of Governor. We prayed with all our hearts about this and in the end Solomon stood for the election and God gave him the victory. He became the first civilian Governor of Plateau State.

It was during General Obasanjo's time that Solomon's talents were recognised. He was appointed a member of the Irikife Panel for the creation of more States in the country. He was also appointed Chairman of the African Continental Bank as well as carrying on his legal practice in chambers. He championed a programme in Nigeria called 'Legal Aid' which is mainly to assist poor citizens who cannot afford to hire the services of lawyers. This programme is still of great help to the poor in Nigeria, but is now known as the Legal Aid Council of Nigeria and run by the Government.

By the special grace of God after four years serving as Governor, he was re-elected for a second term of four years. It was during his second term that the military struck again - on 31 December 1983 all politicians were taken into custody. He was accused of overspending the security money. He was singled out for punishment because he was said to have challenged some 'big powers'. Later, another panel was set up which found him 'not guilty'. When the military government of General Buhari came into power in January 1984 I thought Solomon was going to be released from the evil of politics, but the military government seemed all out to destroy him. Solomon was in detention for four years.

Solomon Freed and Reinstated

General Ibrahim Babangida's regime came into power in August 1985, and freed Solomon on 1 October 1987 after four years of torture in prison. A new panel was set up to review Solomon's case and he was discharged and acquitted in September 1986, although not released for another year.

Solomon organised a thanksgiving service in March 1988 where he gave testimonies of how God kept and used him in prison. He was like a Chaplain to the detainees. Those who had been discharged earlier called to express their gratitude for what Solomon had done to keep their spirits up in prison, and some sent us gifts.

Solomon seemed lost at the beginning of his freedom, but was happy to be flanked by people every day, many of whom gave him financial support. Then he started to revive. He formed a company called Pangna Nigeria Limited which kept him going from 1988 to date. His house is like a consulting room - people are always there, day and night. This became so unbearable that I had to complain bitterly to him on behalf of the family about our lack of his attention.

I was in London in December 1993 when Solomon rang to inform me that the Head of State, General Abacha, had selected him to serve as a Minister in his Cabinet. 'How do you feel about it' I asked. 'I feel I should respond to this national call' he answered. Although I did not share this view, I kept silent. I knelt down and prayed. My prayer was simple: 'Lord, you who know everything about us, give me a heart to accept your will for us'. My children were not excited either. It was not long after this that we left London and Solomon met us at Lagos airport. He came as the Minister of Police Affairs accompanied by a few policemen. He was given a minister's quarters in Assokkoro in Abuja, an exclusive area for government top level officials. After the thanksgiving for my recovery from ill health, I found Abuja peaceful and refreshing. Then suddenly one day during the 4 o'clock news in Jos, I heard that General Abacha had dissolved his cabinet. I drove quickly to Abuja to stand by my husband. We had a time of prayer and thanksgiving. One is never sure of the mood of the country.

I later learnt that the Head of State had initially wanted people of integrity to help him form a government, so that it would be accepted by the nation. As soon as the government seemed stabilised, he did not waste time in sacking these selected politicians.

After a careful study of the situation, I realised that God had used Solomon's position to bless many during this short stay in government. It was during some of the quiet moments of rest in Abuja that the Lord gave me some challenging visions.

Evangelism

First the Lord spoke to me one night that I should get all members of the Lar Mbamzhi's family together, starting with Grandfather Lar who was the first to receive the Gospel of the Lord Jesus, the act which resulted in the burning of his house. His grandchildren are richly blessed - some are lawyers, doctors, architects, teachers, accountants etc. The family had multiplied to more than a hundred. One of them, Mrs Cecilia Sheni, became the leader of the Women's Fellowship of the Church of Christ in Nigeria (COCIN) for over ten years. She worked relentlessly to extend the Kingdom of God in Nigeria and Africa. Another, Mrs Esther Bali, is a proprietor of two schools in Nigeria.

Mrs E D Aliyu has been an accountant with the Government Ministries of Plateau State for more than twenty years. Lilian has been a nursing sister for over twenty-five years and is very active in Sunday School work. Both male and female members of the family have been wonderfully blessed.

The Lord put it into my heart to go back to the village where my father was born to give special thanks and glory to the Lord God, our Father. I invited the whole family and more than 50 of us went in a hired bus. We had several prayer meetings to ask the Lord to use us to reach that village for Him. People were invited from around the village and old and young turned up to see the grandchildren of Lar Mbamzhi. The village church could not contain us all, so chairs were arranged outside the church. The Chief of the entire district, the *Ponzhi Zinni*, Mr Jeremiah Goselle, was there to tell the history of Lar Mbamzhi. We each participated - some gave testimonies, some sang, some recited scripture verses. I spoke on the faithful God, who knows His own and cares for them. I used the story of Shadrach, Meshach and Abednego, and Daniel to show how faithful God has been and will always be to His people. I pointed out that evil men designed that the Lar Bamzhi family should perish, but that God chose to bless us instead. Then we sang 'We are what we are by the special grace of God'. Even though the rains were over, there were some mild showers of blessing. The gentle thunder in the skies around us seemed like the voice of God, as if it were saying 'My children I am pleased with you'. At the end of the programme, 38 people gave their lives to Christ. We prayed for each one of them.

Literacy Programme

One woman approached me with a different problem. She was the leader of the Women's Fellowship of the local church. She said she had received Christ some years before, but she was illiterate. She could not read the Bible or interpret it to the women, and she sometimes felt like committing suicide over this handicap. I assured her that

God had a plan to teach her to read and write. I had already written some primers in my language and Hausa, the dominant language in Northern Nigeria. I taught a volunteer evangelist how to use the primers and gave him some free copies and some chalk boxes. He went back and taught the villagers.

Solomon and I re-visited the village two years later. This woman was all smiles. She could now read the Bible! This started me thinking about others like her. Earlier, two missionary friends had challenged me to organise literacy classes for the large number of women who could not read the Bible for themselves. One of these was a teacher in Gindiri, a Miss Pixie Caldwell, the other missionary was a Nigerian, Agnes. The message was clear. The Lord was directing me to a new area of service and I was able to take up this challenge, because of Solomon's support, particularly financial. The project is called **'Auntie Mary's Literacy Project'**.

Solomon encouraged me to produce hymns sung in my native Tarok language on cassette. This was launched in the Church at Langtang. With this and Solomon's support, the literacy project was launched on the 31 March 1995 by the Honourable Commissioner of Education for Plateau State, Dr Jonah Madugu. The representatives of Adult Literacy Commissions at the State and Federal levels were present and they donated books for the project. Sixty-five people were trained to start classes in Langtang, both North and South and over 600 learners were registered during Solomon's short stay in Government.

Brother Joshua from Lagos said that God showed him two seats of power, one for Solomon and one for Mary his wife. So when Solomon became a Minister, I thought I would be a Minister or be placed in some high position. But then I remembered that brother Joshua went on to say that while he saw Solomon busy with government, he saw me busy watering the garden.

I was able to organise some Tarok women to go home and visit their own village churches. In one of the places, the evangelist said that in his sleep he saw some people descending like angels, bringing them messages from heaven. We praised the Lord for the over 40 who stayed on for counselling. In another village their requests were for Bibles and for classes to learn to read. After these visits we formed a prayer forum for those village Christians.

Although I was not totally sound in health, God gave me enough strength to carry out many of these assignments. During Solomon's short stay in government, we were also able to publish a Tarok dictionary which we had compiled over a period of 20 years. I constantly faced health crises - I wept so much that the Lord had to do something to give me the assurance of His presence. He sent a sister called Agnes. She is of the Seventh Day Adventist Church in Bukuru, but belongs to a Pentecostal prayer ministry. The Lord spoke to her in her sleep to look for the house of Mary Lar and to take a message from Him.

She said 'I do not know this woman, why are you sending me to her?' The Lord said 'Go and look for her. Mary is worried about her health. She need not worry at all, because I have already healed her.' She asked 'Is there no verse for her?' The Lord said 'Share Ezekiel 47:1-6 with her. Tell her that her sickness is like the river which Ezekiel saw. The river wants to take her, but, I have already rescued her and have put her life on the river bank. She should carry on with the work. Tell her that her sickness is gone and pray with her'.

Sister Agnes arrived at our house in the afternoon. She waited for hours for me as I was still away at work. When she shared the message with me I was overjoyed. I prayed 'Lord you are wonderful, you care for a faithless wretch like me. Just forgive me and push me into your service.'

I offered Sister Agnes some money to help her go back to Bukuru. 'No, the Lord has given me enough money to come here and go back. I do not need any extra'. I was doubly sure that the message was from the Lord by this singular act, because in Nigeria these days, even some Christian leaders are tempted to compromise and lose their credibility for money. After this experience I was confident enough to face my responsibilities. I planned more village church visits and the Lord gave us more harvests.

Chieftaincy Title for Solomon

When Solomon was in government, the Ponzhi Tarok (chief of the Tarok people) and his council decided to honour him with a traditional Chieftaincy title. This is in recognition of his role in the ethnic group as a leader, a contributor of outstanding qualities. They conferred on him the title of *Walin Langtang* - that is someone who has excelled in matters of judgement or counselling.

Before the turbanning ceremony, people brought all kinds of gifts to the newly appointed chief, including clothes, money, cows, rams, chickens etc. Most of these were given out by Solomon to the less privileged members of society. The animals were slaughtered for the great feast. I saved a cow for my birthday which was to take place within six months. The day of turbanning came - 3 December 1994. Solomon rode on the traditional white horse for chiefs, specially decorated, and sent to him by the Emir of Wase. It was a grand occasion, a memorable day. Many people came from all over Nigeria. These included representatives of the Head of State, Ministers, members of the Diplomatic Corps, Military Governors, Emirs and Chiefs, top civil servants, heads of parastatals, religious leaders, members of the business communities, members of the constitutional conference, labour congress etc. The town's air-strip was packed with aircraft which had brought people for the ceremony. When it was all over, we knelt down and praised God for letting us see another exalting occasion in our lives.

My Birthday Celebration

When my birthday came on 9 May 1995, I had a special evangelistic birthday for the blind, the lame and the deaf. Leaders of each group were asked to select 25 handicapped people each. Others from the university were also invited. The youth band from my church was there to give life to the gathering and the church drama group presented a special play portraying the love of God, which extends to the down-trodden as well as the rich. Mr Bitrus Gani, a privileged blind man who was trained at Gindiri school for the blind, went to Gindiri Boys' Secondary School and finally went through a training in physiotherapy at London University, was the speaker for the occasion. He is a born-again Christian, endowed with enormous abilities both in speech and skills. The cow I had saved from Solomon's Chieftaincy gifts was slaughtered. My Church Pastor and elders also honoured the occasion. The programme went beautifully. At the end of it, seven people gave their lives to Christ.

Later Response and Conversion

One blind Muslim man, who was trained at Gindiri School for the Blind, heard about the Lord while in Gindiri, but when he went back to his home in Bauchi, he faced so much persecution amongst his Muslim kinsmen that he retracted. He was in his final year in the University of Jos.

He said 'That night I listened to you sharing the testimony of Paul Yonggi Cho. This kept me sleepless as I wondered why I did not give my life to Christ that day!' The Spirit of God spoke to him in the night. He recalled me saying that Paul, in South Korea, out of desperation for his health called out 'Is there a God higher than Buddha that I have not known. Please come and help me'.

It was at that point that God sent a school girl to tell Paul Yonggi Cho about a God he had not known who has power to heal and to do everything under the sun, because He is the maker of heaven and earth. At first, Paul was resistant, but later the Spirit convicted him and he gave his life to Christ. That was the beginning of a new life for Paul Yonggi Cho who now has the largest congregation on earth.

Because I had read Paul's book, I was able to share his experiences at this gathering. Paul Yonggi Cho's testimony was winning souls in far away Nigeria. This is one of the wonderful ways in which God works. The next morning this young Muslim man went to his Christian lecturer in the Special Education Department. He confessed his sins and turned to God. He made public confession in the ECWA church in Bauchi and to his fellow students. He said the Lord had reassured him that the only way to salvation is through Jesus Christ and that he was wasting his time trying to please human beings. He could please people and perish or please God and live forever. He chose the latter and has surrendered his life to Jesus Christ who is 'the Way, the Truth and the Life' (John 14:6) which God used to bring the Gospel to the disabled in Jos.

Solomon Freed Again

I did not feel it was fair for Solomon and his colleagues in politics to be called into office one day and be laid off the next. All the same, the Lord must have a purpose for everything. The prophecies by brother Clifford Hill and brother Joshua about Solomon's coming back into government were fulfilled, even though it was for a short period. Solomon served the government faithfully and honourably. The Military Government of General Sani Abacha sent him out of government in February 1995. As they were still interested in politics, they were encouraged to leave the government and participate fully in politics. What was not clear was that other men who were equally active politicians were invited into the new Military Government.

Now, politicians are re-grouping. Solomon has emerged as the leader of the middle belt zone of his party. Meanwhile, he is busy in politics, studying the transitional programme of the Military Government. It is his hope that things will work out well this time around.

Whether in government or out of government, Solomon is generally respected as a leader of thought and an opinion moulder. He has had the privilege of being called upon at critical moments in the life of the country. For example, in 1992 when there was general dissatisfaction during General Babangida's regime, Solomon was invited by the Head of State to form and lead the Elders Forum. In 1997, General Abacha invited him, among other leaders of thought, to advise the government on what to do following the country's suspension from the Commonwealth.

All these are clear indications that Solomon has a lot to offer the nation. My prayer is that he will be upheld by God's grace and continue to play an honourable part in politics for Nigeria and for the Lord.

Chapter 17

PERSONAL PERSPECTIVES

Many changes have taken place, within the sixty years of my existence. I thank the Lord for giving me the grace to live thus far, so that I can share some of my experiences with the world. My real concern is for the current situation in some parts of Africa. I watch the television and see a sea of heads migrating in millions, some worn out and fallen by the roadside, children crying, the aged tired but unable to rest. I weep and mourn for my fellow Africans. Why is there so much suffering, crying, killing and hunger? Why are there so many refugees? This has posed some serious challenges to the church in the entire Christian world. How can the church cope with all these problems - corruption, materialism, poverty, hunger, inter-tribal conflicts, occultism, all forms of ungodliness and general moral decadence?

When I first went to Britain in 1962, people showered praises on Nigerians. It is now a shameful thing even to mention one's country of origin in any part of the world. Some African Americans who used to claim their origin as Nigeria or West Africa now say they come from South Africa. In those days, it was Asia and India in particular that were known as suffering, hungry countries. Emphasis now has been shifted to Africa. It puzzles me. Asia and Africa were liberated from colonialism about the same time, but looking at them politically, socially, economically and culturally, Asia has gone ahead. What is wrong with the African people? What is wrong with their leaders? Why does Africa not make the same progress? Were we made with less brains? Is the continent cursed? Africa was at some time called the dark continent, when the colonial masters first visited it. What made it dark? Why do the people still sit in darkness and continue serious tribal conflicts witnessed in many of its nations? As I view Africa, I see us living in a world full of stateless people - destitute with no proper shelter. Many are sick and there are no basic facilities to take care of the refugees. Why is there always war in Nigeria, Somalia, Ethiopia, Rwanda, Burundi, Sudan, Chad, Algeria, Zaire, Angola, South Africa and Liberia? Nowadays it seems Africa is the symbol of suffering. When we know the cause we are on the way to finding solutions.

Let us examine some of the problems:

Corruption

Many Africans will agree with me that corruption is one of the root causes of our set back. It has done incalculable damage to the continent.

When I was in school, we were taught to hate corruption. Our leaders lived exemplary lives and we tried to copy them. Progress was on course. Employment, schools admissions, promotions, business, farming etc went smoothly, because everything was fair and justly administered. Then I watched sadly as righteousness, fairness, justice, self-discipline, self-denial and uprightness (which were regarded as virtues and legacies left by our pioneers) disappeared and were increasingly regarded as irrelevant. The same is true in some of the other African nations where there is corruption in its totality, as described by the dictionary, 'wickedness, rottenness, deprivation, bribery, vitiated by errors especially during elections, destruction of purity of language, decomposition, moral deterioration, deformation (of word) (law) and bribery'. I may add, indiscipline, selfishness, materialism, oppression, injustice, deceit, cheating, mockery of all things good, and above all rejection of Christ in our lives.

School and Education

The admission process into schools, colleges and universities used to be based on merit, but now whenever somebody wants to go to any institution, public or private, he starts looking for godfathers who will give him a letter of introduction to the authorities concerned, so that they can be favoured.

Someone pleaded with me to give him a letter to the examining officer so that he would pass his son. I insisted that a note from me was not necessary but this man brought others to help him plead with me. The people are not confident in the system.

We were asked to conduct interviews with those who passed the examination but to my amazement the list of those we gave as having passed the interview were mixed up with names that had not passed the exam or had not passed the interview. These students were from very influential families. When these irregularities were pointed out to the ministry, they said there was nothing they could do about it. Some parents blamed the school for not helping their children to catch up to secondary school level in that year.

In another school I experienced a pathetic case. The daughter of a chief had not got the ability to pass examinations, but the housegirl had. So the housegirl was sent to take the examinations bearing the name of the daughter of the chief. She passed and was invited for interview. The same girl attended for her and passed the test. When she was admitted the girl, who had never sat the examination, nor attended the interview, arrived at school. The school had no way of identifying who was who but the housegirl later wrote to the school. It was a difficult case to decide so the matter was passed over. How many more might have been cheated in the same way? These down-trodden human beings are crying out for justice.

Examination malpractice has started to show its ugly face in many of our institutions. Corruption has caused people to be insincere. This could be the reason why people demand indiscriminate introductory notes, which may not even concern the person about whom the note is written.

The Market Place

More and more people are bribing their way into employment or to gain favour of some sort. People are receiving and giving bribes openly with no one to check the practice. The very people that the government has set up to check corruption have come to participate in it.

In my day the measuring pan was level, nowadays it is knocked upward so as to reduce the quantity of the food, or item, paid for. In the case of tomatoes, potatoes, onions and the like, the sellers start by putting layers of dried grass, then a layer of rotten or small ones, before putting nice ones on the top. In the end the buyer may have received goods worth only half, or less than half, of what he has paid for. In the case of those who sell grain in big bags, they fill half of the bag with rotten or bad grain and just put nice attractive grain at the top. Sometimes the bag which is supposed to contain a hundred measures, may be 5 -10 measures less when taken home. These practices get copied by others, thus creating a social problem.

At a higher level, society is also corrupt. People who are in a position to award contracts often demand a token. A registered contractor told me he had to bribe every desk that is in the ministry, even the messenger who had to carry his file from desk to desk. Another one said he had to bribe the gateman before he could gain entrance into the ministry where he was to be given the contract. The shocking thing is that corruption has even been found among Christians. One expects Christians to live in the light so that others can see the way. In my younger days anything truthful, honest and just was associated with the Christian community. These were the people called upon to give testimonies in the courts, and what a Christian said was usually considered, when pronouncing the final judgement. Christian children were healthier, neat, obedient and well-disciplined. They survived the high rate of mortality from which others suffered. Christian farms yielded more crops; there was no hunger and they were never in need. God blessed everything they did, because they depended on Him. They cared for one another because they loved the Lord. The Christian was admired and respected everywhere.

Then others, who wanted to get this respect, began to join the church. They became baptised and sometimes they were placed in positions of leadership in the church. Such people started to want power and to have a negative influence on the Christian community. They used the church for selfish ends. Their hearts were far from God; they were hypocrites, wolves in sheep's clothing. 'A bribe corrupts the heart' (Ecclesiastes 7:7). If we practise bribery we corrupt our hearts, which affects everything else that we do.

I was in a ministry in Abuja and two young men served me so faithfully that I wanted to encourage them as a mother. The one bearing the Christian name was quick to receive it, as if he were waiting for it, while the nonChristian shook his head and said, 'mama how can we receive anything from you because we serve you doing our duty. You are our mother' and he went away. I was not used to seeing such people, but I know there are very few like this man in the country. Keeping the law in itself is good, but we need more of the power that will sustain us in our faith that is only in Jesus Christ.

During the launching of a literacy project in March 1996, most of the donations were fake, even government contributions were only meant to be heard and not to be received. They were pleased to make an announcement to show the people that they were supporting a good cause. The money I spent in following up one government pledge was almost as much as that which had been promised. One of them told me 'the government did not approve the payment'. Yet it is the same government that assigned this person to represent them at the launching and to promise that exact donation.

My Tuesday prayer partner shared a topic for prayer with me. She said, her husband was awarded a contract by a government official. This government official invited her husband as a friend and gave him the contract. After her husband had spent more than half of his resources on it, the contract was revoked without any payment. Meanwhile he had used the contract papers to obtain a loan from the bank and the interest on the loan was building up. In some places he had completed the contract but government officials have refused to evaluate and pay him. Even where it has been evaluated and accepted, the money has not been paid to him. Has this contributed to our recent banks' failure? There are so many who have registered as contractors, men and women and even children. They storm the offices seeking for contracts.

When my husband was made the Minister of Police Affairs, people used to say his office was like a labour office. Those seeking jobs, contracts, financial help, trooped in daily in large numbers. No wonder many civil servants leave their offices to get away from the chaotic visits. Apart from the job and contract seekers who come in, there are those who come to beg for money or food for survival because they have no livelihood, yet no dole is dispensed and there is no plan for it, as it is in advanced countries like America or Europe.

Those who have not got Christ tend to turn to wicked alternatives such as armed robbery. Is there anyone left who can sit down with God and plead for Nigeria and Africa in the way Abraham did for Sodom and Gomorrah? We are all tangled up in confusion. Who will loose us from these tangles? Sometimes I join in the song of the Evangelical band Langtang who sing in our language:

"Iza ka nfa ya oganan (x 2)
Unam ga nnandar ya kat a,
Ko uda ran go ka nnam iyam gi igwak wo (x 2)
Ayir Inan ya lap kat a.
Amo! Unam ga nnandar ya kat a."

English interpretation:

What is happening brethren (x 2)
Not one single honest man.
Every one is doing what his heart tells him to do (x 2)
No fear of God again in them?
Amazing not a single honest man is available.

There are many, in fact millions of God's people in Nigeria, but their impact is not felt much in society. This is why many wonder whether there are any honest people still left.

Elections

As I watched CNN news in November 1996 in Germany one evening I listened to the reactions of a number of people on the USA elections where Bill Clinton had just been voted as President for a second term. I took more interest in the response of two Cameronians. The lady said, 'I am happy Bill Clinton won the election, but I am also impressed by the straightforward way they did it. I hope to witness this in my country too.' The man said 'I admired the way they conducted the elections. If it were in Cameroon names would be missing, ballot papers short etc. etc.' This made me laugh, not for joy but because it gave the picture of what is happening in my country too. The experience seems to be a common one we Africans have. It is true that voters' lists will be mixed up during elections, some names may appear miles from the actual polling stations of the voters. Some names will be completely missing from the list on the day of the elections or the pages blank, with serial number in order, without the names. The officials may not appear on time in some voting areas, until uncaring voters get impatient and disappear. Under age children have been found voting in some places with nobody stopping them.

The Military Government during the time of General Babangida's regime introduced physical counting of people lining up for a particular candidate's picture. Counting was supposed to start at a particular time to avoid people casting their votes twice. Vehicles were not allowed to move during the voting period. Still this was abused. People were imported from neighbouring states the night before to vote for those who were not popular in their areas of residence. This meant that fictitious names must have been registered earlier so that the voters, who were not known by anyone in the area, could answer these names. Different types of election rigging usually surface on the day of the election. Even when a candidate has clearly won an election he is not always declared the winner, unless by some divine intervention, especially when the winner is not in favour by the authority conducting the election. Solomon was almost deprived of his second victory at the polls in 1983, because he belonged to a different political party from the Government's party. Were it not for the prayers of God's people his opponent would have been declared the winner. The most recent we witnessed was the 12 June, 1993 elections where the results were never declared at the end of the polls.

Justice is the Answer

One could go on enumerating all the ills connected with elections. This has resulted in the general frustration, despondency and insecurity of our nation. As we hurt innocent people their cries reach out to heaven. And God who sees trouble and grief will take it up because He is the father of the fatherless (Psalm 10:14). For the Lord is a God of justice (Isaiah 30:18); ' . . . for the Lord searches every heart and understands every motive behind the thoughts' (1 Chronicles 28:9). 'He watches over the way of the righteous, but the way of the wicked will perish' (Psalm 1:6). All those who are oppressed because of their uprightness or love for Christ will be delivered. 'Because the eyes of the Lord are on those who fear him' (Psalm 33:18-19). He sees all that goes on in this world!

A society which mounts up frustration, despondency and the like will be sure of breeding destruction. There is therefore no short cut to peaceful co-existence. It lies in recognising all the citizens of the country equally. Our government should devise ways of balancing the conflicting needs of our various communities. Their actions must be based on justice and fair play. We are all citizens of this great country Nigeria. Nigerian leaders owe a duty to God to allow each talented citizen to utilise his talents in his country, whether he's in the opposition or not; they are all equal before God. They should inculcate in everyone the virtues of justice, equity and fairness. None should be relegated to the background for their ethnic or religious inclinations. The writers of our National anthem were not wrong when they included 'Though tribes and tongues may differ, in brotherhood we stand. Nigerians all are proud to serve our motherland.'

Doing things wrongly because someone else is doing it, is not the solution to our problems. Someone produced fake drugs, made a huge amount of money at the expense of many lives, then went to his people and bought a chieftancy title. This kind of thing should not be allowed because 'we shall each give account of each word we utter and do' (Matthew 12:36). 'So then each of us will give an account of himself to God' (Romans 14:12). No matter how long we live in this world, we must at the end give an account to God. What sort of account will it be if we carry on injustice, cheating, dishonesty, oppression, and corruption of all sorts?

The prophet Zephaniah was concerned about the evils he witnessed in his day, so he warned his people 'Seek the Lord, all you humble of the land, you who do what He commands; seek righteousness, seek humility, perhaps you will be sheltered on the day of the Lord's anger' (Zephaniah 2:3) He knew that God would punish their sins, so he spoke out.

We Must Live God's Way

A preacher once preached in church about youths who waste their lives in lust, smoking, drinking, and in sexual immorality. He said God is not happy with them and they must turn away from this before God's anger catches up with them. A young man stood up, gave a big hiss and left the church. 'Why did you do that?' I asked. He said each time he goes to church, the pastors start preaching at him. He could not humble himself to listen to the voice of God. Instead he developed a hatred for pastors. Today he is a wretched man who goes about begging for clothes for himself, his wife and his children. He lost his wife and some of his children in the process. When God is speaking to us as Nigerians, or as Africans, we should humble ourselves, stop, and reason. The Lord will only live within the meek and humble who trust in His name (Zephaniah 3:12). We have all sinned against God in little or big ways. We busy ourselves running after money or power, killing and destroying ourselves in the process.

A lady who lived in South Africa for many years went back to England and said 'I have had enough of all these killings in South Africa'. She said there will always be problems in that country. The factions will never be at peace with one another. She concluded 'Africa, God loves you! If you love Him too, you will embrace His teachings on forgiveness'. We are all brothers and sisters, we have a lot in common. How wonderful to know that we are the same, wherever we live, God made us and called us Africans. Our problem is that we do not forgive, so we continue to fight, but fighting destroys us. This can be attributed to our lack of spiritual commitment to the God who has created us. God values all of us.

We have all watched the dehumanising events in our beloved continent - Africa. We should have a new determination to bring all these to an end through the mighty power of Jesus. '. . . not by might, nor by power but by my spirit says the Lord Almighty' (Zechariah 4:6). The newspapers report horrors about us everyday. The Nigerian Concord of 22 November 1996 reported 500,0000 Rwandan Hutu refugees missing. It said they cannot be accounted for. Only days after, hundreds of thousands of others arrived in Rwanda from Eastern Zaire, where they had fled in the wake of the 1994 genocide. About the same number were still roaming in Eastern Zaire. Some refugees were seen by the local people still fleeing the area westward. Truly Africa is passing through a very rough time. Even those who are not affected should feel it by the mere fact that they are Africans.

Some leaders have rightly called for prayers for divine intervention. But can God intervene while we continue in sin, ie throwing each other in jail, criticising out of jealousy, leaders and followers being dishonest in their lives, hiring people to kill on their behalf, relegating useful members of our society, oppressing them, causing political instability, taking the law into our own hands, hoarding, or hiking prices, so that the common man cannot afford to live.

Treating each other unjustly is causing our downfall. Some people who may reject the idea of turning to God have failed to present a better solution, because there is no other solution than to turn to Jesus the Saviour of the world. They say 'God is not responsible for our woes so why must we call on him to deliver us'? Humanly speaking we cannot, we always fall because man has fallen short of the glory of God. Man is doomed to condemnation by God. It is as a result of Africa's rejection of God, and of His salvation provided for man through Jesus Christ, that the continent is suffering so much. These are the things that are causing us all the chaos, anarchy, depression, instability, lack of progress and insecurity. No leader, no individual has a solution, because we are suffering the consequences of our stubbornness. 'If you do not listen and if you do not set your heart to honour my name, . . . I will send a curse upon you and I will curse your blessings. Yes I have already cursed them because you have not set your heart to honour me' (Malachi 2:2).

A Message to Africans

I admire an African leader, President Frederick Chiluba of Zambia so much, that I pray for him as often as he comes to my heart, because he has recognised the sovereignty of God. He pleaded with God for his people. This leader could carry all his people and together come before God Almighty and plead for mercy. He had God's forgiveness. I was not surprised his people re-elected him president. When the going was good he gave God the glory and when something went wrong like the loss of their national football team, together with his people they bowed before God and pleaded that he take not His blessings from them. Continue to let your light shine, President Chiluba, not only in your own country, but to other African countries as well. May God prosper your kingdom to the glory of the one you love and serve.

I urge all African leaders to turn to the Lord in penitence so that He will give them the heart to treat all their citizens as equals. 'Have we not all one Father? Did not God create us? Why do we profane the covenant of our fathers by breaking faith with one another?' (Malachi 2:10). Africa, your citizens are not so much concerned about the gigantic promises you make for developing their land. They want you to utilise them fully for their nation's development. Give them an example of a God-fearing life. All other things will follow.

Encouraging African citizens to keep the laws of God will naturally lead them to keep the laws of the land too. Leaders set an example in everything you do!

We need now to get out of the wrath of God, which means turning away from anything evil, and giving our hearts to the Lord Jesus Christ. The difference will be very clear. And those who feared the Lord talked with each other, and the Lord listened and heard. A scroll of remembrance was written in His presence concerning those who feared the Lord and honoured His name (Malachi 3:16-18). 'They will be mine', says the Lord Almighty, 'in the day when I make up my treasured possession. I will spare them just as in compassion a man spares his son who serves him. And you will again see the distinction between the righteous and the wicked, between those who serve God and those who do not.'

The only alternative left for Africa is to turn to Jesus. If you are African by birth or history start to meditate on these things. I offer the only alternative left for Africa to restore its glory. The only alternative to a way forward. Otherwise we shall continue to suffer. It is not God's will that we should suffer the way we are suffering now. That is why He provided a way out by sending Jesus Christ. He alone can give us the pure heart which we need for advancement. May these truths be opened to all Africans and indeed to all the suffering world.

Chapter 18

AFRICAN WOMEN

Women in Nigeria have struggled and to some extent have achieved a degree of social recognition. Traditionally they were supposed to be seen and not heard. They were there to satisfy men. Whenever there was an important men's gathering they were there to look after the men's food. Right from the start the mother trains her children by their sexes. The girl learns to cook and the boy to go on errands outside the family circle.

The girls were made to respect the boys, because they were the ones who would carry on the family name. The boys were taught to protect the girls. Certain expressions were allowed by girls and certain expressions were exclusively for boys. In my ethnic group the woman had to walk bending her back in respect for where the men were seated. The place of the woman was in the kitchen even though she participated fully in the family farm.

When there was a death, the men would sit outside to be consoled while the women would sit inside and receive their fellow women. The women were given less status in the community, but they seemed to have accepted their role without any resentment. Even in the first African churches men and women were segregated, but with time there seemed to be less distinction. Christianity and education have rightly affected this attitude.

Christian Teaching on Gender

God created men and women as equal bearers of his image

(Genesis 1:26-27). Both are accepted equally in Jesus Christ. 'In Christ there is neither Jew nor Gentile, slave nor free, male nor female for you are all one in Jesus Christ' (Galatians 3:28). We are told of the promise of the Holy Spirit ' . . . I will pour out my Spirit on all people. Your sons and daughters will prophesy . . . ' (Joel 2:28-29). This is without discrimination. Then Acts 2:17-18 repeats the same thing. Therefore Christians being influenced by the word of God believe that the woman is not inferior to the man. But biologically they are not the same, the two have distinctly different roles. The Bible also states that women should submit to their husbands as to the Lord, for the husband is the head of the wife, as Christ is the head of the church. The submission here is in love. It is not enforced or seen as an inferior position. This refers to family life which is important in raising a decent God-fearing family. Yet God in his wisdom gives the gift of the Holy Spirit to both men and women. He gives as He determines (I Corinthians 12:11).

A Message to Plateau State

God has used women and is still using them to save mankind. I had a convincing experience on 12 March 1996 that God is no respector of people based on their gender. A sister from Makurdi, whom I had met earlier, said God had been showing her visions. She had to abandon her work as a nurse to give herself full-time to the messages God had given her for different people and organisations. She arrived at my house in the company of two other women. She had come all the way from Makurdi to share God's message for Plateau State. She knew I was a believer. God had asked her to see the women in Plateau State where his name is honoured. She said that when people walk closely with God He speaks with them and in these last days God wants to use women. They have to give themselves completely to Him so that He can give them directives.

Things are happening in Nigeria that are contrary to the good development of a nation. Nigeria, she said, has enjoyed good facilities like water, light, and petrol, but these days water does not run easily from our taps - most people, who can afford to, dig their own wells. Electric lights are rare - rich people use generators. Most petrol stations have gone dry. The devil, she said, knows that peace exists in Plateau State. This has angered him with the result that he has centred his attacks on Plateau State, which used to be identified with peace and unity but since 1994 has experienced religious conflict. Women should be more active in prayer for the state and the nation.

She said she was shown dead corpses in some parts of Jos. People were preparing for battle to confront Christians in the state. She was warned that there would be bloodshed, unless the women prayed for the Lord's mercy. If they do this earnestly, God will divert the situation.

In Ezekiel 8 and 9 God's anger was on His people because of their evil doing. God is angry with Nigeria because He wants to use Nigerians, but the people are going in a different direction. She said we should plead for mercy that we women should stand in between, praying only for God's will to prevail in Plateau State. She was shown the horror that was to befall our State.

The prayers of God-fearing mothers are heard by God. Today the women of Plateau State are to serve as the Jehoshaphats of our day. We needed to organise prayer and fasting for Plateau State, so that the Lord will intervene. After God has heard our prayer we needed to organise a thanksgiving to God and to commit the future to the Lord, she added. The women who know the Lord are to do this without any further delay. Many, she said, know the stories of the Bible, but they do not know the power of God behind the stories.

The all-knowing God had given her this message. She has delivered the message to me so that the Christian women of Plateau State should rise and pray for the deliverance of the state and the nation. The Lord said, He will start a good thing from Plateau State where His name is being called upon and honoured. After she delivered this message, the Lord led some of our church women's fellowship members to pray. Other churches also organised prayer. I shared the vision with my church and they decided to make it our church prayer concern. Some women's fellowships around Jos were sent prayer circulars, and prayers were uttered by 'Women in Prayer' and the women's fellowships of their various churches.

Some few weeks after this, an ugly scene manifested itself, and indeed we all knew that it was the answer to the prayers of God's people. People were battle-ready to destroy and kill as the corpse of the son of a retired evangelist was being conveyed for burial. He had been killed during a local government election. Many people would have been massacred on that day but for the Lord's intervention. Women receive messages from the Lord and act upon them even though they are not pastors or men, which proves to me that God uses human beings irrespective of their gender.

On one occasion, the Lord showed me five people in darkness. I could not recognise them, but he said, 'Go and minister the word of God to them'. 'Who are they?' I asked. He brought one of them closer and shone the light on her, then He asked me. 'Don't you know this one then?' Looking at the lady I knew her, so I answered 'Yes I know her'. 'She needs to be ministered the word of God,' he said. He asked me to turn round. When I turned round I saw a pile of clean white linen. He said to me, 'take this and clean the lady with it'. I asked Him again, 'Is there anything that cleans sin apart from your precious blood, Lord?' The voice was clear, 'go and minister to this lady'. I woke up and praised the Lord for the fellowship I had had with him. I was hesitant to go to this lady, but the Lord reminded me that I had not done what He asked me to do. I made an effort to meet with this lady and God greatly blessed our meeting.

On another occasion, I saw a beautiful mansion. Turning my eyes a little to my right I saw a lady asking a man how to get there. But the man answered 'I do not know'. A voice said to me, 'you go and show her how to get there'. I woke up. 'Lord thank you for this assignment, I go in your power'. I obeyed.

Nowadays women are in all professions, medicine, law, banking, engineering, university professors, politics, the forces, administrators, pilots etc. One day my brother wanted to board a plane for Lagos to Jos, a one hour flight. As he queued for the plane he noticed a woman pilot sitting in the cockpit ready to take off. He quietly pulled out of the queue and postponed his journey. He had to spend an extra night with extra expense because of his prejudices. His fear did not stop the lady pilot from reaching her destination and she still flies safely around! Christians should not have such a strong bias against women. The Lord has used women in the past and He is still using them today, provided such women are upright and are living within the will of God.

African Families

The family is instituted by God. It is God's plan for human beings. The family is the closest unit of individuals. When a child is born into a society, his first contact is with his mother, then as he grows, he relates to his father, brothers and sisters. In an African society he relates to the extended family as well. Then he gets to know his neighbours, his church, or other associations, to which the parents belong. His school follows, then his ward, village, district, local government, state, nation, continent and the wider world.

I did not see myself clearly as an African until, in 1962, I left Nigeria and went to college in London. It was then that I associated myself with any African as a brother. In the same way, it had taken me a long time, at the age of 15, to identify myself as a Nigerian. I left home to go to school in Gindiri, where I met with other Nigerian students and people. Hitherto my thinking and scope had been of myself and my family, within the context of my tribal people. Today following years of travel, I see myself as a citizen of the world - someone whom God has brought into the world, through my parents, placed in a particular part of the world, to fulfil a certain function that God has designed for me, and to his glory. And wherever I go I know that God has a function for me to fulfil there as well. Wherever I go, my mind goes straight to my home, my people, my state, my nation. I marvelled at my presence in other countries. But the earth is the Lord's and everything in it. I am sometimes tempted to feel insignificant but then I am reminded that

God has brought me into the world to achieve his purpose and so I am important to him, if not I would not be here. I am significant within the purposes of God. Whatever I do I remember my family, my ethnic group, my nation. And this has checked my behaviour on many occasions. Sometimes it is the thought of a relative, a teacher, a pastor or a friend whom I cherish that holds me together.

When I attended a 'Man of War Bay' leadership course in the Cameroon, and went back home, the chief of my ethnic group said 'Thank you for carrying my name so far. I know that wherever you go, people will ask you where you have come from, and once you answer 'Tarok', you have carried my name there'. Back in Nigeria, people like to know whose offspring you are. Especially when your behaviour is good or bad. Sometimes your behaviour blesses your family, sometimes it does not. If anything should happen to anyone, the first thing anybody asks is, to whose family does this person belong? In the same way Christians carry Christ's name wherever they go.

The family forms the basic foundation for teaching standards of morality in society. A disciplined family usually produces disciplined children and vice-versa. This is not to say there are no exceptions. Traditionally the African family is an extended family. A child born to a member of a clan belongs to the whole clan. They all live together. Families could be nuclear and could be polygamous. Divorce is not a common feature and loose living is not encouraged. Children are commonly treated and disciplined by the older members of the group. The morality of the family members is strictly checked.

Today

Nowadays, things have changed. As people have travelled to other parts of the world and come back again, they have returned with a new outlook. Those who went to college abroad, felt that they knew better than those whom they had left at home. Instead of resisting this new morality, they joined in and many more fatherless children have been born into society.

What used to be shameful is no longer considered shameful. All sorts of crimes are now indulged in. People spurn the traditional way of life and embrace new life styles. Young people want a good life, seeking pleasure, nice clothes, driving cars, living in good houses, eating fancy foods and generally enjoying themselves, such as they have seen in the western world. Along with loose morals, violence and crime are on the increase. There is a craving for material things. Unhealthy competition has been introduced and young people will not wait for these things, they want instant gratification. Girls no more value their virtue, boys no more care for their lives. Village parents seem powerless, unable to control their children. No one cares anymore whose children they are. The girls are no longer ashamed of being called prostitutes, and in fact boys and girls live openly together, even kissing in the streets, the way they see the western world behaving. Those who are not able to travel abroad, see all these things in films or on television.

I met a girl in America who was from Nigeria. I was shocked when she showed me her three children, each by a different father. She was not married. Each father paid for the upkeep of his own child. Did they tell their parents back home that they had fathered a child? Would the parents even care? Once a son or daughter leaves home they take up smoking, drinking or drug abuse in their adopted country. It would have been better if they had not left home. They were supposed to have picked up the good habits in Europe or America, and to have discarded the rest.

There are about one and a half million single parents in England alone. Why should the governments of the western world decide to pay all these single mothers? Are they not encouraging their immorality? One hears so much about sexual promiscuity and homosexuality. What a rebellion against God! His word is clearly against such practices. Our bodies are the temple of God and must be kept pure for God's use only. He is a holy God and nothing unholy can come near him. If African people want God's blessings, they must keep themselves away from any form of immorality.

Being away from home can certainly produce some

loneliness and homesickness. The solution does not lie in taking up vices. All these things are the devil's way to destroy God's people. I have seen many African people die of such diseases as Aids from sexual immorality, also causing infertility, lung cancer from smoking, or alcohol addiction, and tuberculosis from drinking unclean water. What a loss to Africa are all these broken lives!

If you are a child brought into the world by two unthinking adults, do not turn hostile but tell God about it. It is not your fault, and God who allowed you to be born loves you. God will deal with the guilty ones. Live close to God and pray for your parents too.

People get married today for the wrong reasons and the marriage is not strong enough to hold them together for long, so a broken home is the result. Some societies accept trial marriage and if the object were to have children and the woman does not conceive, then they send her back to her parents. This is showing a lack of respect for God who instituted marriage.

God's Ideal

The family unit is God's design for the continuation of the human race. God's plan is one man and one woman, living together for life. God said 'It is not good for man to be alone' and he made a helper for him, not helpers. This rules out all other practices such as polygamy, homo-sexuality, lesbianism, bigamy, concubines, trial marriage and leather marriage (marriage suddenly decided upon and the girl moves in to live with the man). Christian marriage is for life. It is based on mutual love, first to God and then to one's chosen partner. It should be full of respect for one another and dignity. It should be entered into prayerfully, seeking God's approval. Christian marriage is done publicly because it is of the light, not of the darkness. Our church takes every precaution to interview intended couples to make sure their motives for marriage are in accordance with biblical principles before being announced to the church. Then the whole church is asked if they know any reason why the two should not marry, before the wedding can finally take place.

They are advised how they can grow together, overcome their problems and serve the Lord together.

When children come along, they are seen as God's gifts. They are received in love and great care and training is given to them. Above all they are trained in the knowledge of God. However, a childless Christian marriage is also a complete family. God may want to use these families for a different purpose.

A baptised man by the name of Moses was planning to get married in November 1996. He was probably afraid to make this commitment and on the first Sunday in September he was struck dumb. There was no hospital or doctor in the town. I asked him if he was a Christian, a communicant, and if he had been witnessing to Christ? He was hesitant about the latter. I told him that today God would release his tongue to witness for Him. Was he willing to do this? He nodded 'yes'. Then we all laid hands on the man as the Scriptures instructed us to do in James 5:13-15. Each one of us prayed for Moses but he said nothing. 'Moses why are you keeping quiet' I asked, 'God has already released your tongue. Open it and praise the Lord!'. At this point in faith Moses opened his mouth and said 'Praise the Lord!'. When he realised what had happened, he jumped up with excitement. 'Praise the Lord! - Praise the Lord!' he shouted, embracing each one of us.

What God wants from each one of us is faith and also making ourselves available for his service. African families should invite Jesus into their lives, so that he can save them from the agony of broken homes, which is causing so many children and indeed parents so much emotional disorder. Keep your marriages sacred before God! Do not forfeit Biblical moral teachings for your homes and families. Without the family there can be no decent society.

It is my prayer that as Africans strive to advance and make their continent prosper, they should let the doctrines of Ephesians 5:1-6:4 guide their family units. Clifford Hill in his book *Shaking the Nations* (Kingsway; 1995; p111) disclosed that the average marriage in Britain today lasts only nine years. This will not be the case if the marriage is covered by the Lord. Lives that are deeply rooted in God's grace can never be uprooted. Malachi 2:13-16 'You flood the Lord's altar with tears. You weep and wail because he no longer pays attention to your offerings or accepts them with pleasure from your hands. You ask 'Why?' It is because the Lord is acting as the witness between you and the wife of your youth, because you have broken faith with her though she is your partner, the wife of your marriage covenant. Has not the Lord made them one? In flesh and spirit they are his, because he was seeking Godly offspring, so guard yourself in your spirit, and do not break faith with the wife of your youth. 'I hate divorce' says the Lord God of Israel'.

African families, keep your God given families together in the fear of the Lord. Teach your children the fear of the Lord. What a difference this would make to Africa!

African Widows

A widow is a woman who has lost her husband. It is a very traumatic experience and affects every area of her life, spiritual, social, emotional, mental, physical and practical. Her stress is greater than losing any other member of her family. It could mean the lack of a steady income. The woman is suddenly responsible for everything including house rent, electricity bills, water rates, telephone bills, school fees etc. All these are heavy responsibilities for a woman to bear especially when she has no income of her own. She may also be lonely and feel dejected. There is no one to share with; no listening ear.

Every woman in Africa is a potential widow, especially where there is so much bloodshed, as a result of tribal wars, religious uprising, political unrest, stress and tension, claiming many husbands who became victims of these difficulties. Where there is so much suffering from poverty, disease and a lot of dishonest practices, death is rampant. There are also more deaths from air and road accidents. Is God angry with us? This cannot be ruled out.

The blood of those who have died has left a stain on the land. Nations who want God's blessings should avoid the shedding of blood. African nations should rise up and intercede for their peoples and ask God's mercy for so much bloodshed. They must learn to forgive one another and move forward in love for one another. There are too many widows in the land. Shall we leave them to suffer their plight? Or shall we try to minimise their sufferings. This would show our repentance.

In the past, the woman who had lost her husband in my ethnic group was in for a very bad time. Close relations of the dead man might move into the house and take the property, including the man's wife. Women and children could be inherited in this way. If the woman objected she would be turned out of the house and sent back to her own family. In some cases she would also be deprived of her children. Her only hope would be when her sons were grown up, they might be able to take back the property of their father and the mother could take shelter with her sons. Some widows would fall apart under this system, others who were Christians would put themselves into God's care and maintain their dignity.

The Bible warns 'Do not take advantage of a widow or an orphan. If you do and they cry out to me, I will certainly hear their cry. My anger will be aroused and I will kill you with the sword; your wives will become widows and your children fatherless' (Exodus 22:22-24). We should not arouse God's anger by the way we treat widows.

Some churches have organised widow's programmes. The Church of Christ in Nigeria formed a five man committee in 1991 to take care of women who have lost their husbands. This committee is known as *Komitin Zumunci*, which literally means the 'Committee of Fellowship'. They facilitate fellowship amongst widows and encourage them to share their experiences and pray for them. Some widows would appreciate it if church members visited them in their homes and prayed with them. The committee discovered that the majority of members were young. But we praise the Lord for their maturity in Christ. The fellowship encourages the women to look up to Jesus for everything in their lives. They shared testimonies of how the Lord had helped them. One woman shared how the Lord answered the prayers of her family who were badly in need of their house rent. Another gave testimony that since the death of her husband over nine years ago, God has been zealously protecting the entire family with good health.

I want to invite all the women who have lost their husbands, young or old, to join a widows' fellowship or to start one. Some wives of heads of states have built centres where widows can be trained in some skilled work, so that they can be employed or start a business on their own. Some have organised the services of doctors or lawyers to be available free of charge when required. It is important for widows to find some interest to pursue, eg Bible Study, evangelism, enhancing themselves professionally, like involving themselves in some trading activities, or acquiring skills in sewing, knitting and weaving.

The Bible says 'Religion that God our father accepts as pure and faultless is this: to look after orphans and widows in their distress....' (James 1:27). In 1 Timothy 5:3 Paul instructs us to 'Give proper recognition to these widows who are really in need.' 'But for those widows whose children or grandchildren are grown up, they should take care of their parents and grand parents, who are widows, for this is pleasing to God.' (I Timothy 5:4).

It also has instructions for widows themselves. 'The widow who is really in need, and left all alone, puts her hope in God and continues night and day to pray and to ask God for help. But the widow who lives in pleasure is dead even while she lives' (I Timothy 5:5-6).

The Lord has special concerns for widows and if we forget this, we are hurting God himself, and adding more curses on ourselves. Every widow should know that the Lord is aware of the struggles she endures in adjusting to life without a husband. The Lord himself defends the cause of the widow (Deut 10:18). What can a widow do to repay the Lord's goodness to her? The Psalmist asked 'How can I repay the Lord for all His goodness to me?' (Psalm 116:12). 'I will lift up the cup of salvation and call on the name of the Lord, I will fulfil my vows to the Lord in the presence of all His People' he answers (vv 13-14). In Exodus 4:31 we read that the Israelites 'bowed down and worshipped' the Lord when they recognised he was concerned about them. The widow should also declare the goodness of the Lord in the presence of all His people. She should worship the Lord her God with all her heart and serve Him with all her might.

I remember that when we were on a pilgrimage to Jerusalem in 1992, we passed through the valley of Jezreel. I noticed beautiful flowers blooming there. Then I remembered a story that I had read about the Lord being called the 'Lily of the valley'. Hunters used to go hunting for prey in the valleys of Israel. They usually took dogs with them to help them locate the prey by smell. But when the lilies were in bloom the whole valley was filled with the sweet odour of the flowers, so that no dog could locate the prey. During that time the animals would come out of their hiding places to play and were protected by the sweet odour of the lilies. That was how the Lord Jesus came to be equated with the name 'Lily of the valley'. Widows also can live safely so long as they remain in the Lord's valley. The widow is assured of God's help and so she can rise and face the world confidently.

Conclusion
God has placed us in this beautiful continent, but we have allowed evil to overcome us. We need to plead for Africa as Abraham pleaded for Sodom and Gomorrah. We should stop blaming our condition on governments, religious leaders or some distant peoples. We should recognise the present plight of Africa caused by each one of us, and repent and seek God's mercy together.

I identify fully with the objectives of PACWA in Nigeria, that is to:
•   Stop the tide of ungodly liberalism and secularism with its resultant materialism.
•   Assert the true dignity of women as found in Jesus Christ and contained in the Bible.
•   Inject into African Society biblical morals and values through women who are the mothers of any society.
•   Deliver Africa from moral decadence and ultimate collapse.

- Make disciples of African Nationals for Christ.

What I do in Nigeria that brings out these objectives unites me with the women of God in Africa. All Christians in Africa should write and fight against ungodly practices in their various nations, because God wants us to be holy, to be pure in thought and conduct, so that He can bless us. United and in strong solidarity we should dispel prayerfully, with the help of the Holy Spirit, all forms of worldliness, rebellion against God in whatever form, be it traditional religion, witchcraft, divination, spiritualism, gnosticism, or occultism. We look forward with greater hope for Christian victory in Africa. For the Lord has plans to give us hope and a future (Jeremiah 29:11). All of us have sinned, we have come short of the glory of God. We have behaved like Jonah, but Jonah came to terms with the Lord. He obeyed God and God used him to minister to Nineveh. God has already provided a hope and a new life for us in Jesus Christ.

Africa's sons and daughters arise, claim your new life, have your hope! For 'there is surely a future hope for you and your hope will not be cut off' (Proverbs 23: 18).

A nephew of mine once said he would give himself to Jesus when he is old. 'I must enjoy my youth first, then later I can put things right with God', he said: But remember that in giving someone an old gift, it may never be found useful again. For example, if I have some ripe bananas to give my family and I do not give them to them until the bananas become soggy then my family would certainly not eat them. Even so, God does not reject us whenever we come to Him, but a deliberate rebellion and refusal may cause the one who holds us to let us go, because we have deliberately chosen our own timing. The Lord would rather have us in our youth, when we are strong and healthy. There is so much to accomplish, but if our youths are rebelling, who will take the Gospel to the hungry dying Africans?

Chapter 19

PACWA AND POLITICS

Can African women deliver the goods as politicians? The answer was proved positive at the Pan-African Christian Women Alliance consultation on Christian women and their participation in politics, in Nairobi, Kenya, 1993. We praise the Lord for the African women who gathered there to deliberate on this very important topic.

It was interesting to see the background cultures and colours of the women. Whites from South Africa and blacks from the majority of African countries. Even amongst blacks there are several shades of black. Our Lord Jesus Christ, in whom everyone is bonded together in His love, has filled us with His spirit that brings forth unity. To him be the glory, honour and majesty.

Messages from the Conference

Very often when we talk of politicians we think of men. Until recently, it was rare to talk about women in politics.

Should African women run for political office? When we think of women like Margaret Thatcher, Aquino of the Philippines, and the late Golda Meir of Israel, we are convinced that women can be quality leaders. But why is it that Africa has not produced a single African woman leader? This could be due to cultural and traditional constraints from a child's upbringing. It appears that African children raised by their mothers have been made to believe that the position of leadership is not for the female. Thus, the children grow up with this teaching and are quite satisfied with it. Some countries even go as far as legislating against women, and banning them from participating in politics. Therefore, the African woman seems to receive no encouragement from society.

When children are inappropriately trained in managing their responsibilities, they find it difficult to handle public responsibility properly. Journalists in some countries have not helped the situation. Their publications about women have been negative in many ways.

Christian Women in Politics?

Many countries are now experiencing civil strife. Women and children are usually the victims and they are the ones who will be left as refugees. Usually, they die as a result of malnutrition and other diseases and are often left to fight without any encouragement. We must remember that David was a child when he saved his people the Israelites, and Deborah was a woman whom God used to conquer battles for her people.

It is because of the absence of the voice of Christian women in politics that some countries succeeded in passing laws that are damaging to women, for example the legalisation of abortion and pornography. Certain aspects of life mainly affect women and it is women who could adequately handle such matters.

The Bible tells us that women such as Deborah and Esther were used mightily by God and God is still looking for women who are available for Him to use. Christian women, like their menfolk, are called to go into the world and preach the Gospel. That includes the world of politics which can become a mission itself for those God has called into it. A Christian woman in politics can reach people, even men, through other wives and children.

The Need to Integrate Politics and Religion

Other religions know the importance of integrating religion with politics and have used politics to promote their religion. It is the Christian who says 'Give unto Caesar that which belongs to Caesar and to God that which belongs to God.' (Matthew 22:21; Mark 12:17; Luke 20:25)

A non-Christian who was in power in Nigeria decided to take away schools and hospitals from their owners. This was aimed at crippling the spread of the Gospel through these means. The consequences of this act can be seen throughout the country - ungodliness, indiscipline, economic disaster, etc.

PACWA determined to remind Christian women of the need to be women created by God with a mission for the age and to move in faith. God who created us has a right to call us to himself and to place us where he wants us to be. If God has called you to be a woman in politics, step out in faith. Your talents will be maximised by Him and He will endow you with the wisdom to cope. You need to understand why you are running for office. Be confident. Be single-minded.

Sister Eva, chairman of PACWA Continental, ran for the post of deputy mayor. She stood with a man from a highly traditional church, 'You cannot be voted for, because you are a woman' he said. She replied, 'It is OK. What I know is that my God is the God of Deborah. It is not my fault that I am a woman and God will not use that against me'. The Lord knew her feelings and was encouraging her; he led her to victory. When we feel we have a calling into politics, our responses should be like those of Nehemiah. When Nehemiah had a vision with a concern for the walls of Israel, He prayed and God gave him favour; He was granted permission to go and rebuild the walls of Jerusalem, and the daughters of Jerusalem also participated. Christian women should take advantage of democracy and the multi-party system and participate in transforming Africa. The challenge is to rise - will you respond by saying, 'Here I am, send me into politics, Lord!'

Some Obstacles

Women are prone to facing humiliation. Many women are not rich and their priorities do not lie in politics so they would rather use their small resources on their families. Women may not be supported by 'big' men because these big, rich men will prefer to be in the game themselves. In some cases, there is a fear of an unhealthy, immoral relationship developing between the man and the woman. Society finds it difficult to recognise qualities in women, such as being a good public speaker, great freedom fighter, etc.

PACWA has recognised that Christian women have a stronger faith in God than many men. Hence they are likely to be guided by Him and are less likely to go astray. Christian women have virtues which are paramount for African politics and good governance - humility, fairness, love for humanity and seeking God's will in all that they do. Being in a public position does not place anyone higher before God. It is an opportunity to reflect on what is in the constitution which guarantees the participation of all. It is therefore left to women to prove themselves by presenting their worth to the electorate and letting the public choose.

It is equally important for women to get over their own problems before moving into politics. 'Euodia and Syntyche, please I beg you, try to agree as sisters in the Lord' (Philippians 4:2). Paul saw a lot of quarrels over issues amongst women, in market places and elsewhere. Sadly, Christian women were not exempted from this. We must first accept ourselves, so that we can approach politics with a sense of togetherness and pride. We must be ourselves and pick up the cross to follow Christ earnestly. Christ has given us the power to be more than conquerors, but, we must remain in Him. Therefore, Christian women should use their virtues to improve first their nation and then their continent.

Africa has been plagued with a large number of ills. We face a scourging refugee problem, and hunger and malnutrition are widespread. This does not make us proud of our continent. Christian women cannot afford to fold their arms and watch things go from bad to worse. Politics in Africa has been characterised by selfishness, tribalism, and greed, while the rest of the world looks on in contempt. We need to resort to serious prayers for this weakness on our part in order to make Africa great.

The Role of Christian Women in Politics

Different women shared their experiences in politics at this conference:

1. A sister who contested for Parliament in Kenya, felt she was walking on rocky ground. Politics was seen as

something predominantly for men. However, she was encouraged by Esther of the Bible, and that gave her peace. Politics with her heart in the Lord, was very assuring to her. Despite the danger of being ambushed, with threats to her house, and working with hypocrites who behaved as if they had no conscience, she was committed to follow her calling.

In her village, she had seen the activities of darkness, jealousy, hatred, poverty, disease and barely basic subsistence of life. She felt committed to uplift the lives of her people. Although she lost the election, she rejoiced in the Lord. She smiled and people were surprised at her peace. She trekked the hazardous path because she believed that some one had to sacrifice their life for others in order to reap the benefit. If the Lord means much to us then we should bear His cross and move into the world of politics.

2. Another woman was a successful candidate. The party to which she belonged asked her not to stand in the elections, because they feared that she would not win because she was a woman, and that would bring disgrace on the party. She prayed about it and God urged her to take her Christian ethics and join another party. Her constituency was solidly behind her and they followed her into the new party. The opposition was greatly angered by this and they attempted to kill her - they fired at her but the shots missed. She kept on carrying the cross into politics. Out of the 21,000 voters, she had 12,000 votes. She rejoiced in the Lord's protection and power which saw her through.

3. M believes politics is a great means of bringing negative or positive changes to the affairs of men. Being a member of the electoral commission in Kenya, she believed that Christian politics should result in people having good food, education, health, houses, water, etc. She recalled that at one time the battle in Africa was to have our own national flag, but now that we have it, we have breached its meaning and instead of building ourselves up, we fight each other about who should rule, while there are people suffering silently with no one to care.

4. A Minister of Education and Culture said that Malawi still runs a one-party system as the people's choice. They have never had the experience of a vigorous campaign as experienced by other countries. After the election, the President appoints his Ministers and she was appointed as Minister of Education. There were six women and four men in the President's Cabinet. There were 173 Members of Parliament, out of whom 17 were women.

Earlier, she was one of those Christians who did not favour the participation of Christians in politics. She had gone as far as rebuking her father for participating in politics. When she was offered the appointment, it was a great challenge which she found difficult to accept. The grace of God however assured her to accept her appointment. She encountered several problems which were the experience of women ministers generally. Whenever she wanted to address the men, they looked down on her. Therefore the women came together and prayed over their problems; God answered their prayers and the situation changed.

She then headed the largest ministry in Malawi. She recalled the time when she was a civil servant and proposed that the 'Jesus film' be shown in all Malawi schools, her request was rejected. She had been quite vocal on some issues, but previous leaders had not considered her suggestions. She knew now therefore that as a head of a ministry, she had to manage her responsibilities with caution so as to glorify the name of the Lord. Therefore, she demanded that the proposal she had sent on the 'Jesus film' be brought to her. She found that, just before she took up office, the proposal had been immediately approved without her knowing. A Christian brother told her that God was going to use her, but she had to learn to be patient and wait upon the Lord.

5. A Dean of the Faculty of Agriculture and Rural Work in Zimbabwe spoke on the role of Moses' sister who was a 'baby-sitter' to this special child. God was preparing her for a great service. God wants to use willing hearts to accomplish his purpose in politics. He is a God of justice and He chooses someone, irrespective of gender, to deliver His people. We should therefore be willing to be His 'baby-sitter'. We should help to promote and extend His ideology. The case should not be that we are too busy even to identify or play our role. The Lord is looking for a believer who will carry the Gospel of light into the politics of our various countries. It could be you!

6. A former Minister of Information and Education in Ghana, for eight and a half years had many forces against her but she believed that her total liberation as a woman took place 2000 years ago when Christ came into the world physically, and so she did not feel that Christian women needed to struggle to defend any rights. As human beings made in the image of God we have already got every right. Politicians make all sorts of promises, eg that they will build dams, universities, etc and because people do not have any information about their national problems, they tend to believe them. We are only catalysts and facilitators. Good politics encourages people to take up their own initiatives, using their own God-given talents to make their lives better, without too much dependence on provision from the government.

7. P was a worker in the Ministry of Home Affairs in Kenya. She was later called into full-time Gospel ministry. She also referred to the book of Esther. Esther was an orphan and was brought up by a guardian in exile. She rose to the position of a queen. She was married for nine years, when she was faced with a challenge that could have marred her whole future. She was in the Persian empire when the news came to her that her people were being threatened. The document for the destruction of the Jews had been taken to the King and had been signed but Esther had not disclosed to the king that she was a Jewess. Facing him with this issue was the most dangerous thing Esther could do as her husband was a very wicked king. It is no wonder that she said, when going to him, 'If I perish, I perish'. Esther was like Moses because she identified with and loved her people. She was ready to sacrifice her life for them. Christian politicians should follow the

example of God - 'For God so loved the world that he gave His only begotten Son' (John 3:16). Christian women politicians should take a cue from Esther, who though she was well looked after, did not forget her people. Humanly speaking, people in Esther's position may be reluctant to speak on behalf of their people. Doing that could be risky for them.

We are asked 'When the foundations are being destroyed, what can the righteous do?' (Psalm 11:3). Since the Lord sees the heart of all, we need to report to Him and He will take action on our behalf. He has the power to change hearts in our favour. Isaiah 61:1-4 describes all that our Lord Jesus Christ has done for us. He did all that so that we could become righteous.

What Can Women Do?

We are told what to do when foundations are being destroyed. We should rebuild, restore and renew (Isaiah 61:4). We are God's workmanship. God has assigned different jobs to us. As Christian women, we need to know our assignments and to stick to them with all our strength. We cannot do everything, but we must identify our calling and prayerfully be involved in it. If we are called into politics, then we should ask the Lord for direction in it. He calls us into special fields for a purpose as William Wilberforce was called specifically for the abolition of slavery. Once we identify a calling, we should go to God and let Him tell us the specific role He wants us to play. These roles may not be in the areas of our inclinations but we must remember that when God calls, He equips. If we refuse to obey, God will choose others to carry out His assignment and those who refuse will be the losers.

In conclusion, It is certain that a woman is endowed with rich and valuable human qualities, especially in her role as a woman. Whenever one talks of motherhood, one thinks of the nature of life, the care for life, and the qualities that transcend life. It can be argued that some men have more motherly qualities than women. In the book of Hosea, God described his own loving care for Israel in terms similar to that of a mother when He said to them, 'It was I who taught

Ephraim to walk by taking them by the arms' (Hosea 11:3). In Exodus we see how God fed the Israelites in a motherly way. He was the provider of food. He cared for them. When the Lord cares, He really cares and when He loves, He really loves.

It is hoped that the readers of this report will ponder upon it, and will pass it on to other Christian women, who will use it to effect a peaceful and progressive political machinery, ordained by God, in our various countries, and our dear continent, Africa.

I believe that African people should be repenting of their ignorance and selfishness. When education first came to the land men ignorantly kept it from women. I recall my own personal experience. My father did not know that I, as a woman, had the same talent as a man, which would benefit me, and even my parents and my people. He had two misguided thoughts. First, that as a woman I would be married into another family. Why should he spend money on what would be given away to someone else? Secondly, they were quite ignorant of later women like Mrs Margaret Thatcher of Great Britain, the late Mrs Golda Meir of Israel, the late Mrs Indira Ghandi of India, the late Mrs Banderanaika of Sri Lanka, Mrs Benazir Bhutto of Pakistan, Mrs Aquino of the Philippines and other women who were leaders in their own right. All these women served not only their families but their nations and indeed the whole world by their leadership. If they are not satisfied with the example of the women of the Bible whom God has used, they should look around the world and see what God is doing now with women, so that African people can learn to give equal opportunities to women. I believe my father realised this before his home calling.

African women are not just good for marriage, caring for children and looking after the kitchen. God sometimes calls them for other specific duties. And usually he endows them with the talents to cope with those duties. No African should allow himself to stand in the way of what God wants to do with African women.

Chapter 20

CULTURE CLASH

Most traditional religions in Africa believe in a supreme being who is believed to be the creator of the universe. This being is not considered as all-knowing or personal. They also believe in the spirits of their ancestors who are considered to have great influence on the lives of the people. An African university lecturer made up his mind that his preferred religion was in this tradition. He explained that he believed in the spirits of his ancestors, who are constantly watching, protecting and checking his own life. He said he has to be careful that the spirits don't get angry with him in all that he does, or else he would miss their blessing. The believers in this religion make every effort to maintain harmonious relationships with these spirits. In many ethnic groups it is believed that the spirits of the ancestors have a direct bearing on their communities. In every community there are priests who lead the people in consulting and worshipping the spirits.

This belief shifts the emphasis from God, who they believe has created the universe, to the spirits of ancestors. They believe that it is not enough to know that there is a father in the house and then to ignore him. They must take instructions from him, and respect him and there should be a relationship with this father. No father will be happy to see his children respecting and obeying themselves and not him as the father. If this God, whom they believe has created their ancestors who are no more, exists, then should we continue in ignorance to worship the dead?

The instruction of the Father who has created all human beings is clear. 'Salvation is found in no-one else, for there is no other name under heaven given to men by which we must be saved' (Acts 4:12). Jesus Christ died and rose again. He alone has victory over death. Through His death and resurrection we have a new life. Christians praise God for giving Jesus to bring us closer to Him. 'Praise be to the God and Father of our Lord Jesus Christ in His great mercy. He has given us new birth into a living hope through the resurrection of Jesus Christ from the dead, and into an inheritance that can never perish, spoil or fade kept in heaven for you who through faith are shielded by God's power' (1 Peter 1:3-5). God provided Jesus, not the spirits of our ancestors, to atone for our sins. This is the work of God. It is a miracle. Should we rebel and prefer the spirits of our ancestors, if God the Father of our Lord Jesus Christ who knows everything about human beings, made this perfect plan to restore our relationship with Him?

Sunday after Sunday I witnessed many who walked forward before the congregation of God's people and testified to their new found faith saying 'I have forsaken my old ways and have found faith and salvation in Jesus Christ. Pray for me brethren.' Many found a personal joyful relationship with the Lord and have kept to it and died in this faith. When they denounced their old ways, some of them did not find it easy at first. Many suffered persecution from their people but God gave them the grace and the power to overcome such persecutions.

Some, due to persecution or who were still attracted by worldly things, divided their loyalty, half in Christianity and half in the world. Some because they were not deeply rooted in the Bible could not identify what is truly of the Lord and what is of the devil, so they stood between two masters. Either he will hate the one and love the other, or he will be devoted to the one and despise the other. You cannot serve both God and money' (Matthew 6:24).

Today I watch African churches growing very fast. In fact they are among the fastest growing in the world. In some places it is clear that a higher proportion of the total population are found at church services on Sundays than in countries traditionally Christian like in the West where only a tenth or less of the churches may be full on Sundays. The church by numbers is very large in Africa but in reality only a few may be for the Lord among them. Church-goers may not necessarily have a personal relationship with their Lord. They may be going to church for other purposes, varying from socialising, or spying to cause problems for Christians, or just a convenient venue for the display of material wealth. Yet there are many who go to church sincerely to worship the true God of the universe. The problem with many of our churches is not so much empty pews, but keeping purity in the Church.

For many years Rwanda, where we have recently seen chaos and disorder, has been known as a Christian state. If this is a Christian state then what has gone wrong? Some Christians who tried to find out the reason discovered that the Christians who actually know the Lord and are walking close to Him formed only 8% of the Christian population, which means that Christians who are supposed to stand out clearly as believers in the Lord have failed to do so. They use the church as a cover, while their activities are still in darkness.

These are the things that stand in the way of the church's effectiveness. Love, peace, joy and tranquillity should overcome hatred, evil, cheating, and killings. If we profess Christianity, then God desires that we seek him in all we do, and live for Him only. The little hatreds and ill feelings we have against each other are not of the Lord. He will teach us how to forgive one another, no matter how much it hurts. We should remember that the Lord Jesus Christ went through more suffering for us, yet He forgave us and continues to forgive us. So why should we not learn from Him to forgive each other and let His light shine through us. The time has come for Africans to forgive one another for the sake of the one we love and worship.

To let peace reign in our continent, we must keep purity in the church. We cannot be in the church and at the same time partake in the activities of our traditions such as witchcraft, idol worshipping or any non-Christian rituals, sacrifices to appease gods, festivals or ceremonies. This is syncretism and pollutes the church. It blocks the flow of God's blessings on us. God does not find pleasure in our insincerity or double dealing with Him ' No one who puts his hand to the plough and looks back is fit for service in the Kingdom of God' (Luke 9:62).

People of Africa, make your choice. As Joshua presented a choice to his people, I present the same to you, 'But if serving the Lord seems undesirable to you, then choose for yourselves this day whom you will serve, whether the gods your forefathers served beyond the river, or the gods of the Amorites, in whose land you are living. But as for me and my household we will serve the Lord' (Joshua 24:15). For those of you who have made this choice and those who will make the choice, make sure you stand clear of all this devil worship.

Unity of God's People in Africa

Without a clear stand on the side of the Lord, there can be no real unity. We shall continue to take different directions where there is neither strength nor power. The devil will find God's people easy to influence. They will be at each other's throats. Armies that do not co-operate with themselves can never win a battle. They may end up bombarding themselves.

I Corinthians 12: 12-31 clearly instructs that every believer is a member of Christ's body with a definite ministry. If we are members of one body who will share eternity together, then why can we not support each other to promote the Kingdom of God here on earth? I believe efforts have been made in various nations of Africa to unite the people of God to do what needs to be done here on earth. In Nigeria we have several organisations that aim at uniting Christians such as 'The Christian Association of Nigeria' which is more like the association that speaks on behalf of Christians in the country on political matters. I wonder how many churches are giving this organisation full backing. We have 'New Life for All' which brings all evangelical churches together unitedly to propagate the Gospel, and also the Bible Society, which aims at making the Bible available to all. There are several others.

Instead of support, some individuals or churches prefer to criticise. It could be that those placed in a position of leadership do not have time to consult with the different churches as they should. People start with zeal and later disassociate themselves for one reason or another. There is a need to examine this area of unity closely.

At the continental level there are such organisations as the 'Association of Evangelicals in Africa' with its headquarters in Nairobi, and the women's section of it, the Pan-Africa Christian Women's Alliance (PACWA), found in twenty five African Countries, as revealed by the co-ordinator Mrs Judy Mbugua in the World Evangelization magazine on Women's Missions June/July 1995 series. African Countries should support such organisations for a united common effort to promote the Gospel in Africa. If countries like America can see the gravity of the African problem and even form chapters in their country to give their support (and Britain is thinking of doing the same), we Africans should see the urgency, and come together and play our own role.

Chapter 21

AFRICA – THE WAY FORWARD

It is not the intention of the author to condemn anyone in my country or in Africa. Nigeria and the entire continent of Africa is dear to my heart. Those are my roots. My identity and genealogy can only be traced in this wonderful great land created by God. No Nigerian or African or anybody in the world can claim that he witnessed the creation of Africa, or saw it when God brought in all the people to live in it, and only God knows the exact number of people who have lived in that continent since its inception. Now we find ourselves in the land, but who knows for how long? We might all disappear and others take our place. I often wonder what the coming generations will think of us? Will they see any virtue in us? Will they be able to maintain our National Anthem in Nigeria which says *the labour of our heroes past shall never be in vain?* Will they read our history and say 'surely our ancestors lived enviable lives that are worthy of emulation?' If they fail to find anything good in us who should they blame?

The truth is that all of us have done wrong things. We cannot start to single out any individual or group. The wrong thing does not have to be big, before we are found guilty. The Word of God says 'If we claim to be without sin we deceive ourselves and the truth is not in us' (1 John 1:8). Aiding wrong in any form is sin, even keeping mute when we should speak. Each one of us should now fall into a state of serious reflection and meditation and repent. When the Pharisees brought the woman caught in adultery seeking the Lord's opinion on whether or not she should be stoned according to Moses' law, Jesus simply replied 'If any one of you is without sin let him be the first to throw a stone at her' (John 8:7). They dispersed one by one, because they knew that they were not clean either. But then shall we go on sinning so that grace may abound? I believe this would provoke God even more and he would let his wrath fall upon us. 'The wages of sin is death' (Romans 6:23) and because God is holy and he does not condone unholiness we deserve this punishment. When we sin God rebukes us and wants us to change. 'Those who sin are to be rebuked publicly, so that others may take warning' (Romans 6:23). Sometimes the rebuke takes the form of death or suffering of all kinds.

What then shall we do in the face of God's anger on us as a people? Have you felt the guilt? Everyone knows something is wrong with our nation. Shall we just be content and watch Nigeria get worse day after day? Even this attitude is sin. What then shall we do? The directive is clear: 'If my people who are called by my name will humble themselves and pray and seek my face and turn from their wicked ways, then will I hear from heaven and will forgive their sin, and will heal their land' (2 Chronicles 7:14). The directive is:

(i) **humble ourselves,** Old and young, leaders and followers, wealthy and poor, sick and healthy ones, all men and women who live in the land, must humble themselves before the Almighty. We must recognise His sovereignty - His Lordship; He alone have we sinned against. We need to surrender all our wicked ways, lift our faces towards this God in humility and with a deep feeling of guilt kneel before Him.

(ii) **'Pray and seek my face'.** What shall we pray about? Pray the prayer of Daniel 9:3-19, replacing Judah or Jerusalem with our own country. Pray with our whole heart. Seek God's face in earnest. You know that if there is any sin in your life, your prayer may not be sincere enough for the

Lord to listen to it. We have to confess our sins to God. If we sin against a brother or anybody, we must confess it, to allow them to forgive us.

I watched a video cassette of Mother Basilea and her Evangelical Sisterhood of Mary in Darmstadt, Germany. I saw the battle they had to fight with the devil, before the Lord made things easier for them. The sisters were nursing little sins in their lives, like not loving themselves as Christians, not accepting one another truly in the spirit of sisterhood. This caused them so much trouble, including their printing machine which broke down without a cause. Everything seemed to work against them. When they realised what had gone wrong they sat down in sincerity, asked one another for forgiveness, and without any repairs their machines started to function again!

All the hardship we encounter is because God's hand has withheld good things from flowing in our land. If we confess, and plead for ourselves and on behalf of other members of our community, God will have mercy on us and forgive us.

The next action from Daniel demonstrates our state of repentance:

(iii)'And turn from their wicked ways.' It is not enough to come before God, confess our sins and go back to doing these things over and over again. This amounts to deceiving God. It shows we are not sincere. We mock God. We are not serious people. We play with God, which is worse than playing with fire. We must turn away completely from our wicked ways! Our wicked ways differ, each one of us needs to go into our heart of hearts and ask ourselves 'What have I done, or am doing, that is, or can add to, God's wrath on me and my people? From this day I will give this up. I shall seek God's face in all I do'.

The sins of one person can cause an entire people to suffer the wrath of God. This is the most fearful thing about sin. When the Israelites could not defeat Ai, it was because of the sin of one person, Achan. Achan admitted that he had sinned against God, but that was after he had been found out. It is more dangerous to wait until we are found out.

When Achan's case was dealt with, the people of Israel became acceptable to God and He gave them victory over Ai (Joshua 7-8). When we forsake our wicked ways we feel at ease. We have peace of mind. The atmosphere around us changes. Why? Because after we have taken these steps God promises that he 'will hear from heaven and will forgive our sins and heal our land' (2 Chron 7:14). What a great promise! It is a promise by God the Almighty. He does not change as we do. God has all the blessings ready to pour on mankind. But we stop these blessings by our deeds. As a brother once said. 'Pouring blessings on mankind is not a problem for the Lord. He has it all at his fingertips.' It is mankind receiving that is the problem. It is like a rebellious child who never enjoys the wealth of his father because he is far away from him. God has promised he will forgive us and heal our land. So why do we still choose to live away from Him? Why do we choose to stay with this suffering we have brought on ourselves? The wealth of our father's is ours. Should we not come back to our senses and rise and go back to our father and say to Him, 'Father we have sinned against heaven and against you . . . ' (Luke 15:11-24)? There is no record in the Bible of anyone who has turned to God being disappointed. He is the God who pardons sins and will put a new garment on us for Jesus came to take away our sins and to give us new life.

One of my heart's desires is to translate some Old Testament books of the Bible into my language (Tarok). These are the books of Isaiah, Jeremiah, Daniel and the Psalms. After the foundation books of Genesis, Exodus, Leviticus and Deuteronomy which gave the miraculous way God created the world and the laws to govern it, I found that these four books helped me to see clearly how God dealt with a rebellious nation. I see His power, compassion and love in restoring this rebellious nation to Himself. In the book of Daniel, I see the faithfulness of God in dealing with those who honour Him. This could happen in my situation and my people.

Many African people are scattered all over the world. Some went for adventure, while others are refugees or people seeking asylum in other countries. Has the time not come for us to behave like Daniel, Shadrach, Meshach and Abednego wherever we may be, so that we shall obtain the mercy of God, and conditions would be made favourable for us to go back and help in the building of our various nations? Pray like Daniel, stand firm for the Lord wherever you are and we shall all have the experience of the Prophet. The God of the Prophet and the Psalmist is the God who answers the prayers of His people. He is also the God of Africa. That is why I want to translate these books into my language, so that my people may also experience His power, compassion and forgiving nature.

One of the lessons I learnt was from 'The Park' at Moggerhanger, Bedfordshire, in England, where I stayed for three weeks in quiet and meditation to finish this book. I read Rev Dr Clifford Hill's book *Shaking the Nations*. The Bible, he says, is one of hope in the midst of chaos, 'The biblical prophets and the teaching of Jesus point to the God of history still being in control and working his purposes out despite the clamour, confusion and violence of the nations'. He further points out what Jesus said, 'We should rejoice when things begin to get really bad, as this is a sign that the day of liberation draws near' (Matthew 24). He affirmed that 'the global world situation is beginning to show the signs to which Jesus referred.' I believe that the forces of the enemy in destroying Africa, and the entire world, which we are witnessing today, cannot be stopped by human powers. Only God has the power to overcome them.

So where can we find the solution to our political, economic, social and educational problems? The solution can only come from God. It is only in God that we find those truths which can sweeten society. The attributes of God such as love, compassion, justice, kindness and patience are the solutions we need for Africa's problems. If we try to find the solution in politics we shall see nothing but more hatred, killings, oppressions etc. It is only the touch of God that will enable our leaders to govern justly and honestly. It is only the leaders with the attributes of God who will respect the freedom which God has given to mankind to choose to worship Him for good, or to rebel and lose eternal life. When the leaders of Africa can learn from the way God is dealing with mankind, then they too can give freedom to all men in their jurisdiction, to worship God the way they are convinced to do. They will allow God to convict their hearts rather than forcing, or oppressing those that are not of the same religion as they are.

The Future

When the God of love and justice reigns in our hearts, we are able to take the different groups in our nations seriously and address them genuinely. The fears of the minority in the land, the fears of the differences existing in our nations, would disappear as our God-fearing leaders would then be able to invite all these sectional interests for serious meaningful dialogue, with positive action to dispel the fears of every party. The leaders would be able to show by their actions that, even though we differed in tribe, creed and traditions, we could still be united and achieve a better future for Africa.

Dear fellow Africans, IF we fulfil the conditions God has set for all who recognise His Lordship then we could enjoy the land He has given us. We would be proud to be Africans because God's hands would be wide open to pour disciplined sanity and blessings into our society.

Yes, there is hope . . .

Appendix

History of the Tarok

The word describing the Tarok as a people originates from *Talok* which means 'the overflow from Tal' so Tal is recognised as the ancient home of this ethnic group. In 1930, Mr A B Matthews, the District Officer of Shendam Division, estimated that the Tarok people settled in their present location around 1730 - others say around 1700, still others believe that it could have been long before this. They settled as far as Wase Tofa, Kadarko, Lamba, Gwiwan Kogi and Damna, before the advent of Madakin Hassan from Bauchi, which is now present Wase.

It appears that they first settled in the hill country, now known as Gazum Chiefdom, as this afforded them a refuge from their enemies. There are a number of stories about why they moved down from the hills and spread out over the plains. One states that this happened when peace had returned to the land; another says that members of the clan quarrelled over a rat they had killed for meat, so the heads of the families moved away to avoid war, leaving their families and some children on the hills; yet another version suggests that they came down from the hills in search of better farmlands. Today there are over 1.5 million Tarok people in Nigeria.

Reverend H J Cooper was a missionary with SUM (Sudan United Mission) in Langtang from 1908 to 1936 and is recognised as knowing more than anyone about the Tarok people.

Oral tradition maintains that the Tarok people originated from the Bantu tribes of East Africa - there are similarities in language grouping which is Benue Congo (a grouping of East, Central and South African languages) and culture, for instance in the practice of mortuary death. When an important person dies, the funeral celebration is usually delayed for about six months or in some cases as long as a year.

Some Tarok women make big holes in their ears which is common with both Bantu males and females. The Tarok people also dress in animal skins like the Bantus - usually that of the leopard, signifying the supremacy of man and his leadership position. The holding of animal tails such as a male horse or buffalo are a sign of victory in life in both tribes. I was reminded of the many physical similarities when I was asked, in London, if I was from South Africa. 'You look like them' I was told. The Tarok people of today are thankful that they share a common language in their local government area but they need to discover and remember some of their historical language roots.

Tarok Religion

The people were originally idol worshippers and there are still some who, although they believe in one supreme God, nevertheless are afraid to approach him directly, so they try to reach him through idols or the spirits of their ancestors, who they believe are watching and controlling their activities here on earth.

The traditional Tarok society today is surrounded by myth and awe in marriage, burials, sickness etc. Women and children are made to fear the spirits of their ancestors and disciplined through the *rim* institution, which is a secret occult society. There are ceremonies for boyhood and manhood. The *Jujus* have to appease these ancestral evil spirits and are not supposed to be seen by women or children. They meet in clusters of trees on hill tops, where the trees are hung with beads. They place food there and offer them to the spirits. They pray for rain before the harvest and before sowing, and drink beer at the ceremonies, which is made by the women from guinea corn and other grains. So much grain is used in making beer that it sometimes results in a famine if grain is short.

The people's morals, customs and patterns of behaviour all reflect their religious beliefs; for example in the names they give to their children. *Nimfa* means that a man has been born, while *Rimdan* means that the spirit has been re-incarnated from an ancestor.

Tarok Customs

Marriage: The people are guided by high morals. A young woman is not supposed to have intercourse with a man without a proper marriage. Customary marriage means that the young bride can steal away to her husband's house when her dowry and other customary requirements are fulfilled. Sometimes she is advised to do this by her friends or relatives, or even her mother, and the mother would pretend not to have any knowledge of her daughter's behaviour. This custom has given way to rampant elopement by many young people.

Whenever a girl loves a boy, the girl will introduce the boy to her parents. The boy's parents would then start to present gifts to the girl's family. These gifts take the form of rams, wrappers, clothes, jewellery like *jigada* (waist beads) etc. The demands from the girl's family are numerous and may include building a house for the mother and father, farming for them and bringing the equivalent farm products such as rice, soup ingredients like *azul* (melon seed) and izhin (beniseed). Money is sometimes given but is usually for the payment of dowries. When all are satisfied the girl becomes an adult and is in a position to decide for herself; she can then arrange to elope with her boyfriend.

After this she moves to the house of the boy and becomes a bride. She has to exhibit shyness, hard work and not much interest in food! She sweeps the compound alone and does all the housework. When there is a young bride, people take their grinding and pounding work to her to be done; she cannot refuse to do this and thereby she earns a good name. In some communities the young wife does not speak to her parents in-law until they have 'opened her mouth' by a gift of red kola nut, soup ingredients, clothes or money. Sometimes the girl's silence toward her in-laws could mean that what was given to her was too small, and continued silence means that more is required. However, the idea of continued silence meaning asking for more is not common amongst the Tarok people. It seems to be a mixed idea borrowed from a neighbouring ethnic group. During the silent period the girl serves her parents in-law and those around her faithfully. She sleeps in a separate hut (bridal suite) called ijini, where her virginity will be broken by her husband. A token is paid for this in some families, because it is a proof that the girl has kept herself pure for her husband. Someone would then go to the girl's family and inform them of her whereabouts. Usually the parents now feel relieved that their daughter is properly married to a man they all know.

Sometimes the girl goes to a different person after all the labours of the right man. When this happens, the house the girl chooses would arrange to pay back all that the first man had spent on her but usually it leaves bad feelings.

After a week or two, the girl will go back to her parents and live with them for about a year. The parents decide when she should go back to her husband. The girl's family will cook the traditional amwam (Hausa people call it amora). It is some kind of starchy food cooked with the soup seeds brought by the husband during his courtship. This bride's food will be distributed to all relatives and neighbours. It is a way of announcing that the wife of Mr X has finally arrived. In appreciation, they put a token gift in the dish used to give them the food. It could be money, or the same soup ingredient eg azul (melon seed) or abai (cheese made from locust bean seeds) and izhin (beniseed) to help the young bride to settle in her new home.

Marriage for a young girl can be a trying period and mothers usually prepare them for this. It is a period when the girl can prove to the community that she has been well trained by her parents. She would work like a donkey without complaining; she would pound, grind, sweep, fetch water, wash her calabash and pots including her cooking stove area, usually made of pots. She would wash the pots after cooking, and put oil on them to make them shine before the next meal. Her calabash must especially be spotlessly clean and dried on apakun which looks like a high table - one for the dishes/calabash and one for the pots. When she is used to the area, she will fetch her own firewood. These are evidences of a good house wife. There will be plenty of food for the house like *nkpan* (special thick porridge eaten with soup), and special soup to eat early in the morning. Her in-laws will be given hot water to bathe with or clean up early in the morning. So being a bride in Tarokland is hard work!

Many young girls are afraid of this period. They could succeed or fail. Some lazy brides might sleep through the morning and the community would sing songs to ridicule them. This would leave a stigma on her in that community, while those who succeed receive songs of praise.

With the coming of Christianity, the traditional wedding rituals were mostly set aside. Christians still have to go through the traditional demands and after satisfying the parents of the girl, instead of secretly or quietly arranging to elope, they now decide to let the world know that a good relationship has been established between the two couples and their families, so all should go to witness the wedding and rejoice with them. Some people who are not even Christians may choose to have the Christian wedding today for its prestige.

The Tarok social system is dominated by a matrilineal system. In some rare cases, children bear the name of their father. It is the maternal uncle of the wedded girl that has the right to the dowry, not the father. The male child can free himself from his uncle's rights over him by offering sheep and goats. He can do that himself or his relatives can do it on his behalf. The idea of a male child paying a ransom has been watered down only in cases where the marriage is not Christian. In the matrilineal system, a child belongs to its maternal uncle but with the consent of the uncle such a child can be ransomed, then he goes to his father's family.

Females who marry foreigners ie not of the Tarok tribe, are considered lost and bride money is not paid on them.

This has stopped many young females' involvement in inter-marriages. All females are expected to marry and they usually do so since the extended family system is very strong.

Inheritance: When a Tarok man dies, his wealth will go to his next of kin, who could be either his father, if alive, or to his brother or eldest son, or his matrilineal uncle, in trust for distribution to the male relations. His widows can choose which of his brothers they would prefer to be inherited by. In this case, a woman becomes an inherited commodity. This custom is changing fast today, especially among the Christian communities. Most women prefer to remarry or remain unmarried instead of being bound by affinal ties to a man. They could remain unmarried and still be part of their late husband's family.

Eldership: Respect for their elders is a highly cherished cultural institution and it is out of this respect that discipline, law and order are achieved. Young people mature with full anticipation of becoming elders one day. Formerly it was the collective elders who took decisions on matters affecting the tribe. It is sad to state that the same cannot be said today. The fabric of society is being disintegrated by some educated rich young people who have been affected by selfishness and moral decadence. With the coming of the missionaries however, they now have the word of God to determine their code of conduct, which is the best thing that has ever happened to the Tarok people.

Administration

The highest authority in the land was the institution of the *Ponzhi Mbin* (Religious Leader). Each clan had its own *Ponzhi Mbin* e.g. there is *Ponzhi Mbin Zini, Bwarat, Sa, Tumwat, Kumbwang, Kwallak, Nani* etc. Since the advent of the colonial masters, the power of leadership has been invested in the *Ponzhi Tarok*, traditionally a religious, political and economic institution. Literally the word means head or father of a tribe. His main function is to perform religious rites similar to that of the *Ponzhi Mbin* in each clan.

Before the colonial administration, they used to combine temporal and religious duties but in 1923 *Miri Seldun* resigned from the temporal duties and since then there has been a separation of powers between the religious Ponzhi Mbin and the temporal *Ponzhi Tarok*.

The *Ponzhi Mbin* deals with the performance of religious rites when faced with disasters such as plagues, diseases and drought and performs the rites carried out at the beginning of the dry season known as *ibyari*.

The *Ponzhi Tarok* deals with administrative duties, which may involve touring the whole land to collect tax for colonial administration.

In a letter written by the Secretary of the Northern Provinces Mr E J Lethun to the Chief Secretary in Lagos in 1931, he explained that the Tarok people were administratively divided into two unequal portions. These were the Hill Tarok, who then occupied an area in the Pankshin Division and Plain Tarok, who were grouped in 1911 with the Shendam Division. He thought that the whole tribe should be administered as a single unit and considered that this would be a good time to do it, because the Chief of the Hill Tarok had just died.

The Pankshin Division Tarok at that time covered 271 square miles with a population under 4000. They used to pay £286 tax per annum. They were administered by a district staff, who were paid £100 per annum, while the Plain Tarok of Shendam Division had a population of nearly 30,000 and their tax was £2000 per annum. Mr Lethun suggested that they could be ruled through a council of all clan representatives and asked for the administration to have a treasurer, who could later become the head chief. In 1926, the creation of Plateau Province brought the two sections of Tarok people together under the Resident, even though they still remained in different Divisions until 1935, when Hill Tarok was excised from Pankshin Division and merged with Shendam Division. They finally became the Langtang Native Authority in March 1961, now Langtang Local Government Council.

Occupations

Tarok people are neat, hard working and progressive. Today their sons and daughters occupy high positions in business and government.

Other occupations are:

1.   **Farming:**   This is the main occupation; both men and women farm. It is after the woman leaves the family farm that she starts on her own personal farm, where she grows products such as izhin, ilampyar (red beniseed), azul, aku (a type of potato), ananjol (a long potato), afi (bambora nuts), aturet (potato), aso (beans), ibwam (okra), isanduk (green beans), akpal (spinach) and ngwan (cocoa yam).

2.   **Weaving:**   Tarok people weave their own clothes like ngbat (thin stripes of brown and black on white, on edge) and godo (wide cloth, usually white), both used for wearing around the waist. Ngbat is used by men to cover themselves. Latterly, the women wear patari around their waists.

ngbat

3.   **Blacksmith work:**   Using a locally made izambar (bellows) they produce arrows, hoes, sickles, knives, spears, axes and different types of iron.

4.   **Carving:**   Tarok people carve hoe handles, pestle and mortar hoes, 'ika (sickle), and ikwar (a kind of wooden dibber, used for sowing). They also carve calabashes (made from gourds) and wooden planks for sleeping on, raised at one end called igban.

5.   **Pottery:**   Tarok women are unbeatable at this craft. They make different exciting shapes with clay and their hands are very skilful. They make ideri (a water pot peculiar to the Tarok people), ngbat (another pot), isar (a large waterpot used to make alcohol), isakkur (a three legged pot, peculiar to the Tarok region), asu agantan, (an open topped top) isar-nden (a water pot), and ibici (a gourd shaped pot used for alcohol or gruel).

6. **Raffia Weaving:** Raffia is used to make mats such as ndakal (coloured fine raffia mats), iban (a strong straw mat), ajwar (a mat used on the head of Tarok women in order for them to carry pots), anap (a woven container for carrying winnowed grains), ngan (strong mats to cover doorways, especially to restrain animals), akanshat (a woven sifter for seeds), and avit (a woven hanging bag to take a pot or calabash).

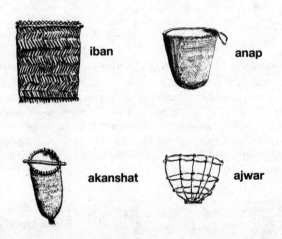

iban

anap

akanshat

ajwar

7. **Tanning:** Tarok elders used to wear animal skins as clothes. Women also used animal skins to carry their babies on their backs, and elders wear animal skins back and front. Today Tarok people dress the same as all Nigerians.